# HUMAN
# SERVICES
# DICTIONARY

# HUMAN
# SERVICES
# DICTIONARY

Howard Rosenthal

Brunner-Routledge
NEW YORK AND HOVE

Published in 2003 by
Brunner-Routledge
29 West 35th Street
New York, NY 10001
www.brunner-routledge.com

Published in Great Britain by
Brunner-Routledge
27 Church Road
Hove, East Sussex
BN3 2FA
www.brunner-routledge.co.uk

10 9 8 7 6 5 4 3 2 1

Library of Congress Cataloging-in-Publication Data

Rosenthal, Howard, 1952-
 Human services dictionary / Howard Rosenthal.
   p. cm.
Includes bibliographical references and index.
 ISBN 0-415-94546-1 — ISBN 1-58391-374-2 (pbk.)
1. Human services—Dictionaries. 2. Human services—
Handbooks, manuals, etc. I. Title.

HV12 .R67 2003
361'.003—dc21

                                        2002012070

# CONTENTS

# ACKNOWLEDGMENTS

Although I take full responsibility for the definitions herein I would like to thank all the people who assisted me including my wonderful wife Patti, Dr. Harold McPheeters, the father of human services, social security expert Bill Hunot, my fellow teachers Dr. Stan Kary, Mary Kay Kreider, Dr. Peggy Tyler, Kathy Petroff, Cindy Shanks-Brueggenjohann, and John Wood. Accolades are also in order for my graduate practicum students, Cindy Daughtery, Stephanie Wideman, and medical students Sara Martin, Kelli Shaon, and Jill Porter. My students Rick Cox and Lou Ann Weyer made a number of important contributions. And certainly, my student Norma Caldwell's work was second to none and deserves special mention.

Finally, thanks to my editor Emily Epstein who made this book a reality.

# INTRODUCTION

## A NEW BREED OF DICTIONARY FOR THE HUMAN
## SERVICE WORKER IN THE 21ST CENTURY

In the mid 1980's I was giving suicide prevention lectures—lots of them. Nearly 10,000 people a year were exposed to my crash courses in emotional lifesaving. I lectured near and far . . . everywhere and anywhere . . . from the 79 acre plant of General Motors in Wentzville, Missouri, to the beautiful Showboat Hotel in Las Vegas, Nevada. Little did I know, however, that the audience that would have the greatest impact on my future career would be the students at St. Louis Community College at Florissant Valley; a school I had attended and snared a liberal arts degree from many years earlier. A school right in my own backyard.

My presentations at the college were enthusiastically sponsored by an angelic woman named Jeanette E. Kimbrough. Jeanette, who ran the 2-year Associate of Applied Science degree in the Human Services Program, embodied every positive quality you would expect a stellar human service worker to possess. She was the perfect role model for myself as well as the students. I discovered that Human Services was an exciting new discipline barely out of its adolescence with less than 20 years of history under its belt. The first human services program was launched in 1966 by Purdue University. The program was intended to train entry-level mental health workers who would be armed with a two-year associate degree.

In my mind, what separated human services from its fellow disciplines was a sense of integration and harmony between the professions. Human Services was the ultimate eclectic interdisciplinary field. This was a field that transcended professional turf wars.

## HUMAN SERVICES: A SAFE HAVEN FOR
## SOCIAL SERVICE AND MENTAL HEALTH WORKERS

Human services was a respite—a safe haven if you will—where social workers, psychologists, counselors, reading specialists, substance abuse professionals, a public health expert, a disabilities specialist, a corrections

1

officer, and even a pharmacist, could teach side by side, in the same department, under one roof, without the slightest hint of discord. Textbooks for the program reflected this multidisciplinary acceptance and were penned by M.S.W.s in social work, Ph.D.s in psychology, a Ph.D. in psychiatric nursing, an Ed.D. in counseling; and of course human services graduates, to name a few. The challenge of human services was and is to retain its own identity as a separate profession, yet at the same time integrate the wisdom of other professions. I liked what I saw, heard, and read. Human services appeared to be doing an exemplary job.

In my mind human services programs were eclecticism personified. All the soldiers on the human services social service and mental health field seemed to be marching in the same direction.

Human services appeared to be espousing the wisdom, usually attributed to Robert Carkhuff, that good helpers of different persuasions seem more alike than mediocre helpers from the same school.

The concept of human services—a discipline that seemed to hold the unwritten patent on the formula for creating harmonious relationships between an array of helping professions—seemed to hold the key to a bright future for myself and my students. In the case of my students the two-year human services degree served as a meal ticket to enter the field in a minimum amount of time and/or continue their education.

I immediately began teaching human services courses part-time for the college in the 80's while I continued lecturing, hospital stress and chemical dependency unit work, and private practice. In 1994, after Jeanette Kimbrough's untimely death, I took over the job of program coordinator for the Human Services Program at St. Louis Community College at Florissant Valley. I have regretted a number of decisions I have made in my life, but taking over the job of running the human services program has never been one of them. I know I am making a difference in my students' lives, and I know my students are making a difference in the people's lives they will be helping.

## THE DAWN OF A NEW DICTIONARY

Some people collect stamps. Others collect coins. I have always been fascinated by social science dictionaries and own a host of them. When I began teaching human services courses I read about a psychiatrist named Dr. Harold McPheeters who helped create this discipline. Some had even gone as far as to dub him "the father of Human Services." Since I had truthfully never heard the name before I began scouring my dictionaries and textbook glossaries of psychology, psychiatry, social work, counseling for an entry pertaining to Dr. McPheeters. Much to my chagrin, I discovered that one did not exist.

I then combed my sources for a definition of human services. When one did appear—which was rare—it was not even remotely related to what the textbooks in the field were saying and it certainly had little or nothing to do with what we were teaching in class! I called all the local bookstores and surfed the net for hours on end hoping to purchase a human services dictionary. The search ended when I realized that I couldn't purchase that which did not exist. I thus came to the inescapable conclusion that **human services needed a dictionary to call its own.** And that, my dear reader, is what you have in your hot little hands!

## THE WORD ACQUISITION PROCESS

I began the long, arduous process of amassing words for this tome in 1994. Since I did not necessarily want to be the sole judge of what was or was not included I enlisted the help of undergraduates, graduate students, and even medical students. Some of the students were typical students, while others had snared distinguished honors. I would assign interested students the task of reading a text (usually a common text used in human services classes) and to let me know what terms or words they did not understand. If the book had a glossary I would have the student assess which definitions they found too difficult to understand. In the case of both graduate and undergraduate students I was often amazed at the simple terms they felt needed to be included and the existing definitions they were unable to comprehend. As professors and seasoned practitioners it is easy to forget that at one time *we didn't understand the meaning of these simple terms either!*

I thus began to see that this dictionary needed to be simple enough for the incoming undergraduate student, yet demanding enough for an advanced graduate student or expert practitioner.

While the students were busy perusing texts I was also burning the midnight oil investigating books that were used (or could conceivably be used) by human services practitioners and students.

3

One thing you rapidly discover when you analyze sources in this field is that the definition or explanation you find in one source does not necessarily match the meaning you will find in another. When confronted with this contradiction I would often try to incorporate the information into a meaningful synthesis or give several different definitions of the term. On a few rare occasions I merely explain to the reader that the definition of the term may indeed vary depending on the source.

Please keep in mind that the final definition you see in this text was often the result of consulting ten or twenty books, dictionaries and study guides. These treatises came from a host of disciplines including human services, psychology, sociology, criminal justice, addictions, psychotherapy, marriage and family therapy, crisis intervention, human growth and development, disabilities, statistics, social work, medicine, alternative medicine, psychiatry, and social welfare policy and politics, to name a few. (You can thank me later for saving you the time, money, energy, and hard work!)

At times I might contact an expert related to the field such as Dr. Stan Kary, a consummate behaviorist, or John Wood, who has been the director of several major hospital chemical dependency programs. Here again, their explanations did not always concur with those found in books, existing dictionaries, or glossaries.

## THE LIMITS OF THIS WORK

An author is often his or her own worst critic. Let me state forthrightly that this dictionary will not—I repeat—will not include every term you need to know. For example, this book will include many terms students need to know for psychology courses, but it decidedly will *not* completely take the place of a dictionary of psychology or text since it will not include the more obscure terms. Yes this book will mention the more popular psychiatric medicines that a human service worker is likely to encounter (e.g., Prozac), but in no way will it cover all of them. The work will define common medical terms such as HIV and sickle-cell disease, nevertheless, it will not and *cannot* cover every disease listed in the *International Classification of Diseases (ICD)*.

At times, you may be surprised by definitions and terms that *are* included. For example, it has been years since Eric Berne's transactional analysis (TA) has been a popular form of therapy. Nevertheless, licensing or certification exams often include questions of this ilk so the decision was made to place them in this book. Other outdated terms—though passé—do indeed pop up in the literature and thus they too became window dressing for some of the pages herein.

Writing a dictionary is not as precise and scientific as mixing specified amounts of a given set of chemicals in a test tube. There are judgment calls that yours truly had to make when picking and choosing words for inclusion. I have an open mind and welcome your input. If you strongly feel that a word, term, definition, or example, is missing that is imperative, I urge you to contact me personally at drhowardr@juno.com so I can consider using your idea for a future edition of this book. Remember to include your definition of the word or term.

## WHY THIS DICTIONARY IS DIFFERENT AND HOW IT WILL HELP YOU!

On numerous occasions a student would approach me and say, "What does this term mean?" I would refer him or her to a typical social science dictionary or text glossary, only to have them approach me again with: "Okay, what does this definition mean?"

I began reading hundreds of definitions from various dictionaries only to ask myself the same question time and time again: "If I didn't really already understand the concept, would I understand it after reading the entry in the dictionary?"

Unfortunately, the answer in a high percentage of the cases was an unequivocal "no"!!!

I thus made a vow to myself that *this dictionary would include definitions that students could understand.* In literally hundreds of cases this meant giving a very simple concrete example as part of the definition. Hence, if you look up the term **task force** the definition includes this example: A college might set up a task force to discover why retention in their human services program is so poor, set a goal for acceptable retention, and specify steps to keep students from dropping out of the program. If you go to the definition of **ice-breaker** you will receive a definition or explanation and then the example of a leader using an ice-breaker who might put the participants in smaller groups and say "If you could talk to anybody who ever lived for an hour who would it be?"

5

Another pet peeve I had about dictionaries was that their definitions often failed to cover typical questions about the term that appear on most exams. My background for tackling this task was ideal. In 1993 I created a text entitled the *Encyclopedia of Counseling*, a tutorial to pass the National Counselor Examination that became a Brunner-Routledge bestseller. I updated the book for 2002. Thus, using my vast experience in this area to write this dictionary, I ameliorated this weak link by **providing critical information to help you on exam questions as part of the definition**. Thus, if you look up **negative reinforcement** the definition will explain that negative reinforcement is not punishment. If you look up the term **correlation coefficient** you will be enlightened by the sentence: Correlation is not causal. (Incidentally, if I had a dollar for every time a professor or licensing or certification exam asked these questions and the student missed them I'd be rich. Unfortunately I don't! But the good news is that with this dictionary a lot fewer students will be missing these typical popular test questions.)

The text helps you find relevant related information that may be pertinent to your area of study. Hence, if you are investigating psychological testing and you look up the term **face validity** you will be told at the conclusion of the definition to *See validity, content validity, construct validity, and predictive validity.*

This dictionary is also replete with slang so when a client who is a substance abuser uses the term **snow** you will know that he is using **cocaine.**

The text also includes a wealth of popular terms from related courses human services majors must take such as psychology, social work, crisis intervention, sociology, and statistics.

The dictionary has up-to-the-minute avant garde terminology such as Web Counseling or St. John's wort and SAMe, the natural antidepressants. Another innovation is that it includes events that might be considered monumental or milestones in the field such as the Coconut Grove Fire.

Finally, trail blazer and human services pioneer, Dr. Harold Mc-Pheeters was kind enough to give a brief history of human services and define the term.

## SO TO RECAP THE BENEFITS FOR YOU THE READER

- The dictionary is chock full of easy-to-understand, reader-friendly, definitions in human services and related courses you might take such as social work, psychology or statistics.

- It serves as a quick informative reference for the human services practitioner.
- When definitions are not crystal clear an example or several examples are provided to clarify the material.
- Definitions are intentionally worded to help you answer questions that typically show up on tests, quizzes and licensing/certification exams.
- Suggestions for related terms are often cited at the conclusion of a definition.
- Slang used in the field is included.
- The newest and latest nomenclature is depicted.
- Two exclusive pieces written by Dr. Harold McPheeters, clarify what human services really is, and a brief history of the human services movement.
- The Resources section puts a wealth of information at your fingertips. It includes a list of the major statistical tests used in human services, the major psychoeducational diagnostic tools, and contact information for obtaining ethical guidelines and or other key information from the primary professional organizations in this field.
- The Resources section contains a list of popular prescription and nonprescription mental health remedies and a list of prescriptions for common medical conditions.

*This book is the ideal resource for students majoring, taking courses or performing duties in human services, counseling, social work, psychology, psychiatric nursing or any of the helping professions. It will also help you prepare for major and minor exams. It deserves a spot on the shelf in the reference room of every library and human services agency.*

## WHAT EXACTLY IS HUMAN SERVICES?

### Dr. Harold L. McPheeters Defines the Field

When I was coming up with the idea for this book, I wrote to Harold L. McPheeters, M.D. the Father of Human Services, asking if he would be kind enough to give us his personal definition of human services, perhaps distinguishing the field from related fields such as social work. He was kind enough to share his thoughts and what appears below is his unaltered response:

7

I am not sure that I have been that much involved in the full definition of that concept.

Our work at the Southern Regional Education Board was clearly aimed at creating middle level mental health workers who might serve more as the advocates/expediters for clients who often found that services from specialists (psychiatrists, psychologists, social workers, nurses) were fragmented and did not extend far from their hospitals and clinics as the clients required more and more services in the communities rather than in hospitals and mental health centers. The terminology we used was "mental health workers."

However, it soon became apparent that the formal system of job descriptions and required certifications in the defined mental health system often blocked the employment of these graduates—especially in the hospitals and mental health systems that depend on reimbursements for only services by properly certified or licensed professionals. Some of the newer community based programs (halfway houses, psychosocial rehabilitation programs, case management programs) were more flexible in using the new workers, but, we found from our surveys, so were many other "human service" programs who found our graduates helpful and readily employed them. These included special education programs that hired them as teacher assistants, nursing homes and community-based child welfare and corrections programs etc. Calling the educational programs "mental health" was misleading since the graduates were working in a wide variety of human service agencies. Several colleges, subsequently, began to change the titles of their programs to "Human Services." We were not among the initiators of that trend, but we could see their point (even if our grant support from NIMH called for developing "mental health workers)."

I never took part in any of the debates about the title changes nor of the conceptual differences of what a discrete "human servcies" profession might be in contrast to the established professions. Later on there came the question of getting our workers recognized with a title and job definition in the Department of Labor's *Dictionary of Occupational Titles.* I submitted my recommendation for what that title should include.

Basically, my personal concept is that human service workers should function more as "generalists," like general practitioners, who are the primary contact persons for clients with the human services system. They make evaluations and solve the problems if possible and refer clients to appropriate specialists when necessary while still providing the coordination of care for their clients in the community. They are not intensive counselors, caseworkers, or therapists, but they need a broad understanding of the human service systems and sufficient knowledge of the bio-psycho-social needs of clients to help clients resolve their community-living problems. Obviously their spheres of operation will vary with the settings in which they are employed (schools, senior centers, mental health case managers) just as the general practitioner's jobs vary depending on whether they are in the military services, private practices or public health centers.

This is not a highly rationalized concept, and I do not know how it fits with what others claim is unique to human services or how human services differs from social work. It seems that many of the baccalaureate level social workers function in much this same way, while most Master's level social workers strive for positions in either intensive case work or administration. Beyond this, I have little to add.

It should be noted that Dr. McPheeters is a modest man when it comes to his title and accomplishments. In one piece of correspondence to me, he wrote: "I am not sure that I am the founding father of human services; there were other persons who were very active in those early days, especially in developing curricula in their individual college programs."

Here's to a better understanding of human services terminology and a fabulous career! Have a great day!

Dr. Howard Rosenthal
January 2003

# EARLY STEPS IN HUMAN SERVICES EDUCATION

**Author:** Harold L. McPheeters, M.D.

**Profession:** Board Certified Psychiatrist, specializing in mental health administration and manpower research.

**Primary Affiliations:** State Mental Health Director and Assistant Commissioner, in Kentucky and New York; Director of Health and Human Service Programs, Southern Regional Education Board.

**Major Works:**

McPheeters, H. L.(1969), *Roles and functions for mental health workers*. Atlanta, GA, Southern Regional Education Board.

McPheeters, H. L. and King, J. B.(1971), *Plans for teaching mental health workers*. Atlanta, GA, Southern Regional Education Board.

In the early days of the Great Society program of President Lyndon Johnson there was a huge expansion of all kinds of health and human service programs, especially targeted to serving clients in the communities where they lived rather than in large institutions. It became apparent that there was no way all of those new programs could be staffed using only the traditional, professional level workers.

In 1965 the Mental Health and Human Service Program of the Southern Regional Education Board (SREB), an interstate contract program of the 15 Southern states concerned with higher education in the Region, received a grant from the National Institute of Mental Health (NIMH) to explore whether it would be possible to train a new level of mental health worker in the new community colleges at the Associate Degree level and what roles such workers might play. That conference report declared that it was feasible to train such workers and identified several possible jobs they might fulfill (e.g. community support workers, after-care workers). The report also suggested that some organization should undertake a major effort to help develop such training programs and their curricula,

11

and help develop job descriptions and establish positions for the new workers in the work force.

SREB subsequently received an additional series of grants from NIMH to do just those things in the field of mental health. The major issue to be decided before any new occupation could be developed was exactly what will these new workers be expected to be: would they be just assistants to one or another of the established professions (social workers, psychologists, nurses) or would they have entirely new roles? A symposium of experts from the mental health fields of practice and education was convened and formulated the concept of the mental health generalist in the publication *Roles and Functions for Mental Health Workers* in 1969. Then a second symposium made up primarily of educators was convened and issued *Plans for Teaching Mental Health Workers* in 1971 based on that same generalist worker concept. These two publications became the conceptual base for the establishment of the Human Services profession—the training programs and the job descriptions.

By this time NIMH had made grants to six colleges across the nation (mostly community colleges) to start mental health worker training programs at the Associate of Arts level. While those pilot programs initially had differing theoretical models for what their graduates would become, they gradually modified their curricula as they participated in the SREB projects. Several more community colleges both in the Southern region and throughout the nation became interested in undertaking such programs based on the models formulated at SREB, and new programs were undertaken in several of those colleges either with NIMH support or with the colleges' usual resources.

Throughout the ensuing years SREB hosted many conferences for faculty persons from those colleges (only Southern colleges at first, but then nationwide after NIMH requested SREB to expand its scope to a national program). Those conferences explored such matters as teaching materials, field training, and collaboration with state and local mental health treatment programs for clinical training of students and for the development of jobs for graduates. SREB also kept and reported data about the new training programs, their faculty qualifications, their students, their curricula, and the fate of their graduates after graduation.

Once there were sufficient numbers of graduates out in the work force, it became apparent that many of the graduates had obtained jobs in a variety of community programs in which they used the knowledge and skills for which they were trained, but the jobs did not carry "mental health" titles (e.g. jobs in senior centers or assisted living facilities, youth development programs, advocacy programs), and so it seemed wise to broaden the title of the training programs to "Human Services." This change took place over a period of years.

With later grant support from NIMH, SREB brought together educators to create the National Organization of Human Service Educators (NOHSE) and a National Organization of Human Service Workers and a program for certifying the competence of those human service workers. Both the organization of workers and the certification program were later abandoned after the SREB projects ended, and the workers found they were unable to financially support such organizational programs on the somewhat slim salaries that many of them earned as entry-level workers.

By the time the SREB projects ended, there were approximately 400 Human Service training programs across the nation—nearly three fourths of them at the Associate of Arts level in community colleges, but many at the baccalaureate level. Many of the graduates of those early programs had obtained appropriate human service positions in a very wide variety of public and private agencies; some had risen to supervisory and administrative positions; many others had gone on for further education to specialize in social work, psychology or counseling.

In the 1980s the nation went through a phase of social conservatism during which funds for human service programs were cut back, and many human service institutions and agencies were shut down. Some human service education programs were cut out or combined with related programs; and a fair number of workers lost their jobs. But despite those problems the Human Services movement has continued strong as newer agencies have been established at the community level. NOHSE has continued and carried the responsibility for further refining the education programs, establishing a Code of Ethics, and establishing Human Services as an independent occupational/professional entity.

**A**
(1) In research and behavior modification, a baseline measure. (2) In rational-emotive behavior therapy, an activating event. *See AB/ABAB design, A-B-C/A-B-C-D-E theory, and baseline.*

**AA**
*See Alcoholics Anonymous.*

**AACD**
*See American Association for Counseling and Development.*

**AAMFT**
*See American Association for Marriage and Family Therapy.*

**AB/ABAB design**
A two-phase continuous measurement research design popular with behaviorists in which A equals the baseline and B the intervention/treatment process. Can be extended to an ABAB format in order to rule out confounding variables by noting whether the second AB pattern mimics the first AB pattern. Generally used with a single subject.

**ABC model of crisis intervention**
A model suggested by Kristi Kanel for dealing with clients immobilized by an emergency. The practitioner should: A, use basic attending skills to establish rapport with the client and maintain contact; B, identify the problem; and C, explore new coping skills with the client.

### A-B-C/A-B-C-D-E theory
A principle of Albert Ellis's rational-emotive behavior psychotherapy in which A equals an activating event, B the individual's belief system, and C an emotional consequence. At D the counselor then disputes B if it is irrational or illogical (i.e., D stands for dispute), which results in E, a new healthier emotional consequence.

### abandonment
(1) Occurs when a helper terminates a client without informing the client of this fact. This is generally considered an ethical violation. A helper can ethically terminate a client (i.e., it is not abandonment) even if the client insists on returning for services if the helper believes he or she has genuinely tried to help the client for a reasonable period of time but cannot, or if the helper believes another provider would be more competent. (2) In child abuse, the act of leaving a child alone.

### abasement
Henry Murray's term to describe the need to comply, atone, confess, surrender, or even accept punishment due to feelings of inadequacy.

### abatement
To reduce or eliminate unwanted symptoms or pain.

### abclution
To reject the process of acculturation.

### aberration
(1) A tendency to depart or stray from normal thoughts, feelings, or behavior. (2) A disorder.

### ability tests
Used to determine one's talents and proficiencies. Measures of aptitude assess potential performance, while measures of achievement assess current skills. In some of the older literature, the term is loosely used as a synonym for aptitude.

### abnormal
(1) Thoughts, feelings, and/or behavior that deviate from the normal adjustment process or cause problems for the individual and/or society. Often abnormality is defined in relation to a given theory of personality or culture. (2) Can also refer to a statistical score outside of the normal range and includes positive attributes such as genius.

**absent parent**
A parent who is not living with his or her children.

**absolute poverty**
The notion that a given (i.e., numerical) income is necessary to reach a minimal level of subsistence. Often contrasted with "relative poverty" which implies that the person's standard of living exceeds the subsistence level but is below others who live in the community.

**absolutist thinking**
In rational emotive behavior therapy created by Albert Ellis, the notion that thinking in terms of absolutes ("I must do this," or "I should do that," or "I ought to be able to") is unhealthy and leads to human unhappiness.

**abreaction**
A psychoanalytic term that describes a client's expression of a repressed emotion. Originally used to describe a release via hypnosis. In the popular press the term "catharsis" is often used synonymously. The emotional release is viewed as curative.

**abscissa**
The horizontal reference line on a graph often used to plot the independent/experimental variable. Also known as the $x$ axis.

**abstinence**
The practice of voluntarily refraining from a given action (e.g., not drinking alcohol or not engaging in sex).

**abstract**
(1) The ability to understand symbolic concepts. (2) A brief synopsis of a journal article that appears just under the title of the article and before the actual article begins. By reading the synopsis, the human services worker can usually ascertain if the article is pertinent to one's area of interest.

**abuse**
To mistreat or harm another individual (e.g., child abuse) or yourself (e.g., self-mutilation or substance abuse) in a physical or emotional manner.

**ACA**
*See American Counseling Association.*

**accelerated learning**
The act of giving a child learning experiences that are usually reserved for older children. Intended primarily for gifted or talented children.

**accommodation**
(1) In Piaget's theory, the act of accommodating/modifying cognitive patterns (known as schemes) to understand new objects and/or experiences. A breast-fed baby, for example, will need to alter a cognitive scheme to begin drinking from a cup. *See assimilation and equilibration/ equilibrium.* (2) Counselors loosely use the term to describe a change in one's way of thinking or behavior to fit a new situation.

**accountability**
(1) Implies that human service workers can document or calculate the effectiveness of the treatment process. (2) The notion that counselors and clients are responsible or accountable for their actions. Documentation for insurance companies or third-party payors to verify that a given course of intervention was necessary and which is then provided as an example.

**accreditation**
A process by which an agency or association recognizes that a program has met certain established qualifications, requirements, and standards. A human services program in a college might seek accreditation via the Council for Standards in Human Service Education (CSHE), while a graduate counseling program would seek accreditation from The Council for the Accreditation of Counseling and Related Programs (CACREP). The American Psychological Association (APA) accredits psychology programs. Social work programs would be evaluated by the Council for Social Work Education (CSWE). Hospitals are accedited via the Joint Commission on Accreditation of Hospitals, while suicide and crisis hotlines/helplines generally use Amercian Association of Suicidology (AAS) standards.

**acculturation**
The process of learning the behaviors and expectations of a culture. This is an anthropological term that is sometimes used to describe the process an individual goes through when he or she transfers into a new culture and attempts to assimilate new customs.

**A-head**
Slang for an individual who uses amphetamines. *See amphetamines.*

**achievement test**
A measure of what a person has already learned or achieved in terms of knowledge, performance, or skill. Achievement tests can be contrasted to aptitude tests (or ability tests in earlier literature), which measure an individual's potential.

**acid**
Slang for LSD. *See LSD.*

**acid freak**
Slang for an individual who uses LSD. *See LSD.*

**Acquired Immune Deficiency Syndrome (AIDS)**
At present, a disease which is considered fatal inasmuch as the immune system shuts down and any infection can prove deadly. The HIV virus, which is transmitted via sexual contact or through the blood stream (e.g., blood transfusions or substance abusers sharing needles), is thought to cause the disease.

**acquisition**
(1) Learning a new thought, behavior, or feeling. (2) The strengthening of a new thought, behavior, or feeling through learning. (3) Thoughts, feelings, and behaviors which are not innate or inherited. (4) The process of gaining goods or possessions.

**acrophobia**
An exaggerated irrational fear of high places.

**acting out**
(1) (Psychoanalytic theory) Acting as if a current situation is the situation that originally caused the strong feelings being expressed. Acting out is symbolic of an earlier life experience and is controlled by unconscious conflicts. A counselee's feeling of transference to a counselor, for example, could relate to a strong feeling toward a parent or caretaker initially manifested at an early age. (2) A dysfunctional expression of a repressed drive or wish. The person will often display irrational violence or act in an irresponsible manner.

**action**
Slang for the act of gambling or placing a bet.

**active crisis state**
The point at which an individual who is experiencing a crisis realizes that his or her modalities of coping are ineffective and is motivated to secure or accept help.

**active-directive counseling/therapy**
Any approach in which the counselor actively directs the topic and the nature of the session (e.g., rational-emotive behavior therapy). Directive approaches are sometimes labeled didactic since the counselor acts as a teacher and suggests specific strategies for the client. Active-directive interventions can be contrasted with passive nondirective models such as person-centered counseling.

**active listening**
(1) The process of listening and then responding to the client (e.g., asking questions or reflecting) in a manner that lets the client know you are truly listening. Active listening conveys an attitude of respect. (2) Attending to the client's verbal and nonverbal actions without judgment to enhance rapport, self-disclosure, and exploration.

**actualization**
Insight regarding one's full potential or the acts of trying to achieve such potential.

**acute**
A serious mental or physical disturbance that comes on suddenly but that has a short duration (i.e., generally less than six months). Acute conditions are often contrasted with chronic long-standing problems which are not short term.

**acute leukemia**
The uncontrolled production and accumulation of immature white blood cells from cancerous blood-forming tissues. The progression of this form of leukemia is much more rapid than other forms. Common symptoms of leukemia are anemia, pale skin, weakness, bruising, and bleeding. *See chronic leukemia.*

**adaptation**
Changing thoughts, feelings, and behaviors to meet the environment. The word "adjustment" is often utilized. *See adjustment.*

**adapted child**
In transactional analysis, the Child ego state is the part of the personality that houses the natural child impulses and experiences of infancy and early childhood. The Child ego state can be further broken down into the Natural Child, the Adapted Child, and the Little Professor. The Adapted Child is the entity that alters and modifies behavior as a result of parent or caretaker demands. The Adapted Child tries to please parents or adapts by whining, procrastinating, and/or withdrawing. *See Transactional Analysis (TA).*

**ADC**
*See TA and TANF.*

**addiction**
A physical and/or emotional overdependence on alcohol or other drugs. Technically, a pure addiction is characterized via an abstinence syndrome in which the individual experiences withdrawal symptomatology. The World Health Organization recommends the term *dependence.* Recently popular behavioral science literature has utilized the term *codependency* to suggest that an individual has an addiction to another person. A person may also be addicted to an activity such as sex or gambling.

**ad hoc**
Comes from the Latin, "for this purpose." In human services the term is generally used in research when a hypothesis is developed after the data have been collected. Can also refer to a hypothesis that is created to explain data which does not fit into a current theory.

**adjunct to counseling/psychotherapy**
Therapeutic measures that supplement or aid the helping process such as recreation therapy, art therapy, or parenting classes.

**adjustment**
Living in harmony with the environment while satisfying one's needs. The word *adaptation* is often utilized, although the term is intended to convey positive connotations and serve as a goal for the client. Human service workers are critical of the fact that all too often adjustment implies conformity.

**adjustment disorder**
A category used in the *DSM-IV-TR* to delineate a reaction which can be traced to concrete life circumstances. Such a reaction abates as the person is better able to cope with the circumstances.

**Adler, Alfred (1870–1937)**
A Viennese psychiatrist who founded comparative-individual psychology, which is more commonly referred to as *individual psychology*. Most of the literature simply refers to the term *individual psychology*. This school asserts that behavior is an unconscious result of attempting to compensate for feelings of inferiority. When an inferiority complex results from feelings related to a given body part it is termed organ inferiority. Overcompensation for a perceived deficiency is seen as neurotic. Adler's therapeutic intervention stresses one's lifestyle (e.g., social and vocational facets).

**Adult ego state**
Transactional analysis structural theory conceptualizes the personality using three ego states: the Parent, the Adult, and the Child. The Adult ego state roughly corresponds to Freud's ego and is the rational, accountable, unemotional, thinking and processing center of the personality that operates on logic. The Adult ego state is also called the *neopsyche. See Transactional Analysis (TA).*

**adventitious disability/handicap**
Any disability or handicap which develops after birth. Often contrasted with congenital conditions which are present at birth.

**adverse**
A negative or unwanted side effect or condition.

**advocate/advocacy role**
To plead for the rights of a client or a group of clients. The worker assists, defends, or represents the client so he or she can obtain services, a job, fair treatment, etc. The helper might even attend a public forum or a legal proceeding. This term is often used in conjunction with intervention for the disabled.

**AFDC**
*See TA and TANF.*

**affect/affective**
Refers to emotions, feelings, pleasantness, unpleasantness, or mood. On occasion counseling literature uses the word affect in place of the word emotion. Affective processes and disorders are seen as separate from those of a cognitive (i.e., thinking and/or intellectual) nature.

**affective disorder**
A disorder involving one's mood. Often means depression.

**affiliation**
The need for association, closeness, love, friendships, cooperation, or group involvement. A popular term in social psychology and personality literature. Henry Murray saw affiliation as a basic human need.

**affirmative hypothesis**
*See alternative hypothesis.*

**aftercare**
Intervention or follow-up procedures utilized after a hospital, day hospital, or inpatient program; often referred to as continuing care.

**ageism/agism**
(1) A tendency to look upon the elderly in a negative manner or discriminate against older persons based on their age. (2) Prejudice or discrimination based on one's age.

**age regression**
A procedure whereby an adult is hypnotized such that he or she experiences life at an earlier age. The technique is often used to help the client recall information repressed during a childhood trauma.

**aggression/aggressiveness**
(1) A tendency to express hostility or hurt people and/or things. (2) To dominate, insult, or injure others in a sadistic manner. (3) In assertiveness training, a communication that puts down or hurts another person such that the person feels his or her rights have been violated; the recipient of the aggressive communication may feel humiliated. (4) A natural reaction to frustation according to the frustration-aggression hypothesis. Some helpers feel that if clients believe in this notion it will lead to dysfunctional behavior and is not accurate.

**agitated depression**
Depression with extreme restlessness.

**A-ha experience**
Also known as insight, the term describes a reaction at a given point in time when an individual puts two or more factors together and subsequently understands or solves a problem.

**agoraphobia**
A fear of open spaces. Often clients with agoraphobia dread leaving home or going outdoors. Persons with this affliction usually suffer from panic disorder (i.e., panic disorder with agoraphobia); however, this is not always the case. Those who do suffer from panic disorder often fear that help might not be available should they have a panic attack.

**ahistoric counseling**
A counseling technique or theory that does not emphasize the past but rather focuses on the here and now. An ahistorical approach does not assume that early life experiences need to be examined in order to change current behaviors.

**ain't it awful**
In transactional analysis, an unproductive pastime that consists of complaining about a situation rather than engaging in productive activity.

**airhead**
(1) Slang for an individual who is not very intelligent or does not use commonsense. (2) Slang for a person who uses marijuana.

**Al-Anon**
A voluntary support group for family members living in a household with an alcoholic.

**Alateen**
A voluntary support group for teens with alcoholic parents or caretakers.

**Alcoholics Anonymous (AA)**
A voluntary worldwide supportive fellowship founded by Bill Wilson in 1936. Self-help groups in the program use a 12-step model and sponsors. Though the program emphasizes spirituality and a higher power, it is not associated with any religion.

**alcohol dependence/alcoholism**
(1) A condition that results from excessive habitual, compulsive, or addictive use of the drug alcohol. In its most severe form it can lead to alcohol psychosis (e.g., Korsakov's psychosis characterized by confabulation and memory impairment or delirium tremens in which trembling and hallucinations occur) or death. (2) According to the joint committee of the National Council on Alcoholism and Drug Dependence, Inc. and the American Society of Addiction Medicine, alcoholism is a primary, chronic disease with genetic, psychosocial, and environmental factors influencing its development and manifestations. It is often progressive and fatal. It is characterized via continuous or periodic drinking, using alcohol despite adverse consequences, and distortions in thinking, generally denial.

**alcoholomania/alcoholophilia**
A pathological craving/love for the drug alcohol.

**alcohol withdrawal**
Refers to any physical and/or psychological symptoms that occur as a result of curbing alcohol consumption or totally abstaining from the drug. Weakness, nausea, depression, tachycardia, increased anxiety, shaking (i.e., tremors), and delusions are commonly experienced.

**Alexander, Franz (1891–1964)**
A Hungarian psychoananlyst associated with the University of Chicago who helped popularize the concepts of brief analytic therapy and psychosomatic medicine.

**alexia**
Loss of ability to understand written words and/or sentences.

**algorithms**
A procedure in which an individual considers every possible solution to a problem.

**alien**
This term is used in multicultural counseling to describe an individual who is living in a given country but is not legally a citizen of that country.

**alienation**
(1) In existential therapy, the feeling that life is meaningless or that one is separated from society. (2) A feeling of being alone; having no friendships with others.

### alloplastic/alloplasty
The process of coping with a situation by attempting to change the environment rather than making changes in yourself. In psychoanalysis this denotes that an individual is turning the libido toward the environment. Can be contrasted with autoplastic/autoplasty in which the individual makes changes in the self.

### Allport, Gordon Willard (1897–1967)
A U.S. psychologist who taught at Harvard and stressed conscious rather than unconscious processes. He believed in idiographic research (i.e., studying individuals) rather than nomothetic research (i.e., studying groups of individuals to create general principles). He is best known for his "psychology of individuality." The theory postulates that the personality is psychosocial (i.e., molded by psychological and physical factors). The personality is also viewed as dynamic, meaning it continuously changes and adjusts to the environment. He emphasized that personality traits (called personal dispositions in his later writings) cause individuals to behave in predictable ways (e.g., an aggressive person views a myriad of situations as calling for aggressive behavior). According to Allport there are (a) common traits that appear in everyone, (b) personal traits, and (c) a cardinal or dominant trait. His "Allport-Vernon Study of Values" measures the values/traits of religion, aesthetic, theoretical, economic, social, and political orientations.

### alms
Giving money, services, or gifts in kind to the poor. A charitable donation.

### almshouses
Shelters that resulted from the 1601 *Poor Law* for individuals who were unable to care for themselves. Sometimes referred to as *poorhouses*.

### alpha alcoholism
Espoused by the Jellinek Model of Alcoholism, excessive or inappropriate drinking without any loss of control or the inability to abstain. The person is said to use alcohol as a means of trying to cope with life stresses.

### Alpha Delta Omega
*See National Human Services Honor Society Alpha Delta Omega.*

26

**alpha error**
The probability that a researcher will reject a null hypothesis when it is actually true. Also known as a Type I error, the alpha error factor is numerically equal to the signficance or confidence level.

**alpha level**
Also called the level of significance or the level of confidence. The probability of committing a Type I error (i.e., rejecting a valid null hypothesis). In human services research the 05 level, and the 01 level have been the most popular alpha levels.

**alpha rhythm/alpha waves**
A biofeedback term used to describe brain wave frequencies of 8 to 12 cycles per second (cps) or 8 to 12 Hertz (Hz). The reading and feedback are provided by an electroencephalogram (EEG). Alpha waves are also known as Berger rhythm and are associated with relaxation but not sleep, hence the term *wakeful relaxation* has been used to describe the state. *See beta rhythm/beta waves, biofeedback, and delta rhythm/delta waves.*

**altered state**
Any state of consciousness that deviates from the normal conscious experience. This state could be induced via drugs, medicinals, ecstasy, meditation, biofeedback, autogenic training, illness, a near death experience, or a peak emotional experience.

**alternate forms**
An interchangeable version of a test that will yield equivalent results. Alternate forms are also called *comparable forms, parallel forms,* or *equivalent forms* and must have similar, if not identical, statistical properties (i.e., mean, standard deviation, and standard error of measurement). Test reliability can be assessed by administering alternate forms of the same test to the same group of individuals and computing a correlation coefficient.

**alternative hypothesis**
A research term. (1) The experimental hypothesis sometimes known as the *affirmative,* or *empirical hypothesis.* (2) An hypothesis which asserts that the null hypothesis is not true.

**altruism/altruistic**
A term coined by the French philosopher Auguste Comte (1798–1857). Altruistic behavior can include any action that is intended to help another person but offers no extrinsic reward (e.g., making an anonymous donation to charity which does not result in a tax deduction). Caring about others' needs and welfare more than your own. Altruistic individuals are never selfish and often behave in a self-sacrificing manner (e.g., attempting to rescue a pet in a burning building).

**Alzheimer's diease**
A dementia causing senility in which brain cells deteriorate at a rapid rate. It is progressive and currently irreversible. Although it is more common in those over seventy years of age it can occur in those who are younger. Common signs include impaired memory, confusion, marked personality changes, and very poor judgment. The etiology is unknown but researchers suspect genetic factors and the toxic inorganic form of the trace mineral aluminum. A diet rich in the nutrient folic acid seems to provide a mild protective effect in regard to the condition.

**ambidextrous**
A person who is able to use either hand equally well. Not having a hand preference.

**ambiguous stimulus**
The term generally refers to a picture or design used in a projective test (e.g., the Thematic Apperception Test or the Rorschach Inkblot Test). Since the stimulus is vague the assumption is made that the individual's personality determines what is perceived. Often the figure, picture, pattern, or design can seem to change as the individual looks at it. Hence, a drawing of an old woman may appear to be that of a young woman if the person continues to stare at it.

**ambivalence/ambivalent**
(1) A state in which two opposite or otherwise contradictory emotions exist simultaneously. A suicidal individual who wishes to die may, for example, telephone a counseling center or a crisis hotline for help. (2) A tendency to shift emotions rapidly in regard to another person or situation. For example, a husband breaking up with his wife can't decide whether he loves her or hates her.

**ambiversion/ambivert**
Carl Jung's term for an individual who has nearly identical introverted and extroverted tendencies. The two forces are balanced.

**ambulatory**
(1) In rehabilitation counseling, the ability to walk. (2) Treatment and/or care which is not characterized by confinement or institutionalization.

**American Association of Counseling and Development (AACD)**
*See American Counseling Association.*

**American Association for Marriage and Family Therapy (AAMFT)**
Originally founded in 1942 as the American Association of Marriage Counselors, this organization is open to professionals of various disciplines interested in marriage and family therapy. Student memberships for those in graduate school are available but require the signature of two clinical members as well as a signature from a department chairman in an accredited program of marriage and family therapy. Student membership is terminated when the person receives a graduate degree and/or has been a student member for five years. The organization disseminates information via the "Journal of Marital and Family Therapy" and the "Family Therapy News." Members must abide by the AAMFT Code of Ethics.

**American Counseling Association (ACA)**
A national organization for counselors offering professional (i.e., a master's degree or higher) and regular membership. All members must abide by the association's ethical standards. The organization was originally formed in July of 1952 and called the American Personnel and Guidance Association (APGA). In July of 1983, after a member vote by mail, the APGA board changed the name to the American Association for Counseling and Development (AACD). On July 1, 1992, after a membership vote, the current name American Counseling Association (ACA) went into effect. The new name is intended to clarify the identity of the association's members and what they do. The organization has 17 divisions or organizational affiliate selections for members: (1) Association for Assessment and Counseling (AAC); (2) Association for Adult Development and Aging (AADA); (3) American College Counseling Association; (4) Association for Counselors and Educators in Government; (4) Association for Counselor Education and Supervision (ACES); (5) Association for Gay, Lesbian, and Bisexual Issues in

Counseling (AGLBIC); (6) Association for Multicultural Counseling and Development (AMCD); (7) American Mental Health Counselors Association (AMHCA); (8) American Rehabilitation Counseling Association (ARCA); (9) American School Counselor Association (ASCA); (10) Association for Spiritual, Ethical, and Religious Values in Counseling (ASERVIC); (11) Association for Specialists in Group Work (ASGW); (12) Counseling Association for Humanistic Education and Development (C-AHEAD); (13) Counselors for Social Justice (CSJ); (14) International Association of Addictions and Offender Counselors (IAAAOC); (15) International Association of Marriage and Family Counselors (IAMFC); (16) National Career Development Association (NCDA); (17) National Employment Counseling Association (NECA). In 2002 the organization had approximately 55,000 members.

### American Personnel and Guidance Association (APGA)
*See American Counseling Association (ACA).*

### American Psychiatric Association (APA)
National organization for physicians who specialize in psychiatry. The organization was founded in 1844 as the Association of Medical Superintendents of American Institutions for the Insane. The organization changed its name to the American Medico-Psychological Association in 1891, and took on its current name in 1921.

### American Psychoanalytic Association (APA)
An umbrella organization for psychoanalysts who practice interventions based on or derived from Freudian theory. The organization was established in 1911 and helps to maintain standards for training analysts.

### American Psychological Association (APA)
Also known as the big APA since it has a larger membership than the other two APAs (the American Psychiatric Association and the American Psychoanalytic Association). A national organization for psychologists founded in 1892.

### Americans with Disabilities Act (ADA)
A 1992 act that stipulates that qualified individuals with disabilities cannot be discriminated against, especially in job situations.

### amnesia/amnestic Disorder
An inability to remember or recall. A loss of memory. *See anterograde amnesia and retrograde amnesia.*

**amphetamines**
A class of stimulant drugs (originally used as bronchial dialators) that energize the individual, increase alertness, ward off sleep, and induce euphoria. Amphetamines such as Benzedrine and Dexadrine have been used to fight fatigue and curb appetite. Ironically, amphetamine-like medicinals (e.g., Ritalin) are also prescribed to control hyperactivity in children. Some experts are critical of both of the aforementioned procedures, though the practice does often produce the desired result. Amphetamines are also known as *uppers, beans, beenies, truck drivers, white crosses, dex,* in the case of Dexadrine, *crystal* for Desoxyn, or *speed.* They are addictive and the dosage required often increases (i.e., habituation occurs) with tolerance. Amphetamines tax the circulatory system and can induce psychosis and death.

**anaclitic**
Being dependent on one's mother or mother substitute for a feeling of well-being. A normal stage of early development.

**anaclitic depression**
Depression abetted by the loss of a mother or father.

**analogy**
A relationship between two things or events that are in one sense the same yet in another different. For example: Glasser is to reality therapy as Perls is to gestalt therapy. In this case both men created a school of counseling, though the schools themselves are different. Counselors sometimes use an analogy to explain a principle to a client and analogy questions are common on many tests and exams (e.g., Glasser is to reality therapy as Perls is to _____.)

**anal expulsive character**
According to psychoanalytic theory, a generous, messy, aggressive individual fixated in the anal stage. Theoretically, such an individual found defecation intensely pleasurable.

**anal retentive character/anal character**
According to psychoanalytic theory, an obstinate, orderly, stingy, individual fixated in the anal phase. Theoretically, such an individual fought his parents by trying to retain feces during toilet training.

**anal stage**
The second stage in Freud's psychosocial developmental theory (i.e., oral, anal, phallic, latency, and genital) which takes place during the second and third years of life. The individual receives gratification via defecation.

**analysand**
Someone who is undergoing psychoanalysis.

**analysis**
(1) Short for the procedure or personality theory of psychoanalysis. (2) The first step in E.G. Williamson's directive counseling approach in which data are collected. (3) Investigating and explaining data revealed through observation or statistical techniques.

**analysis of covariance (ANACOVA/ANCOVA)**
An inferential statistical test used to test a null hypothesis between two or more groups. The analysis of covariance is an extension of the analysis of variance (ANOVA) that controls the impact that one or more extraneous unstudied variables (known as covariates) exert on the dependent variable. It is a parametric statistic indicating whether differences in the dependent variable are greater than chance. *See analysis of variance.*

**analysis of variance (ANOVA)**
Also called a one-way analysis of variance, this inferential statistical test is used to determine whether two or more mean scores differ from each other. The ANOVA examines a null hypothesis between two or more groups. An ANOVA provides $F$ values. An $F$ test is used to discover if significant differences are present. It is a parametric statistic indicating whether differences in the dependent variable are greater than chance. A counseling researcher, for example, might compare anxiety levels in a control group, a group receiving six sessions of gestalt therapy, and a group receiving nine sessions of gestalt therapy. The ANOVA would examine whether a significant difference existed between the groups.

**analytic psychology**
The school of psychology created by the Swiss psychiatrist Carl Gustav Jung focusing on the collective unconscious. *See archetypes.*

**androgynous/androgny**
(1) Having both male and female traits and characteristics. (2) Expressing both male and female qualities or roles. (3) A hermaphodite with an excess of male characteristics.

**anecdotal report**
A written or verbal account of one's observations. Generally anecdotal reports are not accepted as scientific experimental data since replication is nearly impossible.

**angel dust**
Slang for the hallucinogenic drug PCP (phencyclidine). PCP also goes under the street name of Love Boat. It is highly addictive and can cause psychotic-like symptoms.

**angst**
A German word meaning anxiety or psychic pain. Primarily used in the literature discussing psychoanalysis and existential therapy. A condition in which an individual does not experience pleasure from situations which would normally evoke it. A symptom often seen in depression and schizophrenic states.

**anhedonia**
Occurs when one is unable to feel pleasure when experiencing situations that usually elicit it. Can be abetted via drug use, especially cocaine and crack.

**anima**
In Jung's theory, the feminine archetype or side of the personality. Can be contrasted to the *animus,* the male archetype or side of the personality. Jung suggested that both archetypes are present in both sexes.

**animal magnetism**
A term coined by Friedrich (Franz) Anton Mesmer who felt that a person could use a magnetic universal force to influence others. The procedure was later refined by Mesmer's students and labelled *hypnosis.*

**animism**
Attributing human or personal characteristics (e.g., spiritual elements) to inanimate objects. This is common in young children. A child, for example, might say, "My doll has fun when I take her to the zoo."

**animus**
In Jung's theory, the masculine archetype or side of the personality. Can be contrasted to the *anima,* the feminine achetype or side of the personality. Jung suggested that both achetypes are present in both sexes.

**anniversary reaction**
A reaction, feeling, behavior, or mood, related to a previous event or set of events. An individual, for example, who killed another individual in an auto accident might become depressed or wish to take his own life on the anniversary date of the event.

**anorexia nervosa**
An eating disorder characterized by a dire fear of obesity and/or a preoccupation with one's weight. Anorexia literally means "lacking in appetite." Failure to eat or a tendency toward self-starvation are typical symptoms. Can lead to malnutrition or death. Afflicts primarily females in the teen years and is much rarer in those over 30. Anorexic conditions are more common in middle-class and upper-class families. In the counseling setting, the anorexic client will often feel fat even when his or her weight is ideal.

**anorexia, sexual**
This term implies a loss of appetite for sex or a lack of sexual desire.

**anorgasmia**
Generally used in sex counseling/therapy, refers to a client's inability to achieve orgasm.

**antabuse**
The brand name for the drug disulfiram, which is used to treat alcoholism. The drug normally does not induce discomfort; however, when alcoholic beverages are ingested nausea, vomiting, dizziness, caridiac awareness, and headache generally occur. Success using antabuse as an aversive stimulus has been disappointing. Treatment via this method is not always safe.

**antecedent**
A common term in behavior modification that refers to a condition that precedes (i.e., comes before) a phenomenon. A positive reinforcer, for example, is said to raise the probability that an antecedent (i.e., previous) behavior will occur. Giving the reinforcer before the behavior occurs is often termed a bribe and is very ineffective if it works at all.

### anterograde amnesia
A memory disorder often abetted via a traumatic experience and characterized by the inability to store information after experiencing amnesia. Prior memory is not altered. If, for example, an individual is sexually abused and experiences anterograde amnesia, the memories prior to the abuse will still be retrievable and intact. The phenomenon is also termed "continuous amnesia." *See retrograde amnesia.*

### antianxiety drug/medication
A class of drugs/medicinals (e.g., major and minor tranquilizers) that reduce or abate anxiety. Popular major tranquilizers used to control psychotic symptoms include Mellaril, Thorazine, and Stellazine. Valium, Librium, Xanax, and Tranxene are popular minor tranquilizers used for anxiety conditions. Some of the literature uses the term *anxiolytics. See benzodiazepines.*

### antidepressant
A nutrient (e.g., L-tyrosine), an herb (e.g., St. John's Wort), or more likely a drug (e.g., Zoloft) which helps reduce or eliminate depression and improves mood. Antidepressant drugs do not alter the mood of those who are not experiencing a depressive episode. Three popular categories of traditional antidepressants include: Mononamine oxidase inhibitors (MAO's) such as Nardil; trycyclics such as Imipramine; and serotonin blockers such as Prozac. Human service workers as well as licensed counselors, social workers, and psychologists are not qualified to give prescription medicinals and thus must ethically refer the client to a physician (e.g., D.O. or M.D. psychiatrist) when antidepressants are deemed necessary. Some states may allow psychologists to prescribe in the near future.

### antideterministic
Purports that individuals are not merely the result of biological and genetic factors and therefore can influence their own destiny. This view also stipulates that environmental factors can be extremely important.

### antisocial behavior/personality
A behavior carried out without conscience. A person with an antisocial personality can commit crimes (e.g., murder) without feeling a sense of guilt, remorse, or anxiety. The literature will often refer to those with antisocial tendencies as psychopaths or sociopaths.

**anxiety**
(1) A feeling of dread or extreme fear without awareness of what is causing the distress. Often distinguished from a phobia where the person is
aware of what is causing the apprehension (i.e., a phobia of furry white
animals). (2) Often used in a loose nontechnical manner to mean scared,
afraid, or nervous.

**anxiety attack**
A state of extreme anxiety generally accompanied by cardiac awareness,
tightness in the chest, sweaty palms, inability to breathe properly, and
trembling. Persons having an attack often secure medical help believing
they are having a heart attack. The duration of the attacks is often brief,
but several attacks can occur daily. Anxiety attacks are often called *panic
attacks* or *panic disorder.*

**anxiety disorder**
In the *DSM-IV-TR,* a condition that is primarily characterized by an anxiety reaction. This would include panic disorder with and without agoraphobia, agoraphobia without any history of panic disorder, simple phobia,
social phobia, obsessive-compulsive disorder, post-traumatic stress disorder, and generalized anxiety disorder.

**anxiety hierarchy**
This concept is associated with Joseph Wolpe's systematic desensitization.
The client and the counselor work together to rank order anxiety-producing
situations. Ideally, the hierarchy will include 10 to 15 items spaced equidis-
tant in terms of the anxiety each induces. The client is then asked to relax
(training in relaxation is provided) and imagine each item beginning with
the one which produces the least anxiety and working up the ranks until
the most difficult scene can be imagined without anxiety. In-vivo or "live"
desensitization is often implemented after the client has successfully mastered most of the hierarchy in the imagination. *See systematic desensitization.*

**APA**
In human service literature this abbreviation will most likely refer to the
American Psychological Association, but could also refer to the Ameri-
can Psychiatric Association, or the American Psychoanalytic Association.
*See American Psychiatric Association, American Psychoanalytic Association,
and American Psychological Association.*

**apathy**
A lack of emotion or indifference. A common symptom of depression.

**aphasia**
Loss of language/speech abilities due to organic cerebral damage. In visual aphasia the individual cannot comprehend written information. In auditory aphasia there is an inability to understand that which is heard, and in amnesic aphasia language cannot be remembered.

**applied behavior analysis**
A scientific approach to behavior modification. A target behavior is measured via a baseline, a treatment goal is set, and then variables are manipulated using operant conditioning procedures to secure the desired results.

**appraisal**
The practice of assessing or evaluating an individual.

**approach-approach conflict**
A situation where an individual is confronted with two equally attractive, positive, gratifying options (e.g., choosing between two top-rated graduate programs in counselor education that have accepted you).

**approach-avoidance conflict**
A situation where an individual is both attracted to and repelled by a course of action (e.g., a new counseling group member wants to get to know others but is afraid she will be rejected if she attempts to do so).

**aptitude test**
Measures potential, capacity, future performance, knowledge, or skill in a given area. Often loosely called *tests of ability*. An aptitude test predicts probable success or lack of it in a new skill. Aptitude tests are often contrasted with achievement tests that assess actual (i.e., current) behavior.

**archetype**
In Carl Jung's analytical psychology theory, an archetype is an unconscious idea, symbol, or pattern which is contained in the collective unconscious. Archetypes have existed since the beginning of time and are passed from generation to generation. Jung felt he validated the concept by pointing out that certain symbols are universal and have remained constant over time regardless of one's culture. Primal symbols such as the cross appear in every era of history and mythology.

**arthritis**
*See rheumatoid arthritis.*

### art therapy

The client in art therapy either creates a work of art (e.g., a painting or sculpture) or is exposed to artwork. In both scenarios, the focus is on the client's reactions and feelings toward the artwork. Art therapists often need to meet the standards of the American Art Therapy Association (AATA). This organization also sets practices for art therapy training programs.

### Asch situation

A test of conformity named after social psychology researcher Solomon Asch. An individual is placed in a group setting and falsely led to believe that others in the group perceive a given situation in a different manner. An individual placed in this situation often conforms and agrees with the other group members even if they are obviously wrong!

### Asian American

A U.S. resident who identifies with Chinese, Vietnamese, Japanese, Filipinos, Thais, Laotians, Koreans, Samoans, or other Pacific Asians. Sometimes called *Pacific Islanders*.

### assertiveness training

A behavioristic procedure used to train persons to discriminate between nonassertive, assertive, and aggressive modes of communication such that the person can learn to respond in an assertive manner. Modeling, role playing, and behavior rehearsal are used to instill new behavioral patterns. Assertive behavior occurs when a person stands up for himself or herself without violating the rights of others. A refinement of Andrew Salter's conditioned reflex therapy delineated in 1949.

### assessment

Individual or group evaluations using formal (e.g., standardized tests) and/or informal (e.g., observations, interviews, checklists, etc.) methodology. Often used as a synonym for evaluation.

### assimilation

In Piaget's theory, the act of acquiring new information using one's current cognitive patterns or schema. *See accommodation and equilibration.*

### assistant

Sometimes known as an aid, such individuals help professionals provide services to clients.

**association**
(1) A psychological connection between two ideas or things. A client, for example, could dislike her boss because she reminds her of (i.e., she associates her with) her abusive mother. (2) An organization.

**assurance**
A statement or intervention on the part of a counselor that removes a client's doubts and uncertainties and enhances confidence (e.g., "I'm certain your decision to assert yourself is a step in the right direction"). Some of the literature uses the term *reassurance*.

**ataxic aphasia**
An inability to speak or articulate.

**Atlas script**
In transactional analysis, a life theme when an individual tries to carry the weight of the world, company, department, etc. on his or her shoulders. Such an individual will overwork and try to be everything to everybody. Persons with an Atlas script often complain but secretly derive pleasure from this self-perpetuated victim role and misery.

**at-risk**
A person who has a high probability of developing a problem due to genetics, behavior, or environmental conditions. A woman, for example, who smokes, uses drugs, and drinks alcohol throughout her pregnancy will have a child who is at-risk of having birth defects. At-risk individuals are often called "vulnerable" populations in the literature.

**attempter**
Short for a suicide attempter who has attempted to take his or her own life but has failed. Often confused with the term *survivor,* which refers to an individual who has lost a friend or loved one via suicide.

**attending/attentiveness**
Behavior on the part of a counselor that enhances the communication process and thus builds rapport (e.g., open posture, active listening, and good eye contact). The counselor gives the client his or her complete attention such that the client is aware that the counselor is listening.

**attention deficit disorder (ADD)**
A *DSM-III-R* diagnostic category. *See attention deficit hyperactivity disorder (ADHD).*

**attention deficit hyperactivity disorder (ADHD)**
Older literature may refer to this problem as *attention deficit disorder, hyperactive child syndrome,* or *hyperkinetic reaction.* This disorder can begin in infancy, childhood, or adolescence. Symptomotology includes an inability to concentrate, a short attention span, impulsivity, an inability to wait one's turn, and excessive motor activity. Ironically enough, in addition to counseling, biofeedback, and/or behavior modification, Ritalin (Methylphenidate), a central nervous system stimulant, has been widely used to treat the disorder. The practice of giving an amphetamine-like compound to young children has been a source of ongoing controversy, although is seems to be highly effective in some cases. Some experts believe this diagnosis is utilized too frequently and that many of these children are victims of other problems or food allergies (especially sugar).

**attitude**
A set of ideas or beliefs toward another person or object which cause us to behave in a certain manner. A human service worker, for example, who has the attitude that hyperactivity in children is purely biological might refer a hyperactive child for medical treatment without utilizing any form of counseling.

**attribute**
A characteristic, trait, or property of a person or object.

**attribution theory**
A theory of social psychology postulating that individuals are prone to give a reason, interpretation, or a cause to one's own behavior or that of another person (e.g., she quit her job due to low self-esteem). F. Hieder suggests that we evaluate others and respond to them based on our perception of their motives (i.e., why we assume they behave in a certain manner).

**atypical**
Uncommon behavior, feelings, symptoms, or thoughts; especially related to a given diagnosis (e.g., atypical psychosis).

**audit**
Refers to the assessment of an agency, hospital, or practice from a financial or a treatment perspective. The term "independent audit" implies that the audit is conducted by someone (usually an accountant) who is not associated with the organization being audited.

**audiology**
The science and study of hearing.

**augmented family**
A family situation where unrelated persons such as friends or boarders are living in the household.

**authentic/authenticity**
A helper who is genuine, real, sincere, honest, and does not put up a facade. Also called *genuineness.*

**authoritarian leadership style**
A group leadership style that is often compared and contrasted with the democratic and laissez-faire styles. Sometimes known as *autocratic leadership.* A facilitator utilizing this persuasion makes decisions for the group and limits group interaction and input from members. Although overall the democratic style is probably the most effective, an authoritarian style can be the most efficacious when an immediate decision is necessary or an emergency or crisis situation exists. *See democratic leadership and laissez-faire leadership.*

**autistic child**
A withdrawn child preoccupied with daydreaming and fantasy. Such children do not seem interested in reality and do not communicate well with others. They show an overall lack of appropriate affect and they are abusive to themselves and often aggressive toward others.

**autobiography technique**
Any strategy in which a counselor or client is asked to provide a written or verbal autobiography/personal life history. In the case of the counselor, the strategy helps the helper get to know himself or herself better. The knowledge helps the counselor understand how personal issues will impact upon topics which surface during counseling and therapy sessions. When clients are asked to perform this activity they can discover personal strengths, weaknesses, and roles. The activity also helps clients predict what will likely transpire if changes are not made and whether the present is being experienced as if it is the past.

**autocratic leadership style**
*See authoritarian leadership style.*

**autoeroticism**
Self-initiated erotic behaviors such as masturbation or sexual fantasies.

**autogenic phrases**
The practice of saying or thinking phrases which induce relaxation or self-control (e.g., My forehead is relaxed and my right hand is warm.) This practice can also be termed *self-suggestion* or *autosuggestion*. Clients utilizing autogenic phrases often use biofeedback devices to determine whether the phrases are indeed having the intended effect. *See autogenic training and biofeedback.*

**autogenic training**
A procedure that combines aspects of self-hypnosis, psychoanalysis, and yoga to learn relaxation and self-control. Although the procedure was created in 1910 by the German Johannes Schultz and became popular in Europe, it's use in the US has been primarily limited to comparing its effects to biofeedback training. Many clinicians believe that biofeedback is more scientific than autogenic training and works faster inasmuch as it provides objective physiological feedback. *See autogenic phrases and biofeedback.*

**autohypnosis**
Self-hypnosis (i.e., a state of hypnosis that is self-induced).

**autonomic nervous system (ANS)**
The portion of the nervous system that controls the smooth muscles and the glands. Autonomic nervous system functions are bodily functions that occur without any conscious or voluntary control such as breathing, pulse rate, or control via biofeedback training. Some of the literature refers to the ANS as the *automatic nervous system.*

**autonomous morality**
In Piaget's theory of morality, the second stage of moral development (the first is heteronomous morality) beginning at approximately age 8, in which rules and regulations are viewed as relative and can be changed. Actions are judged partially on intent.

**autophobia**
A fear of being alone.

**autoplastic/autoplasty**
The process of coping with a situation by making changes in yourself rather than attempting to change external circumstances. Can be contrasted with alloplastic/alloplasty in which the individual takes steps to change the environment. A human service worker is thus faced with the dilemma of whether to utilize an autoplastic or alloplastic intervention in a given situation. *See alloplastic/alloplasty.*

**autonomy versus shame and doubt**
Erik Erikson's second stage in his eight-stage theory of psychosocial development that occurs from age one and a half through approximately age three. The child struggles to achieve self-mastery, self-control, and autonomy. If the child is punished for the aforementioned behaviors the child feels shame, and doubt, often lacks assertiveness, and becomes dependent on the parents.

**autosuggestion**
The act of saying or thinking suggestions to alter one's own mood or behavior. This technique was popularized in the 1920s via Emile Coue, who advised individuals to say "Every day in every way, I am getting better and better" at least twenty times daily. Also known as self-suggestion, the technique can be used to induce a state of autohypnosis/self-suggestion. *See autogenic phrases and autogenic training.*

**auxiliary ego**
In Jacob Moreno's psychodrama, the client plays the role of another individual.

**average**
A descriptive statistic. (1) The mean or so-called arithmetic mean computed by taking the sum of scores and dividing it by the number of scores (e.g., 5 + 10 + 15 = 30; 30, the sum, divided by 3, the number of scores, yields a mean of 10). (2) The mode is also sometimes referred to as an average. It is the most frequently occurring score or category. (3) The median, too is often called an average. It is the middle score or hypothetical score when the data are ranked from highest to lowest (e.g., 1,2,3,4,5; the median is 3). (4) That which is typical or normal. *See mean, median, and mode.*

**aversive therapy**
The term *avoidance learning* is also used to convey the same meaning. A procedure that pairs an unpleasant (i.e., aversive) stimulus (e.g., an electric shock) with an inappropriate or maladaptive behavior. Aversive stimuli are sometimes called *noxious stimuli* and can be real or imaginary.

**avoidance-avoidance conflict**
A situation where an individual is confronted with two negative, unattractive, or repulsive situations (e.g., paying a stiff fine or spending time in jail). He or she tries to decide on the lesser of two evils.

**awareness**
A state where one is alert, cognizant, and conscious of the self, others, and the environment. A goal of gestalt therapy is to enhance present moment awareness of the "what" and "how" of experience. Thus gestalt counselors and therapists ask "what" and "how" questions rather than "why" questions to promote awareness.

**awfulizing**
Albert Ellis' term for irrationally believing that a somewhat minor situation is a catastrophe. Also called *catastrophizing* or *terriblizing. See rational-emotive therapy (RET)/rational-emotive behavior therapy (REBT).*

**axes of the DSM**
The DSM uses 5 axes to diagnose and assess the personality. Axis I is used to report clinical disorders or other conditions that may be a focus of clinical attention (except for personality disorders and mental retardation); Axis II, Personality Disorders and Mental Retardation; Axis III, General Medical Conditions that are relevant to the mental disorder; Axis IV, Psychosocial and environmental problems that could affect the diagnosis (e.g., housing problems, educational problems, economic problems); and Axis V, Global Assessment of Functioning (GAF). *See Diagnostic and Statistical Manual IV-TR, Global Assessment of Functioning (GAF) Scale, and diagnosis.*

**B**
(1) In behavior modification, research, and policy evaluation, B stands for the treatment, policy, or intervention. (2) On a graph depicting an AB, ABA, or ABAB research design, B signifies the period during which the treatment, policy, or intervention was being administered. (3) In Albert Ellis's rational-emotive behavior therapy, B is the belief system manifested by a client regarding an activating event. *See AB/ABAB design, A-B-C/A-B-C-D-E theory, rational-emotive therapy (RET)/rational-emotive behavior therapy (REBT), and irrational beliefs (IB)/thinking.*

**babbling**
In human growth and development, prelinguistic speech composed of meaningless sounds. Babbling generally begins at approximately four months of age.

**bachelor's degree**
A four-year college degree such as a bachelor of arts (B.A.), bachelor of science (B.S.), or bachelor of social work (B.S.W.). Often called an *undergraduate degree* or a *baccalaureate degree.*

**background check**
An investigation into the person's past to see if he or she is accurately representing himself or herself. Many agencies will run a police check and/or a child abuse check prior to hiring anybody for a human services job.

**backward conditioning**

This term is used to describe a classical conditioning situation in which the unconditioned stimulus (known as the US or UCS) comes before the conditioned stimulus (CS). In the classical or so-called forward conditioning experiment by Ivan Pavlov, for example, the CS, the bell, would be introduced before the US/UCS, the meat. In backward conditioning, the meat would precede the bell. In most cases backward conditioning is ineffective. *See Pavlov, Ivan.*

**bag lady**

Slang for a homeless woman who lives out of a shopping bag.

**bailout**

In gambling addiction treatment, the notion that someone else covers the gambler's losses, which helps lower the gambler's level of stress and financial pressure.

**barbituates**

A class of physically and psychologically addicting sedative-hypnotic drugs from barbituric acid used to induce sleep, relax muscles, and curb convulsions/seizures. Such drugs interfere with REM sleep and are physically addictive. Clients often experience habituation and thus need higher dosages to produce the desired effect as time goes by. Often known as *downers.*

**barriers to treatment**

Any factor within the person or the environment that interferes with treatment or access to services (e.g., lack of transportation or distrust of human service professionals).

**bartering**

Occurs when a human service worker provides services and takes goods and/or services from the client as payment. For example, "I will keep your child at my day center for a week if you fix the leak in our sink, give me free tires from the tire center you own, etc." Bartering is generally considered a special form of a dual relationship and thus is deemed unethical. *See dual relationship.*

**baseline**

This term is very popular in behavioristic literature, especially in cases where a single subject or client is monitored. A baseline reading is a record of the frequency, quantity, or strength of a behavior prior to intervention (i.e., before treatment). Hence, a baseline reading often serves as a pretest measure in research. It can also denote a period of time when there is no intervention. The baseline procedure is often signified by an upper case letter A. When the term is spelled as two words (i.e., base line) it usually refers to the abscissa, or the $x$ axis, which is a horizontal line on a graph. *See AB/ABAB design.*

**BASIC ID**
*See multimodal therapy.*

**basic skills**
In school counseling and educational guidance work, relates to reading, writing, language, and arithmetic necessary for success in advanced educational settings or future school performance.

**battered child**
A child who is the victim of physical abuse.

**battered spouse**
A wife abused by her husband or a husband abused by his wife.

**battered woman**
A woman who has received physical and emotional abuse.

**battered woman's shelter**
A service that provides shelter specifically to women who have been in domestic violence relationships. Such shelters often provide linkages to other resources such as educational, mental health, or employment opportunities.

**batterer**
An individual who is physically abusive. Often called a *perpetrator* of abuse.

**battery**
(1) A group of tests. The results can often be combined to produce a single score which is assumed to be more accurate than merely assessing the individual with a single measure. (2) In abuse counseling, the act of violating the law by hurting, battering, or physically assaulting another person.

**beamer**
Slang for an individual who uses crack.

**bean counter**
In an agency or organization, slang for the accountant or the individual who makes monetary and fiscal decisions.

**becoming**
A term associated with humanistic/existential psychology (especially Carl R. Rogers) that describes the process of moving toward a self-actualized state where a person reaches his or her full potential.

**bed-wetter**
A child or adult who loses bladder control while sleeping. Also referred to as *enuresis* or *functional enuresis.*

**Beers, Clifford (1876–1943)**
Often cited in human services literature as the person who pioneered the mental hygiene movement. His book *A Mind That Found Itself* is considered a historical classic that depicts the terrible conditions in early mental institutions. In 1909 he created the National Committee for Mental Hygiene.

**behavioral medicine**
Using emotional helping strategies with medical patients since their problem may be exacerbated by emotional difficulties. For example, an asthmatic child might receive counseling about how to deal with asthma in physical education class. A cancer patient might be taught how to use creative visualization to possibly enhance the speed of recovery. Pain management and prevention programs aimed at stress reduction also fall into this category. Hospitals often house or own behavioral medicine units.

**behavioral rehearsal**
The act of practicing a behavior in the helping session that can be beneficial in the client's life. For example, a client who is afraid to ask for a raise could role play the situation in the safety of the interview and could receive feedback regarding his or her approach. Also called *role playing.*

**behavior counseling/therapy**
(1) The act of applying behavioristic/learning psychology to the individual, group, or family counseling or therapy process. Behavioral methods attempt to focus on the symptom (e.g., a fear of elevators) rather than postulating that the symptom is the result of a deeper cause (e.g., an unconscious conflict) or a hypothetical construct (e.g., weak ego strength).

This approach puts little stock in catharsis, free association, the unconscious, symptom substitution, childhood exploration, and transference. At times, the client/counselor relationship is stressed less than the behavioral strategy. Behavior therapy is based on scientific studies, and doing behavior therapy is said to be analogous to doing a scientific experiment with a client. The outcome of the treatment should be measurable. Behavioral intervention has been criticized on all of the aforementioned points, and some experts insist such an approach is simplistic and reductionistic, that man is more than a learning machine and thus the model is somewhat dehumanizing. Wolpe's systematic desensitization, relaxation training, implosive therapy, flooding, shaping, covert sensitization, and aversive procedures fall in this category. When the treatment incorporates cognitions (i.e., thought processes) it is termed *cognitive-behavioral counseling or therapy*. (2) Some purists only use the term when it describes a therapeutic technique derived from classical conditioning theory. When the strategy is based on operant Skinnerian principles, the term *behavior modification* is preferred. Thus some purists, for example, would not refer to a token economy setting as *behavior therapy*. (3) Can refer to any helping strategy that relies on operant conditioning, classical conditioning, cognitive-behavioral intervention, and/or social learning theory. When two or more approaches are combined the term *eclectic behaviorism* is sometimes utilized. (4) Loosely used as a synonym for *behavior mod/behavior modification. See behaviorism and behavior mod/behavior modification*.

### behaviorism
Strictly speaking, the notion that only observable behaviors can be examined or investigated. Hence, a staunch behaviorist would not be concerned with concepts such as the unconscious mind or the super-ego. This school of thought was pioneered by John B. Watson in 1913 who felt that the concepts of mind, introspection, and consciousness, had no place in scientific psychology. Behaviorism often relies on data from animal experiments and is concerned with environmental manipulation as a technique for behavioral change. In recent years, B. F. Skinner's radical behaviorism is illustrative of this viewpoint. Today most counselors see strict behaviorism as an extremist position. Counselors who do adhere to behaviorism are generally neobehaviorists, in the sense that they acknowledge that unobservable, covert (i.e., internal) emotional states can and do influence behavior.

**behavior mod/behavior modification**
(1) Generally refers to the use of B. F. Skinner's operant or instrumental learning theory, as well as social learning theory in the helping process. Hence, reinforcement, back-up reinforcement (e.g., tokens), differential reinforcement of other behavior (DRO), punishment, successive approximations, chaining, and extinction would be utilized when adhering to this theory. The approach has been called a "functional analysis of behavior," or an "applied behavior analysis." The notion is that dysfunctional behaviors are not neurotic or sick but rather the result of learning. This approach has been extremely successful when used with mentally retarded and autistic populations; and clients who are cognizant of precisely what behaviors need to be changed and what target behavior is desirable. Humanistic practitioners have criticized this theory for being too simplistic, reductionistic, and not recognizing that man is more than a reinforcement machine or different than the lower animals (i.e., pigeons, cats, and other animals are often used in behavior modification experiments). Moreover, real life situations do not always reinforce desirable behaviors and thus a behavior that is controlled in a behavior modification setting could be inappropriately elicited in other situations. Hence, a retarded individual who is reinforced for not stealing, might steal outside of the treatment facility when this is not the rule. The existentialists point out that this viewpoint ignores man's free will and is futile when the client is suffering from an existential neurosis or does not know what is specifically causing the difficulty. Psychodynamic supporters worry that behavior modification ignores unconscious processes, transference, and an examination of one's childhood and thus could abet symptom substitution.

**bell-shaped curve**
Also called the normal curve or a Gaussian curve. The term refers to the theoretical shape of a normal distribution when it is graphed. Most physical and psychological traits such as height, weight, and IQ are assumed to be normally distributed in the population. The bell-shaped curve is symmetrical in the sense that the right and left sides are mirror images. A bell-shaped curve does not lean to the right or left, and the mean, median, and mode all fall in the exact center of the curve. Since it has a single peak it is said to be unimodal.

**Bell's palsy**
Paralysis on one side of the face that periodically comes and goes. Thus, a person with this condition who smiles would only be able to display the nonverbal behavior on one side of his or her face. Currently the cause is unknown but a virus is suspected.

**Bender-Gestalt Test**
A popular test for brain or neurological damage in which the person being tested is asked to copy a set of figures. A referral to a neurologist may be in order depending on the test results.

**beneficence**
An ethical term that implies that the worker acts in a manner that is for the good of the client.

**benefits**
(1) What the client receives in public assistance, food stamps, social security, etc. (2) What an insurance company will pay for in terms of services. (3) In career counseling, what a job offers in addition to the salary (e.g., health insurance, dental insurance, child care, and educational benefits).

**benign**
*See cancer.*

**benzodiazepines**
Prescription drugs given for anxiety or insomnia such as Valium, Librium, Halcion, Restoril, or Xanax. These medications have physiologically addictive affects and withdrawal properties that rival or exceed street drugs.

**bereavement**
The experience of losing a loved one that typically includes a grief process including denial, anger, sadness, and acceptance.

**Berne, Eric (1910–1970)**
An American psychoanalyst who created transactional analysis (TA). He also authored the popular psychology books *Games People Play* and *What Do You Say After You Say Hello? See Transactional Analysis (TA).*

**bestiality**
The act of having sexual intercourse with an animal. Can also be called *zoophilia* or *zooerasty.*

**beta error**
A statistical term indicating that a researcher accepts a null hypothesis when in reality it is false. Also known as a *Type II error. See Type II error.*

**beta hypothesis**
A behavioristic technique based on the work of Knight Dunlap which asserts that in order to eliminate a bad habit an individual should force oneself to do it when it would ordinarily not occur. A client, for example, who wishes to eliminate blushing or nail biting would be advised by the counselor to deliberately engage in these behaviors repeatedly. *See negative practice.*

**beta rhythm/beta waves**
Generally used in conjunction with biofeedback terminology, a beta rhythm is from 13 to 25 cycles per second (CPS)/Hertz (Hz) as measured on an electroencephalogram (EEG) This is a low amplitude brain wave associated with alertness. *See alpha rhythm/alpha waves, biofeedback, and delta rhythm/delta waves.*

**bias**
(1) A prejudice or unfair attitude. (2) A sample for a research study which does not accurately represent the population being investigated. Generally this is termed as a *biased sample.* (3) An unfair test or test questions.

**bibliocounseling/bibliotherapy**
Utilizing books, pamphlets, and literature as an adjunct to the counseling and therapy process. The counselor selects readings based on the client's specific needs. In recent years, audio and video cassettes have also been used in this respect, although technically the prefix "biblio" refers to books.

**bifactor measure/test**
A measure producing two scores, such as a verbal and nonverbal IQ.

**Big Book**
A guide for Alcoholics Anonymous (AA) members that depicts stories of individuals fighting alcohol addiction. The book was originally published in 1939 and revised in 1955 and 1976. A new edition was created in 2002 with 24 new stories to reflect the social and cultural diversity of AA members.

**bimodal**
The mode is the most common score or score category in a distribution of scores. This is a statistical term indicating that a distribution has two modes (i.e., peaks that represent the most frequently occurring scores or score classes). The two modes (i.e., peaks) need not be identical, they merely need to stand out from the rest of the scores. From a graphical standpoint, the bimodal curve looks like a camel's back. *See average and mode.*

**Binet**
Abbreviation for the Stanford Binet Intelligence Scale.

**Binet, Alfred (1857–1911)**
The French psychologist who along with Theodore Simon created the first standardized intelligence test in 1905. The test was intended to predict which children would benefit from the Parisian school system. Lewis M. Terman of Stanford University later Americanized the test in 1916, hence today it is known as the Stanford Binet Intelligence Scale. Today the test is unsurpassed in terms of assessing extremely high or extremely low functioning individuals.

**binomial variable**
A statistics and research term that implies that a variable can only exist in two conditions. For example, a counselor's state licensing status could be licensed or unlicensed.

**biochemical model/biomedical model**
Asserts that emotional difficulties (e.g., depression, panic disorder, etc.) are primarily caused by biochemical factors and thus counseling and psychotherapy will do little to help the individual. Psychiatric medicinals would thus be the treatment of choice. Counselors often assert that this model is sometimes inaccurate and stressed too heavily, especially by psychiatrists.

**biofeedback**
This approach uses sensitive electronic devices to provide biological feedback to an individual. Somehow, when an individual is given biological feedback regarding bodily functions these functions can be brought under conscious control. A client might wish to learn to control heart rate, pulse, blood pressure, muscle tension, or brain wave rhythm. Prior to the use of biofeedback in counseling and rehabilitation it was erroneously postulated that such bodily functions could not be controlled since they were regulated by the autonomic nervous system (ANS). Biofeedback is used primarily by

counselors who favor a behavioristic approach and especially for clients who suffer from anxiety. The most common types of biofeedback devices include temperature training, brain wave training (Electroencephalogram—EEG), muscle relaxation training (Electromyogram—EMG), and skin conductivity (Galvanic Skin Response—GSR). Feedback can be auditory such as a tone or beeps, or visual, such as looking at a meter. In children, innovative feedback can be utilized as a reinforcer to raise motivation such as when a biofeedback device is hooked to a model train which speeds around a track when the desired behavior occurs.

**biogenic hypothesis/theory**
Also called the *theory of biogenic amines.* A biochemical theory that asserts that biogenic amines such as norephrine and dopamine can cause psychiatric mood disorders. *See biochemical model/biomedical model.*

**bipolar**
Having two opposite poles or traits such as dominant and submissive.

**bipolar disorder**
A psychiatric mood disorder diagnosis in which two opposite personality poles (i.e., manic and depressive episodes) are manifested. A bipolar disorder can be contrasted with a condition that is a unipolar disorder (i.e., the client experiences only depression). Bipolar clients sometimes receive prescription lithium carbonate and other medicines or natural lithium and nonprescription lithium supplements in addition to counseling. In some of the literature the term *manic-depressive* or *cyclothymic disorder* is used synonymously.

**birth order**
The assumption is that one's order of birth (i.e., first born, middle child, third born, etc.) can influence his or her behavior and later success in life. Alfred Adler emphasized this concept in his school on individual psychology, and many family therapists believe in this notion. Some studies show a very small advantage for first borns; however, some human service workers dismiss birth order as irrelevant.

**birth trauma**
(1) Physical damage occurring at birth. (2) Otto Rank's psychoanalytic position that a child is overloaded with stimuli at birth and hence is traumatized.

**biserial correlation**
A statistical technique for computing a correlation coefficient when one variable is on an interval scale while the other is dichotomous (i.e., two valued). A correlation between a counselor's IQ and his or her licensing status (i.e., have a counselor's license or do not have a counselor's license) would require a biserial correlation.

**bisexual**
(1) An individual who has sexual desires for the same sex as well as the opposite sex. (2) Having characteristics of both sexes.

**bivalence**
A synonym for ambivalence. *See ambivalence/ambivalent.*

**bivariate analysis**
In statistics and research, the process of analyzing two variables simultaneously in order to ascertain the relationship between them. A correlation coefficient would be a bivariate analysis.

**blackout**
A nontechnical term for a loss of memory caused by physical or emotional factors. The term is often used to describe an individual who ingests drugs (especially alcohol) and has no recollection regarding a period of time.

**blame**
The act of not taking responsibility for your own behavior. For example, a student might assert that he or she flunked out of college because the teachers' grading systems were unfair. A client might assert that his wife "drove him to drinking." Human service workers feel that blamers generally do not wish to change their behavior since they believe that they are not at fault.

**bleeding heart**
Originally applied to helpers who were extremely concerned about disadvantaged clients, this term can also describe a helper who does too much for the client, often displaying sympathy rather than empathy. When this occurs, the client sometimes lets the human service worker do all the work. This allows the client to remain disturbed or a victim of inaction and inertia.

## blended family
A family situation where a man/woman marry or live together and bring children, step-children, and/or relatives into the family constellation. This has an impact on family dynamics. A woman's daughter from a previous marriage, for example, could now have a step-brother to live with from the husband's previous relationship. *Blend* refers to the combining of two or more families into a single family unit. Older literature uses the term *step-family*.

## Bleuler, Eugene (1857–1939)
Coined the term schizophrenia.

## blind
Legally defined as visual acuity of 20/200 or less in the better eye after that eye is corrected using glasses or contact lenses. 20/200 implies that the eye can see clearly at 20 feet what the normal eye can clearly see at 200 feet. Vision restricted to a field of 20 degrees or less is also considered legally blind.

## block grant
Describes a system in which funds are dispersed for a given purpose; however, the recipient of the funds determines precisely how to use the money. Generally, the federal government gives the money to the states for social programs and each state decides how to use the money. Experts often insist that block grants make budgeting easier for government agencies who are providing the funding, since the government agency will not have to determine the precise dollar amount for each service provided.

## blocking
(1) In group work, any technique used via the leader to stop (i.e., block) a behavior that could physically or psychologically harm another individual. (2) Refers to someone's inability to recall something.

## blood alcohol concentration/level (BAC)
The concentration of alcohol in the bloodstream. Currently a level of .10 (i.e., one-tenth of one percent) is considered intoxicated in most states. The driver of a motor vehicle can generally be arrested for operating a vehicle when the level is .10 or higher. The level can be determined by blood analysis or via an alcohol breath test (using a Breathalyzer). An American Medical Association study panel has suggested that the legal intoxication level be reduced to .05. Other researchers believe that even infinitesimal

amounts of alcohol cause impairment and those laws should ban driving when any alcohol is in the bloodstream. Persons who violate drinking and driving laws can be arrested on a driving while intoxicated (DWI) or driving under the influence (DUI) charge and can be required in some cases to undergo counseling or chemical dependency treatment.

### blue collar worker
An individual or social class of people who work in a factory and perform manual labor. Traditionally, workers in such settings wore blue uniforms or attire. Blue collar workers are often contrasted with white collar nonlaborers or professionals.

### board
Short for board of directors, licensing board, certification board, board of trustees, or advisory board.

### board certified
A helper who has met the requirements of a state or a national certification board. Certifications allow clients and agencies to know that a worker has achieved a certain level of knowledge and/or proficiency. A counselor, for example, who has completed the requirements of the National Board for Certified Counselors (NBCC) can use the designation National Board Certified Counselor (NCC). A certification is not the same as a license (e.g., licensed professional counselor, licensed psychologist, or licensed clinical social worker). A license allows one to take insurance payments, whereas a certification generally does not afford this benefit.

### board of directors
All not-for-profit/nonprofit agencies are required by law to have a board that is responsible for making certain that the agency is operating in an effective manner. The board is also responsible for hiring the top employee to run the operations, such as the executive director in an agency or the chancellor in a college. Board members are volunteers who do not get paid. A good board is diverse. That is to say, it is composed of persons with specialized knowledge that can help the organization (e.g., an accountant or a lawyer with personnel experience) or individuals who are very influential and thus can bring in business, donations, and publicity. Although a board may indeed have some human service workers on it, a good board is not composed merely of human service professionals. Often contrasted with an *advisory board* which merely makes suggestions about programs but does not have the legal responsibility for running the agency.

**body dysmorphic disorder**
A preoccupation with a defect in appearance. The defect can be imagined or concern over a small feature that is exaggerated to the point where it impairs the individual's ability to function. In the older literature this is known as *morphophobia. See body image.*

**body image**
One's own thoughts and feelings about one's body and how others perceive it. Hence, an individual with an eating disorder could be dangerously underweight but still not perceive himself or herself as slender enough when looking in the mirror. This perception, however, would not necessarily apply to viewing others. The same individual could very easily look at another person his or her own height who weighs considerably more and note that the other person does not appear to be overweight.

**body language**
A nontechnical term which refers to the study of nonverbal communication. Experts generally suggest that you must know a given individual before assuming that a gesture has a specific meaning. For example, someone who has his or her arms folded might not be open to what others or saying or this person could merely be cold.

**Bogardus social distance scale**
A measure of social bonding or prejudice toward ethnic or cultural groups that are different than one's own.

**bonding**
(1) A very strong attachment. Usually refers to the mother child connection that occurs soon after birth. (2) In group therapy the process of bonding among group members is sometimes called *cohesion.*

**borderline personality disorder**
Serious personality disorder that includes suicidal behavior, self-mutilation (e.g., cutting oneself), difficulty with anger control, identity disturbance, feelings of emptiness, boredom, and a tendency to manipulate others.

**borderline state/borderline psychosis**
A person who vacillates between normal behavior and psychosis in which he or she is out of touch with reality. Because it is very difficult to tell whether the client is currently psychotic or nonpsychotic, most experts agree that this is a very difficult type of client to treat.

**boundaries**
(1) In family therapy, the rules regarding the amount and type of contact that is allowed between family members. (2) The emotional and physical limits one person places on another (e.g., a counselor only allows clients to call after hours in emergency situations).

**Bowlby, John (1907–1990)**
British psychoanalyst who investigated infant bonding and the impact of maternal deprivation.

**brain damage**
Actual physical or so-called *organic* damage to the brain that impairs a person's abilities.

**brainstorming**
A technique in which individuals (usually in a group setting) suggest ideas to solve a problem. The suggestions are not criticized by others who are present for the brainstorming session.

**breathalyzer**
An electronic testing device that reveals blood alcohol levels, primarily used by police officers who have stopped a driver who may be intoxicated.

**Breuer, Josef (1841–1925)**
Viennese neurologist. Taught Freud the value of catharsis or the so-called talking cure via the famous Anna O. case. Published *Studies on Hysteria* with Freud.

**brief counseling/therapy**
Generally implies that the treatment is goal directed and revolves around a given issue or set of symptoms. Treatment of this sort is usually 15 sessions or less. This form of treatment became popular with managed care companies as a cost-saving measure.

**brief strategic counseling/therapy**
A model of helping that focuses much more on the solution than the problem and exceptions to the rule. For example, a client who says "I've always been depressed" might be asked whether there was a time (even if it was very brief) when she was not depressed. The client would then analyze what was different on this occasion.

**Brill, A. A. (1874–1948)**
Known for being the first analyst to translate Freud's writings into English.

**broken home**
The old term for a family with an absent parent (i.e., a mother or father who is not living in the household). The term *single parent family* is preferred.

**broker**
A human service worker's role that is accomplished by helping clients find and/or take advantage of services. In the broker role the human service worker merely hooks the client up with the appropriate service rather than personally providing the service.

**Brown v. Board of Education, Topeka, Kansas**
Considered a landmark Supreme Court decision in 1954, ruling that "separate but equal" educational facilities were actually unequal and unfair. The separate but equal doctrine implied that African Americans were inferior. *See Plessy v. Ferguson.*

**bruxism**
The act of grinding one's teeth, usually while sleeping. Psychodynamic practitioners often assume this symptom is caused by hostility. Helpers who do not use psychodynamic procedures often use relaxation techniques in addition to traditional intervention strategies when treating bruxism.

**BSW**
Abbreviation for a Bachelors of Social Work degree from an undergraduate program that is accredited via the Council on Social Work Education (CSWE). Hence, a four-year institution that advertises a B.A. in Social Work is implicitly revealing that the program is not CSWE accredited. Some job openings will only accept—or are only funded—for the CSWE degree. Moreover, accredited Master of Social Work Schools give advanced standing to students who have the accredited BSW degree.

**Buckley amendment**
*See Family Education Rights and Privacy Act (FERPA) of 1974.*

**budget**
A document that depicts the income and expenditures that an organization, agency, school, practice, individual, or household will encounter during a specified period of time (usually one year). A budget helps make money management and policy decisions. A budget can refer to a specific program (e.g., the foster care project) or the entire operation.

**buffeted clients**
Clients who have numerous problems as opposed to a single presenting complaint.

**bulimia/bulimia nervosa**
An eating disorder characterized by binge (i.e., pathological excessive) eating followed by forced, self-induced purging (e.g., laxative abuse, fasting, or vomiting) and/or excessive exercise to prohibit weight gain. Guilt is often evident after a bulimic episode. Persons with this condition sometimes suffer from anorexia nervosa. *See anorexia nervosa.*

**burn**
Slang for the act of reporting a drug dealer or user to the police.

**burnout**
Excessive stress caused by one's job.

**bystander apathy/bystander effect/bystander intervention**
A social psychology phenomenon which asserts that persons rarely help a stranger in trouble. Moreover, it has been found that the larger the crowd, the greater the apathy. In other words, the larger the crowd, the smaller the chance becomes that bystanders will provide assistance to the person in need.

**C**
Stands for the emotional consequence in Albert Ellis's A-B-C/A-B-C-D-E theory of personality utilized in his rational-emotive behavior therapy. C is said to be caused primarily by B, the belief system, rather than A, the activating event. *See A-B-C/A-B-C-D-E theory and rational-emotive therapy (RET)/rational-emotive behavior therapy (REBT).*

**CA**
Abbreviation for chronological age, which is a person's actual age in years.

**CACREP**
*See Council for Accreditation of Counseling and Related Programs.*

**cactus head**
Slang for a person who uses peyote.

**CA group**
Cocaine anonymous. A twelve-step group based on Alcoholics Anonymous for persons with cocaine addictions.

**cancer**
A disease that is identified by uncontrolled cell reproduction. *Tumors* are excess tissue that is formed due to uncontrolled cell division in various parts of the body. A tumor that develops and is noncancerous is known as *benign*. However, a cancerous tumor is called malignant. If

the malignant tumor arises from muscle or bone tissue, it is known as a *sarcoma*. If the tumor arises in the lining of organs such as the lungs, liver, or the brain, it is known as a *carcinoma*. Cancerous growths of the skin cells are known as *melanoma*. Cancers related to blood-producing tissues are known as *leukemia. See acute leukemia and chronic leukemia.*

**cannabis**
*See marijuana.*

**capitation**
A method of payment for healthcare services that involves a managed care company paying a health care provider a fixed amount of money per month regardless of the extent of the health services provided.

**carcinoma**
*See cancer.*

**career counseling/guidance**
Any intervention that helps the client pick an appropriate job, career, or occupation and balance the work with his or her leisure, family, and social activities.

**career fair**
An arrangement where a number of employers set up booths in a designated area for a specified time (say a large room in a college or hotel for the entire day) where individuals can see what jobs are available. Literature, representatives from the agency hospital, etc. are present. Job, volunteer, and practicum applications are often available at the event. Academic institutions—though they are not publicizing jobs—often set up displays to help future employees secure programs to give them the credentials they will need for the jobs at the fair.

**caregiver**
Can refer to any professional or paraprofessional helper.

**case**
(1) The client's file or record. (2) In older literature, a client or patient with mental health problems (e.g., "I had a case who suffered from schizophrenia").

**case aide**
A paraprofessional who will be assisting professionals who are working with the client.

**case conference**
The act of bringing in several different human service workers or other professionals (e.g., an attorney or a physician) to help discuss the best methods for intervening with the client.

**caseload**
All of the clients that a given human services worker will be helping.

**case notes**
Also called *dictation* or *narrative entries,* the term describes the worker's written documentation of his or her activities related to the client (e.g., home visits, telephone contacts, release of information forms given to the client, suicide prevention contracts, etc.). At some agencies the helper actually writes in the chart. At other sites the worker uses a computer to input the information, and at still others a tape recording (or dictation) may be given to clerical staff who will then transcribe it into the record.

**caste system**
A system that treats people differently based on their class or status (e.g., those persons with a high income and education might be treated better than those who are poor and uneducated).

**castration anxiety/complex**
A fear of losing one's genitals or dread that one's sexual organs will be harmed. The radical psychoanalytic belief is that this occurs when the boy fears his father will punish him for wanting his mother in a sexual manner. *See Oedipus complex.*

**catalepsy**
In hypnosis, a trance phenomenon where a limb will remain in a rigid position. Also occurs in catatonic schizophrenia.

**cataracts**
An opacity of the crystalline lens that decreases the visual acuity of the eye. Most cataracts are due to an increase in the formation of insoluble proteins. These proteins usually aggregate, creating an opacity that keeps light from reaching the retina, which interferes with vision. This is most commonly found in the elderly population and is often due to the aging process. However, there are several types of cataracts that can be caused by a variety of outside sources such as ultraviolet radiation, electrocution, and trauma to the crystalline lens. Interocular implants are usually utilized to treat patients with advanced cataract formation.

**catastrophizing**
A term coined by Albert Ellis, the father of rational-emotive behavior therapy (REBT), to convey the notion that somebody is exaggerating the emotional pain of a given situation. Also referred to as *awfulizing* or *terribilizing* in the literature.

**catatonia**
A state seen in hypnotic trances and schizophrenia characterized by a lack of movement and rigid, often unnatural body positions. An arm or a leg will remain in a position in which it has been placed.

**catchment area**
The geographical area served by a counseling center or other facility.

**catecholamines**
Biogenic amines such as norepinephrine, epinephrine, and dopamine that impact the functioning of the nervous system. Some antidepressants increase amines.

**catharsis**
(1) Conveys the idea that talking about one's problems is therapeutic. (2) In psychoanalysis, the notion that one expresses a previously repressed incident and that this expression is curative. The term *abreaction* is used in some of the literature.

**cathexis**
Extreme concentration on a person or idea, giving it tremendous importance.

**CAT scan**
In medicine, a computerized method that allows the doctor to see inside the body.

**ceiling**
The highest possible score on a test or examination.

**ceiling professional**
An individual who secures a very high or prestigious job near the beginning of his or her career and feels there is nowhere to move up.

**census**
Data collected from all members of a given population. Often contrasted with survey data, which is acquired via a sample and not the entire population.

**central nervous system**
The brain and the spinal cord.

**centration**
Piaget's term to describe a child in the preoperational stage (ages 2 to 7) who can only focus on a single or outstanding part of an object or situation and ignores other aspects. A child who sees a clown, for example, may notice only the large red nose. *See Piaget, Jean.*

**cephalalgia**
A headache or other pain in the cranial region.

**cephalocaudal**
(1) A developmental term that suggests that the growth sequence is head to tail in the human fetus (e.g. the head would develop more quickly than the legs). (2) The portion of the body between the head and the tail.

**cerebral palsy**
Motor impairment generally caused by brain damage occurring in the prenatal period or during birth.

**certification**
A designation that a practitioner or an agency has reached a specified level of qualifications. A helpline, for example, might be certified by the American Association of Suicidology. In the case of the individual practitioner, it should be noted that a certification is not equivalent to a license. A counselor with National Board Certification but no state counselor's license could generally not take insurance, managed care, or other third-party payments. *See licensure, Licensed Clinical Social Worker (LCSW), Licensed Independent Clinical Social Worker (LICSW), Licensed Professional Counselor (LPC), and Licensed Psychologist.*

**CEU**
Abbreviation for continuing education unit. These units are often required by state licensing boards or certification bodies to retain a credential (e.g., a certified counselor might need 100 CEUs in a five-year period).

**CHAMPUS**
Abbreviation for the Civilian Health and Medical Program of the Uniformed Services. The program provides health insurance policies to current and retired military personnel and their families.

67

**Charcot, Jean-Martin (1825–1893)**
A French neurologist and psychiatrist who convinced Sigmund Freud that hypnosis was a useful form of treatment. Sometimes referenced as the first physician to treat emotional disorders using psychotherapeutic methods.

**charitable gambling**
The use of gambling activities to raise money for an organization. For example, a homeless shelter might hold monthly bingo games to help fund the agency.

**Charity Organization Society (COS)**
Private voluntary organizations that began in the 1800s in England and then the US. The workers, who essentially performed social work functions, were known as friendly visitors. COSs were the predecessors of not-for-profit helping organizations.

**chaser**
Slang for a drug user who continually uses crack.

**cheeking**
Slang for the fact that a patient is not truly taking his or her medicine. Instead, the patient places the capsule or pill inside the cheeks and then expels the medicine when medical personnel are not observing.

**chemotherapy**
To treat a mental or physical disease (usually cancer) with chemicals (i.e., drugs).

**Chicano/Chicana**
Slang. The term Mexican American or Hispanic is preferred.

**child abuse**
*See abuse.*

**child analysis**
Modified procedures of psychoanalysis that can help children with emotional problems.

**Child ego state**
In Eric Berne's transactional analysis, the child ego state is not associated with one's chronological age. Instead it refers to a hypothetical entity in the personality, which houses all the impulses, experiences, and recordings from infancy and childhood. When a person is acting like a

child he or she is said to be operating primarily out of the child ego state. Somewhat analogous to Freud's Id. *See Adult ego state and Parent ego state.*

### childhood
Birth to approximately 12 years of age. Infancy to the start of puberty.

### Chi Sigma Iota (CSI)
An honors society for students who are becoming professional counselors.

### Chi square
In statistics, a mathematical test to determine if observed results differ from chance results.

### chromosome
A biological structure that carries genes. A biologically normal individual has 23 pairs of chromosomes (i.e., 46 total).

### chromosome 21
In rehabilitation and gerontological counseling, the notion that the 21st chromosome is responsible for Down's Syndrome and possibly Alzheimers.

### chronic
A condition that lasts for an extended period of time. Often contrasted with a time-limited acute condition.

### chronic leukemia
The accumulation of mature white blood cells in the blood stream due to prolonged life span of these cells. This type of leukemia progresses much slower because some of the white blood cells can still carry out their normal metabolic functions. Symptoms are similar to acute leukemia. *See acute leukemia.*

### chronic obstructive pulmonary disease (COPD)
A respiratory disorder that is described by chronic obstruction of the airways, which interferes with the proper amount of airflow reaching the lungs. COPD sufferers have complications with breathing due to an increase in airway resistance. COPD usually takes a period of years to develop, which means that most of the individuals who suffer from this disease are older adults and are persistent smokers. The most common forms of COPD are chronic bronchitis and emphysema.

### chronological age (CA)
An individual's actual age (i.e., birth to one's present age). Often contrasted with one's mental age (MA).

### circular causality
In the context of family therapy, the notion that one family member influences the other members in the family and that each family member is impacted by the all the other members in the family. This is known as a systems theory and is said to be reciprocal in nature (i.e., each person influences others while they are simultaneously influenced by others). This is often contrasted with linear causality (e.g., A causes B that causes C) which assumes that causation takes place in one direction.

### claims-based liability/malpractice insurance policy
This type of policy only covers the policy holder during the time he or she holds the policy. Thus, if the policy holder holds the policy during 2002 and a client takes legal action against the policy holder in 2005 for something the policy holder did during 2002, the policy will not cover the policy holder. Often contrasted with the higher priced occurrence-based policy that will cover you during the time you held the policy even if the claim against you takes place years later. The occurrence-based policy is recommended for human service professionals.

### clarification
Asking a client for additional information so the helper can better understand the client's situation.

### classical conditioning
*See Pavlov, Ivan and backward conditioning.*

### claustrophobia
Extreme fear or dread of closed places such as closets, elevators, or rooms without windows.

### client
An individual who is helped by a human services organization.

### client-centered therapy
*See person-centered counseling/therapy.*

**clinical psychologist**
A psychologist who treats people with emotional difficulties or performs research related to such issues. Clinical psychologists focus mainly on diagnosing the client, often using a battery of tests, and then treating the client using counseling and psychotherapy. In general, clinical psychologists have more training in giving projective tests than any other profession. They also work as consultants. *See Licensed Psychologist.*

**closed group**
A group that does not admit new members after the first session or the first few sessions. Most college and graduate classes would fall into this category. Often contrasted with open groups in which new members are permitted to join at any point in the group. The closed group helps abet cohesion, which is desirable. However, the number of members can be unstable since individuals can quit but they cannot be replaced. In addition, the discussion can become redundant since the same group of people have input during each session.

**closed-ended question**
A question that can be answered with a single word or a "yes" or "no" answer. An example would be: Do you like your job? Closed questions are generally seen as inferior to open questions, which require an explanation, e.g., "What has your experience of the job been like?" Open questions generate more information; however, when time is of the essence or specific information is necessary, the closed question could be the question of choice. *See open-ended question.*

**closet homosexual**
An individual who is unaware that he or she is homosexual or who has not acknowledged this fact publicly.

**cluster sample**
Sometimes referred to as a *multistage sample* in which a natural group (i.e., a cluster) is identified and then a smaller subsample is selected. For example, a human service program is selected, and then several classes are randomly selected to represent the human service program as a whole. In cluster sampling a group—not an individual—is randomly selected.

## cluster suicides
Several suicides that seem to be linked via a contagion effect (e.g., the second person who suicided saw an article about the first person who suicided in the newspaper). This phenomenon seems to occur more in adolescence.

## cocaine
Also known as *coke* or *snow,* a highly addictive stimulant manufactured from the leaves of the coca plant that can sometimes induce death. In the late 1800s Freud believed that cocaine could help cure depression, and by the early 1900s cocaine was included in a host of therapeutic products without a prescription, most notably Coca-Cola. In 1914 the Harrison Narcotics Act prohibited the nonmedical use of the drug. Cocaine is one of the most physiologically addictive substances known to man. Cocaine can be inhaled (known as "snorted") from a drinking straw that picks up the drug lined up on a sheet of glass or a mirror. Cocaine can also be injected into a vein (known as "intravenous injection") or smoked (known as "freebasing"). The first high is usually the best; thus the addict chases that sensation again and again. Currently, it is believed that cocaine depletes brain chemicals necessary to fight depression and so the user is left with a condition called *anhedonia,* or an inability to enjoy life. Reversing this condition can often be a lengthy process. Total abstinence is imperative for treatment. *See crack.*

## Coconut Grove Fire
On November 28, 1942, 483 people were killed by a fire in the Coconut Grove Nightclub in Boston. This was, at the time, the largest single building fire in U.S. history. Eric Lindemann of Massachusetts General Hospital helped survivors and later teamed up with Gerald Caplan (the father of crisis intervention) in the Wellesley community project to study bereavement and trauma. This incident is usually sited as the beginning of the crisis intervention movement in the US.

## code of ethics
*See ethics.*

## codependency/codependent
(1) Generally refers to a set of emotional or behavioral problems that an individual has as a result of being in a relationship with someone who has an alcohol or drug problem. (2) Being addicted to a relationship with another person. (3) The notion that an individual's mood is dependent on the mood of another person in the relationship (i.e., a women is happy only when her boyfriend is happy). Codependency is not an official diagnosis in the *DSM.*

**codependency anonymous/CODA Group**
A twelve-step group based on Alcoholics Anonymous for persons with codependency tendencies.

**cognitive**
Refers to thinking, imagining, and reasoning. Often contrasted with affective, feeling, or emotional responses.

**cognitive counseling/cognitive therapy**
(1) Any school of counseling and/or psychotherapy that focuses primarily on helping the client to be aware of cognitive patterns and ways to change them. This approach stresses that cognitions (e.g., thoughts, beliefs, internal verbalizations, and images) help create our emotional responses. In the popular press, cognitions are often referred to as *self-talk*. Hence, to change one's life one must change one's way of thinking about the world. (2) The cognitive therapy model created by psychiatrist Aaron T. Beck.

**cold turkey**
Giving up an addiction completely in an abrupt manner. A smoker, for example, who smokes two packs a day, might completely quit and smoke no cigarettes. This approach usually causes withdrawal symptoms.

**coleadership/cotherapy**
The act of using two or more counselors, therapists, or facilitators to run an individual, group, or family therapy session. Coleadership nearly always applies to group settings.

**collective unconscious**
Carl Jung's theory that humans possess an unconscious that is collected, passed on, and shared by all people. Often referred to as the *racial unconscious*.

**color blindness**
To clarify, color blindness is not a form of blindness in any way. It is an inherited gene that effects the way a person perceives color. A red-green color deficiency is the most common form of color blindness, but there is also a less common form, which is blue-yellow color deficiency. Color blindness occurs when certain cells in the retina do not respond to color as they would normally. Color blindness is generally inherited by men from a color-deficient mother or a mother who just carries the gene.

### coming out
Refers to a homosexual publicly revealing that he or she is gay or lesbian.

### commercialization
The practice of advertising and marketing social welfare services or mental health services.

### commitment
(1) A legal procedure, which varies throughout the country, for admitting an individual into a psychiatric facility. (2) A serious level of motivation or dedication regarding one's treatment.

### communication effective
When an individual interprets a message in the way it was intended.

### communication failure
When an individual interprets a message differently than it was intended.

### communication of intent
When a person gives a message indicating his or her future behavior. Routinely used in suicidology to indicate that a person intends to harm himself or herself.

### compensation
(1) An unconscious ego defense mechanism whereby a person attempts to make up for a perceived deficiency. (2) A conscious attempt to make up for a perceived deficiency. (3) Paying someone for services (e.g., she is paid $10 an hour to work as a case manager).

### compulsion
Repetitious behavior to ward off anxiety. For example, a client may wash his or her hands repeatedly, or check to see if the door is locked again and again. Compulsive behavior usually occurs in conjunction with obsessive thinking.

### concrete operations
In Jean Piaget's developmental theory it is the third developmental stage, where the child can understand concrete situations (i.e., actual experience) but not abstractions.

### Concrete operations stage.
*See Piaget, Jean.*

**conditioned/conditioning**
Learning. These terms are used in behavior modification and behavior therapy.

**conditioned reflex therapy**
A therapeutic approach created by Andrew Salter, often known as the father of behavior therapy, which suggests that people should express all their verbal and nonverbal emotions (known as excitation rather than not expressing emotions which is known as inhibition). Salter relied on Ivan Pavlov and John B. Watson as his theoretical basis. Experts feel that his theory led to the birth of assertiveness training.

**conditioned response (CR)**
*See Pavlov, Ivan.*

**conditioned stimulus (CS)**
*See Pavlov, Ivan.*

**conditioning**
Learning. *See backward conditioning, behavior counseling/therapy and Pavlov, Ivan.*

**confidentiality**
An ethical stance which suggests that nothing discussed during the counseling session can be revealed. In reality, there are numerous exceptions to confidentiality (e.g., child abuse, insurance companies requesting records, clients threatening suicidal or homicidal acts, cases with helpers involved in a malpractice legal battle, etc.).

**conformity**
Doing what most of the other people in your social group, age bracket or society do (e.g., someone wearing a given hair style because everyone in his or her school is wearing it).

**confrontation**
Occurs when a human service worker points out discrepancies between a client's thoughts, attitudes, nonverbals, and behavior. A human service worker might comment to a client that she says the death of her father is not causing her grief, but she cries each time it is discussed during a session.

## congenital

A condition which is present when the child is born, though it is not necessarily inherited (e.g., a prenatal condition could inflict it). Often contrasted with adventitious disabilities/handicaps which occur after birth.

## conjoint counseling/therapy

Seeing both partners together during marriage or couples counseling. Often associated specifically with the treatment paradigm suggested by Virginia Satir.

## conscience

The moral characteristics of the individual. In psychoanalysis this is assumed to be housed in the "super-ego," while in transactional analysis it exists in the "Parent" ego-state of the personality. *See Parent ego state and superego.*

## conscientious objector

A person who refuses to fight in a war or work in the military.

## conscious

A state of being alert or aware of one's thoughts, feelings, actions, and behaviors. Often contrasted with unconscious. *See unconscious.*

## consent

To secure the client's permission to perform an act of service (e.g., give a client's minor child a test or send his record to another provider). *See informed consent.*

## consequences

In behavior modification, the result of a behavior (e.g., a child receives a toy each time he completes a math problem).

## conservation

The notion popularized by Jean Piaget's theory that the amount of a substance does not change when its shape changes. Thus, a child who has not mastered conservation who sees a tall thin pitcher of water poured into a small squatty beaker may insist that the small beaker has less water. Children in Piaget's preoperational stage (ages 2 to 7) cannot master this concept. It is mastered in the concrete operational stage (ages 7 to 12).

## constitution

Refers to one's inherited (i.e., genetic) physical and/or psychological makeup.

**construct validity**
The degree to which a measure (e.g., a psychological test) accurately assesses a hypothetical construct such as ego strength or intelligence. *See validity, content validity, face validity, and predictive validity.*

**consultation**
The process of helping other professionals deal with difficulties so they can perform in a more desirable manner and enjoy their work more. The person who receives the consultation is known as the *consultee*. Thus, a consultant might give a teacher (the consultee) guidance on how to use behavior modification in the classroom to reduce unwanted behavior. Consultation was pioneered in mental health settings in 1970 via Gerald Caplan, who believed that consultation helps reduce stress and should be a nonsupervisory, voluntary relationship. *See Schein Consultation.*

**contagion effect**
Refers to a copy-cat phenomenon (usually suicide or homicide). When a famous person kills himself or herself, the suicide rate will go up as others mimic the self-destructive behavior.

**contagious**
Occurs when a person has an illness that others can contract.

**content validity**
Sometimes known as *rational validity* or *logical validity,* this term refers to whether the test actually assesses the specific content or subject matter it purports to examine. A test on psychoanalysis that had all questions about behavior therapy would have poor content validity. Each item on the test should be assessed for content validity to ascertain whether it should be included. *See validity, construct validity, face validity, and predictive validity.*

**content versus process analysis**
In group work the notion that a leader can focus on content (what has been said) or process (interactions between group members, such as "I notice that Sally always cringes when Jane talks about her husband's abusive tendencies").

### contingency management

In behavior modification this occurs when a client is told in a verbal or written contract that he or she will receive a reinforcer (or consequence) for performing a certain behavior. A young child might be told that he will receive a dollar for each night he sleeps in his own bed rather than his parent's bed. Referred to as *self-contingency management* when one uses the technique on oneself.

### continuing education units (CEU)

Educational training required for human service workers who are who are licensed or certified. The National Board for Certified Counselors (NBCC), for example, requires that National Certified Counselors (NCC) have 100 hours of CEUs in 5 years. Often, the licensing or certification organization will specify that the units—or a certain number of units—are amassed in a given specialty area.

### continuous reinforcement schedule

The act of reinforcing each behavior after it is performed. A child who receives a candy bar after each math problem would be receiving continuous reinforcement. Most experts believe that continuous reinforcement works best when initially trying to shape behavior. However, the helper should switch to an intermittent schedule of reinforcement after a while (e.g., give the child a candy bar after each three problems) so the child will not satiate or habituate.

### contraception

Any method (e.g., condoms or diaphragms) that is used to prevent a woman from becoming pregnant.

### contract

A verbal or written agreement between the human service worker and the client created to delineate a desired course of action. Contracting is especially popular with behaviorially oriented helpers and those who practice reality therapy and transactional analysis. It is also often recommended as beneficial when working with suicidal individuals.

### contracting out the work/contractual work/treatment services

The act of purchasing a service from persons who are not employees. Generally, these contractors will not receive employee benefits (e.g., health insurance or paid holidays). A state child abuse agency, for example, would pay therapists to help abused children by paying them only for the times when services to the clients were rendered. Some of the recent literature uses the term outsourcing.

**contradict and attack**
The third technique or rule of conduct in Andrew Salter's conditioned reflex therapy to restore healthy excitation to the personality. The client is advised that he or she should express disagreement with others openly and freely whenever it is felt.

**control group**
A group of subjects in a research study who do not receive the independent variable (i.e., the experimental treatment). An attempt is made to insure that the control group is nearly identical to the experimental group in every other respect. *See experimental group.*

**controlled substance**
The Drug Enforcement Administration (DEA) has classified drugs that can be abused into levels of control such as: I, high abuse potential with no medical uses (e.g., heroin); II, high abuse potential, but the drug can be used in medicine (e.g., amphetamines); III, moderate abuse potential (e.g., codeine used in prescription cough medicines); IV, low abuse potentials such as weak narcotic or non-narcotic cold medicines.

**convalescent home**
A facility that cares for persons who are too sick to live in their own homes but a not sick enough to be placed in a hospital.

**conversion disorder/reaction**
Also called a hysterical neurosis, this diagnosis implies that the individual has somatic symptoms (e.g., paralysis or blindness) caused by psychological or emotional conflicts.

**cookie cutter reports**
Slang for any report that uses a finite number of stock, generic sentences or paragraphs that apply to a wide range of clients. The person who prepares the report might have 10 different preconstructed paragraphs in a given section to choose from. Hence, two people with cookie cutter psychological testing reports might have several paragraphs that are identical in their respective reports. Since this approach to report writing is not 100% individualized some providers assert it is not nearly as accurate or valuable as a report that is written in a traditional manner.

### cookie cutter treatment plan
Slang for facilities that use a finite number of stock, generic treatment plans for all of their clients. Thus two people with vastly different problems could be receiving identical treatment. Since this approach to treatment is not 100% individualized some providers assert it is not nearly as accurate or valuable as a treatment plan that is created in a traditional manner.

### copayment
The amount owed by the client after insurance pays its part of the client's bill. If a client's bill is $100.00 and insurance covers 80%, then the copayment is $20.00.

### COPD
*See chronic obstructive pulmonary disease (COPD).*

### coping skills
Methods people use to cope with stress such as sports, hobbies, changing self-talk, or meditation.

### core conditions
In person-centered therapy set forth by Carl R. Rogers, the notion that effective helpers are empathic, genuine or congruent, and show unconditional acceptance; also known as *unconditional positive regard.*

### corrections
The study of law enforcement, police work, probation and parole, legal offenses, the family and juvenile court, administration of justice, and corrections facilities.

### correlation
Expresses an association or relationship between two variables. Correlation does not imply causal. When it is raining a high percentage of folks open an umbrella, but opening an umbrella does not cause it to rain. Correlation research is sometimes called quasi-experimentation rather than true experimentation or "ex post facto research," meaning that the conclusion is based on uncontrolled situations that occurred previously. *See correlation coefficient.*

### correlation coefficient
In statistics and research a numerical description of the association or the strength of the relationship between two variables. Correlation coefficients go from $-1.00$ to $+1.00$. A correlation of $-1.00$ or $+1.00$ is said to be "perfect." In the case of the $-1.00$ one variable goes down exactly the same

amount as the other goes up. In the case of the +1.00 both variables go in the same direction at exactly the same amount. In the real world, perfect correlations almost never exist. (An example of a perfect correlation would be a correlation between height in inches and height in centimeters.) A correlation of zero (i.e., 0.00) is indicative of no association between the variables. Correlation does not imply causal. A could cause B; B could cause A; or C could cause A or B. When it rains, many individuals will carry umbrellas, but carrying an umbrella does not cause rain. Correlation is generally expressed via a lower case $r$ (e.g., $r = -.92$). *See correlation.*

### Council for Accreditation of Counseling and Related Programs (CACREP)
An accrediting body that sets academic standards for masters- and doctorate-level counseling programs.

### Council for Standards in Human Service Education (CSHSE)
Created in 1976, this organization is committed to improving the quality, consistency, and relevance of human service education programs. Human service degree programs can be accredited by this body if they meet specified standards.

### Council on Social Work Education (CSWE)
This organization, formed in 1952, accredits social work programs in the US if they meet the necessary standards. Students who ultimately seek social work licensure are urged to attend CSWE-accredited institutions.

### counseling psychologist
An individual who is licensed as a psychologist and specializes in counseling. A licensed counselor could not legally or ethically use this designation unless duly licensed as a psychologist. *See Licensed Psychologist.*

### counselor
(1) An individual who uses knowledge that can help clients improve their coping skills and acquire awareness, and thus enhance their lives. In the past, it was assumed that counselors worked primarily with a normal population, while therapists worked with more disturbed clients and/or administered a deeper more complex brand of treatment. Today—with the exception of group work—the distinction is rarely used and often the terms "counselor" and "therapist" or "psychotherapist" are used interchangeably. (2) An individual who is trained in the behavioral sciences to help others prevent and/or solve or cope with problems of everyday life.

(3) An individual trained to practice counseling or psychotherapy. Work could include information giving, educational and/or career guidance, consultation, testing, and research. (4) An individual who holds a state license to practice counseling (e.g., LPC or Licensed Professional Counselor) or counseling psychology and can thus legally use the title "counselor" or "psychologist."

### counselor educator
A trained professional counselor who educates those who wish to learn more about counseling, become counselors, and/or enhance the education of practicing counselors. The term counselor educator usually refers to an individual teaching counseling courses and/or performing research in a graduate school of counselor education or related counseling training program. Counselor educators also provide workshops for practicing professionals and supervise counselors engaged in a practicum, internship, or working to meet licensing or certification requirements.

### counterbalancing
In research, presenting stimuli in a different order to rule out the possibility that the order of presentation is impacting the experiment.

### counterculture
A term that manifested itself in the 1960s to describe persons whose dress and lifestyle were different than the mainstream macroculture.

### countertransference
When a helper has a problem or an unresolved issue that is preventing him or her from being an objective helper.

### covert
In behavior therapy, a thought, idea, or picture in one's mind.

### CPT Codes.
*See Current Procedural Terminology.*

### crack
A version of cocaine that is smoked (freebased). Crack has been called the "fast food" version of cocaine because of its lower cost. Cocaine is mixed with baking soda and water and the dried substance is cracked into small chunks and smoked. Crack is extremely addictive and can cause death. *See cocaine.*

**crank**
Injecting methamphetamine to experience euphoria. After the drug wears off depression and psychotic-like symptoms can occur. When smoked it is called *ice*.

**credential**
A license, degree, or certification such as Master Addiction Counselor (MAC) or National Board Certified Counselor (NCC).

**criminology**
The study of crime.

**Crips and Bloods**
Two notorious street gangs purportedly involved in the sale of drugs. Crips wear blue, while Bloods wear red.

**crisis**
(1) An event or emergency that has a tremendous emotional impact on the individual, sometimes referred to as disequilibrium (meaning that the person is thrown out of balance). When the individual is not able to use traditional coping skills then he or she is said to be in a situational or accidental crisis. Examples would include a fire, unplanned pregnancy, a flood, a rape, a victim of a crime, or the discovery of a fatal illness. (2) A developmental crisis refers to stress generated by a predictable life change such as puberty.

**crisis helpline/hotline**
A telephone service usually staffed primarily by trained volunteers to help people in crisis. The helpline worker generally has a resource and referral system to help the individual attain continued care after the telephone intervention. Many of the early crisis hotlines focused primarily on suicidal callers, but today many handle a wide range of problems. Some crisis hotlines still focus on a specific group of callers such as a rape hotline or a drug abuse helpline.

**crisis intervention**
Any brief or time-limited strategy intended to help the individual in crisis.

**criterion validity**
The degree to which a measure (e.g., a psychological test) relates to an external, outside criterion. Thus, a test that supposedly tested baseball ability would be said to have low criterion validity if a professional baseball player scored very low on the test. *See validity.*

**Crohn's Disease**
Also known as *ileitis,* this is a form of inflammatory bowel disease (IBD) that affects the gastrointestinal tract by producing chronic inflammation of the lower part of the small intestine, the ileum. Due to the inflammation, the intestine tends to empty more often than normal, which can result in persistent diarrhea. It is thought that there may be some hereditary component, since it tends to run in families.

**cross-cultural counseling**
Counseling in which the client is from a different culture than the counselor. Also called intercultural and multicultural counseling. Most of the literature now uses the term "multicultural counseling."

**cross-dressing**
The act of dressing in clothing of the opposite sex. Also known as *transvestism.*

**cross-sectional research/study**
A study that relies on observations conducted on numerous people at a given point in time. Often contrasted with a longitudinal research that relies on observations conducted on the same people over a long period of time.

**CSHSE**
*See Council for Standards in Human Service Education (CSHSE).*

**CSWE**
*See Council on Social Work Education (CSWE).*

**cultural-familial mental retardation**
Describes mental retardation which is not the result of organic factors. A child who is physiologically normal but is retarded due to lack of environmental stimulation would fit into this category.

**culture**
Shared values, behaviors, and symbols of a specific set of people that is transmitted from one generation to the next.

**culture free test**
A measurement in which the score is not dependent on a knowledge of a given culture. Most experts agree that many tests (e.g., IQ tests) should be culture free, but that it may be impossible to create a test that truly meets this definition.

**culture of poverty**
A theory that poverty is transmitted from one generation to the next.

**culture shock**
The stress induced by living in a different culture.

**culture specific**
A behavior which is typical of a given culture.

**culture-specific disorder**
An emotional disturbance which is not described in the *DSM* but is somewhat typical of a culture outside the US. In the Eskimo culture, for example, *piblokto* refers to screaming and crying while running through the snow naked.

**curative approach to poverty**
Providing skills to the poor such as literacy training and job skills to eliminate the true causes of one's poverty.

**curfew**
A specific time when individuals must not be in a certain area. For example, a homeless shelter might stipulate that all residents must be back at the center by 8 p.m.

**current procedural terminology**
Known in the field as CPT codes, these are codes that list services (e.g., psychotherapy or hypnosis) provided by physicians and other human service providers. CPT codes and a *DSM* diagnosis are required for insurance or managed care firm payments.

**curvilinear model of anxiety**
Too much anxiety is bad; however, a moderate amount of anxiety after an emergency situation often causes the person to grow emotionally stronger. The term is usually used when discussing the impact of crisis intervention services.

**Cushing's syndrome**
An ailment that is common when there is an overabundance of steroid hormones (cortisol) found in the blood. This can be found in people that naturally produce large amounts of the hormones or in people that are taking steroids. Common symptoms of this syndrome include the patient's face starting to look fuller and rounder, a pad of fat developing between the shoulder blades, and bones becoming thin and fragile.

**custody**
The term describes who has legal rights over a child. Usually refers to the legal decision made after a divorce or a death. The term *joint custody* implies that after a divorce both parents have shared obligations in terms of raising the child.

**customary charge**
The fee that is generally charged for a given service in the field. Thus, if most MSW social workers charge $75 for a session of family therapy and a provider is charging $175, the latter social worker is not charging a reasonable fee and will most likely not be reimbursed for the full amount by an insurance company.

**cutback**
A reduction. An agency cutting back on employees might decide that 20 caseworkers could do the work that 35 performed previously. The agency might also cutback on services by, for example, providing food orders but not clothing requests.

**cybercounseling**
Counseling that occurs over the World Wide Web or the Internet using e-mail or another form of electronic transmission. Sometimes called *Web counseling. See Internet counseling.*

**cybernetics**
A popular family therapy term introduced by the eminent anthropologist Gregory Bateson to suggest that a family system is governed by rules and the flow of information by feedback loops.

**cyclical unemployment**
Unemployment that is caused by an economic recession or depression.

**cyclothymic disorder**
Refers to mild cases of bipolar disorder.

**D**

In the practice of rational-emotive behavior therapy, D means that the therapist disputes the client's irrational beliefs at B, the belief system. *See A-B-C/A-B-C-D-E theory.*

**day hospital**

A treatment program that allows patients to go home for the night. Sometimes referred to as *partial hospitalization.* Can be contrasted with an inpatient hospital, where the patient does sleep at the facility, or a weekend hospital. Also different from *outpatient* or *intensive outpatient,* both of which are less intensive.

**DEA**

Abbreviation for Drug Enforcement Administration.

**death instinct**

In Freud's theory, the unconscious drive toward death. Also called *Thanatos,* it is often contrasted with *Eros,* the life instinct.

**decompensation**

Describes a client whose condition is deteriorating (e.g., becoming more anxious or depressed and is losing control of behavior or emotions).

### deductive reasoning
The process of formulating a specific hypothesis or hunch from general principles. A human service worker who believes that all alcoholic males lie, for example, would assume that a new male alcoholic client is not being entirely truthful during the initial interview. *See inductive reasoning.*

### defamation
In ethics and law, making false verbal statements to injure a person's character. Often contrasted with libel, which occurs when someone uses the written word to degrade somebody's reputation.

### defense mechanisms
Freud's notion that the individual unconsciously distorts reality to protect the ego from the unconscious ideas of the id or superego that the person cannot accept. *See denial, displacement, projection, rationalization, reaction formation, repression, and undoing.*

### deficit
(1) Implies that something is lacking. A counseling service, for example, might have a deficit of counselors trained in testing. (2) The client is lacking something from a neurological standpoint.

### deinstitutionalization
Discharging long-term hospital patients who still suffer from severe mental illness into the community. This movement escalated in the 1970s.

### deja vu
The distinct feeling that one has experienced a particular situation before.

### delinquency
Occurs when a person who is under the legal age to be an adult breaks the law.

### delirium tremens (DTs)
A condition caused by withdrawal from alcohol, occurring within 24 to 96 hours after abstinence. Hallucinations, delusions, and convulsions are common. Experts generally agree that such individuals need inpatient emergency medical care.

### delta rhythm/delta waves
In biofeedback, an electroencephalogram (EEG) reading indicating a brain wave of 4 Hz or less that is common during deep sleep. *See alpha rhythm/alpha waves, beta rhythm/beta waves, and biofeedback.*

**delusion**
An obviously false belief. Called *delusion of grandeur* when a person exaggerates his or her importance. A client, for example, may insist he or she is the president when he or she is not. Referred to as a *delusion of persecution* when one feels attacked. A client, for example, may feel that a government agency is watching all of his or her actions.

**demand characteristics**
In research, this term implies that subjects may have clues about what the researcher is looking for. If this is the case then the subjects often behave in a different manner and the experiment is said to be *confounded* (i.e., not accurate). The subjects might try to please or displease the researcher.

**dementia praecox**
An old term for *schizophrenia.*

**democratic leadership style**
A group leadership style that is often compared and contrasted with the authoritarian/autocratic and laissez-faire styles. A facilitator using this persuasion shares authority with the group. Although the leader has the final say, he or she elicits input from the group members before making a decision. *See authoritarian leadership style and laissez-faire leadership style.*

**demographic data**
Agencies routinely use statistical data for the population they are serving (e.g., average age, number of clients in a given zip code, number of African Americans, etc.) to make program decisions or to provide to organizations/individuals who are interested in making donations.

**demography**
The study of population statistics.

**denial**
The conscious act of denying reality, sometimes referred to as *suppression.* This term is often wrongly used for the term *repression,* which is automatic or unconscious forgetting that is beyond the individual's control. Denial is commonly accepted as the most common defense mechanism in chemically dependent individuals ("I don't have a drinking problem.")

### dependent personality
Someone who allows another person or persons to make decisions and take action for him or her. Dependent individuals do not take responsibility for themselves.

### dependent variable (DV)
A variable that "depends" on the independent/experimental variable. In research the dependent variable is the outcome or data variable. If, for example, you run an experiment to see whether cognitive therapy raises IQ scores, then the IQ score is the dependent variable. *See independent variable (IV).*

### depression
A mood disorder characterized by extreme sadness.

### deprivation
To withhold or not provide something that is necessary. For example, a parent who never holds, cuddles, or talks to an infant has created a state of emotional deprivation.

### depth psychology
A school of helping that believes that impulses buried deep in the unconscious mind are responsible for one's behaviors and feelings. Can also be referred to as a *psychodynamic approach.*

### descriptive statistics
Any statistic that describes a property or attribute of a sample. The mean, the median, the mode, and the range would be examples of descriptive statistics. Often contrasted with an inferential statistic, which makes inferences about the population at large by analyzing a sample from that population. A *t* test or an analysis of variance would be an example of an inferential statistic.

### designer drugs
A form of drug abuse in which a prescription or over-the-counter drug is chemically altered to help one experience a drug high. Designer drugs are illegal.

### determinism
A philosophy stating that nothing occurs without a reason. Since this philosophy holds that factors outside of the individual's control influence behavior, adherents of determinism do not believe that human beings have free will.

**developmental psychology**
The branch of psychology that deals with physical and psychological changes that occur throughout the aging process.

**diabetes mellitus (DM)**
A pancreatic disease that leads to elevated blood-glucose levels known as *hyperglycemia.* Common symptoms of DM are excessive thirst, hunger, fatigue, frequent urination, and double vision. There are several types of the disease. Type I is the type of DM that is caused by insulin-producing cells (i.e., Beta cells of the pancreas) being damaged and thus very little if any insulin is being produced. A person with this type of DM requires injections of insulin to control the high glucose levels in the blood. Type I usually impacts individuals under the age of 20, which is why some people refer to this as *juvenile diabetes.* In the case of Type II DM, the body does produce insulin but it is an insufficient amount or it doesn't work properly. Therefore, the glucose cannot get into the cells to produce the energy needed by the body. This form of DM is the most common, and is usually found in adults over the age of 40 that are overweight. A modified diet and exercise normally can keep type II diabetes under control. Gestational diabetes is induced by pregnancy due to the changing hormone levels. The hormones impact insulin's ability to work correctly in the body. Generally, after giving birth blood-glucose levels return to normal; however, women who suffer from gestational diabetes are more likely to develop Type II diabetes later in life.

**diagnosis**
To classify and label a physical or emotional disease or disorder. In order to receive insurance or managed care third-party payment, a provider must assign a *DSM* diagnosis code or ICD diagnosis code to the client. Diagnosis is viewed as a double-edged sword. It is positive in the sense that when one professional speaks of a client with a given diagnosis he will mean the same thing as another professional. Nevertheless, sometimes the person will begin to live up to the label. *See DSM-IV-TR, iatrogenic disorder/illness, and ICD.*

**dichotomous cognitions/thinking**
A form of irrational thinking often seen in depressed individuals in which the person only perceives two, usually diametrically opposed, options. A client might say, for example, "My girlfriend can come back to me or I'll kill myself."

**dichotomous variable**
In statistics and research, a binomial variable that exists in two categories (e.g., male or female).

**differential reinforcement of other behavior (DRO)**
An operant conditioning behavior modification technique in which the human service worker reinforces an alternative behavior to reduce or eliminate an unwanted behavior. In essence, the helper can reinforce any behavior except the inappropriate one. Hence, a child who steals or curses during a given period of time could be reinforced for remaining quiet, working on a scholastic assignment, etc.

**directive counseling/therapy**
Refers to helping approaches in which the helper actually tells the client what to do, how to think, or what steps to take. Treatment modalities that employ advice giving are considered directive. The term also implies that the helper may tell the client what topics to discuss. The directive approach (sometimes called the *active directive approach*) is often contrasted with the person-centered, client-centered, or nondirective paradigms in which advice is rarely if ever given and the client guides the interview.

**direct mail marketing campaign**
Sometimes known as *doing a mailing,* this is a highly effective technique for organizations who wish to sell an item or an event (e.g., a resource guide, fund raiser, or a workshop) or who want to raise money. The technique works best when advertising materials are mailed to individuals who have made donations or helped the agency in the past. Nevertheless, mailing lists may be rented or purchased in order to target other individuals (e.g., a list of state licensed social workers). List brokers can rent to an agency lists of virtually every possible group of individuals. The mailing package usually consists of an envelope which may or may not have teaser copy on the outside of it (e.g., "Your donation can help feed three hungry children"), a compelling letter, and sometimes a return card or envelope. Most small agencies have found that providing a return stamp is not profitable.

**direct practice**
The process of actually working with clients. Often contrasted with tasks that do not involve directly working with clients, such as fund raising or agency administration.

**disability/disabled**
(1) Lacking the ability to function as others do on a permanent or temporary basis. A disability can be psychological (e.g., a learning disability) or
physical (e.g., loss of sight). (2) For social security disability insurance
benefits, an inability to work due to physical or mental impairment that
will last or has lasted over twelve months or will result in death. Must be
substantiated via a medical examination.

**discrimination**
(1) To treat a person differently because of race, sex, ethicity, religion, age,
or gender (e.g., not hiring someone because they are over 50). Often a
form of prejudice. (2) In behaviorism, the ability of a person or animal to
distinguish between two similar stimuli. For example, a mentally challenged child might be taught to get on the purple bus but not the blue
one, even though blue looks similar to purple. To train this child we
would reinforce him when he picked purple but not blue. Often contrasted with stimulus generalization in which we want the person to
respond to a range of stimuli. *See stimulus discrimination and stimulus
generalization.*

**disinhibition**
In Andrew Salter's conditioned reflex therapy, the therapeutic process of
taking an individual who is inhibitory (i.e., not emotionally expressive)
and helping that person to become excititory (i.e., emotionally healthy
and liberated in affect). *See conditioned reflex therapy.*

**disorder**
A disease or something that is not considered normal.

**disoriented**
A state in which the individual is confused about what is going on. A disoriented person may not know where he or she is, the date, the time, the
place, or the year.

**dispersion**
In statistics, the extent to which scores are spread out or clustered in relation to a given value, generally the mean.

93

**displacement**
An ego defense mechanism in which the individual is scared to show anger toward the actual individual he or she is angry at because of the possible repercussions. Therefore, the individual takes his or her anger out on a safe target. A teacher, for example, may be very angry at her principal but might be afraid that if she tells her principal it will jeopardize her next raise or even her job. Therefore, she takes out her anger on her students. The difficulty with the defense mechanism is that since the individual is never dealing with the person who is causing the anger the problem with that person cannot be resolved.

**dissociation/dissociative disorder**
A defense mechanism characterized by a pattern of thoughts or feelings that do not match the actual situation. A soldier in battle, for example, might erroneously think that the gunfire is actually fireworks and that he is attending an Independence Day celebration. Older literature may refer to this pattern as *disassociation*. Amnesia (a loss of memory) and multiple personality disorder (MPD) characterized by two or more distinct personalities, now called dissociative identity disorder, are common examples of dissociative disorders. On occasion an individual will leave his or her environment and take on a whole new life. This is known as dissociative fugue.

**distributed practice**
The notion that spreading practice or learning sessions out is more effective than trying to learn or practice without a break (called *massed practice*). Hence, a client might be advised to study a little each night rather than cramming in a long marathon study session prior to an exam.

**distribution**
In statistics, a graph or other visual representation of the scores.

**disulfiram**
*See antabuse.*

**divorce mediation**
A process, practiced not only by attorneys but also by other specially trained mental health and social service professionals, to help the couple settle matters of custody and possessions out of court.

**Dix, Dorothea Lynde (1802–1887)**
A teacher who helped improve conditions for mentally ill individuals and criminals. She was instrumental in founding or enlarging over 30 mental hospitals.

**dizygotic twins**
Usually referred to as *fraternal twins,* this term indicates that the twins were born from separate fertilized eggs called *zygotes.* Genetically speaking, dizygotic twins are no more genetically alike than brothers and sisters. Contrasted with monozygotic or identical twins born from the same egg. *See monozygotic twins.*

**DM**
*See diabetes mellitus (DM).*

**double-bind**
Also known as a no win or no escape situation, this dysfunctional form of paradoxical communication presents the recipient with two conflicting messages, thus the individual cannot totally comply (e.g., "Don't be so obedient!"). This communication pattern was first illuminated by the eminent anthropologist Gregory Bateson and is said to be fairly common in dysfunctional families. Some experts believe that if parents utilize this form of communication repeatedly children begin to display schizophrenic tendencies.

**double blind study**
An experiment conducted in a manner such that neither the experimenters nor the subjects know who is getting the experimental variable. This type of research is required for studies of prescription medicines. The purpose of the double blind study is to eliminate expectations or demand characteristics from the experiment. *See demand characteristics.*

**downers**
Slang for barbiturates, tranquilizers that induce extreme relaxation or a sleeplike state. Drugs of this nature can be extremely addictive and dangerous, and withdrawal can be difficult.

**downsizing**
Occurs when a business, agency, hospital, or government program reduces the number of staff or employees.

### Down's syndrome
A chromosomal abnormality that can cause retardation, heart difficulties, reduced muscle tone, and a flat nose. In the older literature the term *mongolism* was used, though this condition can occur in any racial group.

### Draw-A-Person Test (DAP)
A norm-referenced projective/expressive test in which the person is asked to draw human figures. It is a nonverbal measure of intellectual ability and can be used as a projective measure of personality. Suitable for ages 3 to 16.

### dream work
(1) In psychoanalysis, making the hidden or so-called latent content of the dream conscious in order to analyze the meaning. Freud felt dreams were very important and dubbed them "the royal road to the unconscious mind." Freudians often refer to dream work as "dream interpretation." (2) In gestalt therapy, analyzing the dream in the present moment to help integrate the personality.

### drug abuse
The use of drugs, including alcohol, in a manner that threatens physical, social, or emotional well-being.

### drug czar
Slang for the individual the president picks as the U.S. director of drug policy and education.

### drug habituation
The notion that more and more of a given drug must be used to produce the same effect. Can occur with prescription or over-the-counter medicinals. An individual, for example, who takes an aspirin a day to ward off a heart attack for a long period of time might need considerably more than one tablet to abate a headache or muscle pain. In street drug users, the intake of higher dosages and more frequent use can cause medical problems or death.

### drug of choice
Drug abusers often demonstrate a preference for one drug over all the drugs with which he or she has experimented (i.e., "Her drug of choice is alcohol.").

**drug paraphernalia**
Items that facilitate the use of drugs such as needles or pipes.

**DSM-IV-TR**
*Diagnostic and Statistical Manual,* 4th edition, text revised. The official book published by the American Psychiatric Association that is used to classify psychiatric disorders. The book lists symptoms (i.e., criteria) so that when one clinician is talking about a given disorder he or she means the same thing as another clinician who is using the same term. Each diagnosis has a number (e.g., 296.22) and a name (e.g., adjustment disorder with mixed emotional features). Insurance companies, managed care firms, Medicaid, and Medicare require a diagnosis from this book in order to pay the provider for services. *See nosology and taxonomy.*

**DSW**
Abbreviation for Doctor of Social Work or, on occasion, Doctor of Social Welfare. Some schools offer a Ph.D. in either of the aforementioned disciplines.

**dual diagnosis**
Used to describe a chemically dependent or addicted individual who also has another psychological disorder such as depression or panic disorder.

**dual relationship**
Occurs when the client's human service worker also has another significant relationship with the client (e.g., related to client, having a sexual relationship, dating, human service worker is the client's boss, etc.). All professional ethical bodies frown on dual relationships, as they get in the way of objectivity. Imagine that you are dating a client; she breaks up with you and now comes to sessions with you to talk about how much she likes her new boyfriend. The term *multiple relationships* can also be used to describe this ethical violation.

**duration**
(1) In behavior modification, the length of time a behavior does or does not occur (e.g., the child engaged in head banging for 45 seconds) (2) In policy, the length of time a program will operate (e.g., a one-year program to help flood victims).

**DV**
*See dependent variable (DV).*

**dyad**
The term dyad literally means *two*. In our profession it generally means a helper and a client. Also called a *one-to-one session* or *individual helping session.*

**dynamics**
The interactions between two or more people. Usually refers to what is transpiring between group members.

**dyscalculia**
The inability to do math.

**dysfunctional**
Unable to function. Disturbed, impaired, or abnormal.

**dysgraphia**
The inability to write.

**dyslexia**
A learning disability characterized by an inability in terms of learning to read. A person with dyslexia will often reverse letters when reading or writing. Mental retardation, lack of environmental stimulation, and organic factors are generally ruled out before using this label.

**dysthymia/dysthymic disorder**
A mood disorder that is like a persistent low-level depression that lasts for at least two years.

**E**
(1) In rational-emotive behavior therapy created by Albert Ellis, E can stand for a new, healthier emotional response. (2) Abbreviation for the word *environment*. *See A-B-C/A-B-C-D-E theory.*

**EAP**
*See employee assistance program.*

**early childhood education**
(1) Educational programs for preschool children. (2) Educational programs for children ages 8 and under.

**Earth Day**
A celebration championed by human service workers and others each year dedicated to the independence and cooperation of all people around the world. The observance also stresses the importance of ecology and not destroying the natural resources of our planet. The first Earth Day was held on March 21, 1970.

**Easter Seals**
An organization with a staff of 13,000 plus volunteers that helps more than 1 million adults and children with disabilities each year. The organization got its name from a fund raising activity that began in 1934 when donors placed seals on envelopes to show their support.

**eating disorder**
Inappropriate eating including anorexia nervosa (severely limiting food intake to the point where it can be life threatening), bulimia (eating huge amounts of food in a short period of time and then using vomiting, laxatives, or excessive exercise to curb weight gain), pica (eating items that are not food such as chalk), and rumination disorder of childhood (ejecting food from the mouth when one is not vomiting).

**ebonics**
A term coined by St. Louis psychologist Robert L. Williams to describe the true language of African-Americans. Sometimes ebonics is referred to as *Black vernacular,* or *Black English.*

**EBT**
Electronic benefit transfer. *See voucher.*

**eclectic**
The practice of using several theories of counseling or therapy when treating a client. A therapist, for example, using reality therapy might also employ biofeedback to help the client cope with severe anxiety. The eclectic approach is often contrasted with any treatment approach that sticks steadfastly to a single approach. Some experts now use the new terms *integrative counseling* or *integrationalism* in place of the traditional term *eclectic.* Other experts insist that integrative therapy goes beyond eclecticism and that the various theories can be unified.

**ecological fallacy**
In research, the tendency to draw a false conclusion about individuals after observing groups of individuals.

**economic policy**
Any policy that concerns money such as how much an agency will pay for rent or how government defense spending will impact education.

**ecstasy**
A so-called rave party or club drug that became popular in the 80s and 90s. The designer drug, which can cause brain damage and impaired memory, is a combination of methamphetamine and hallucingenic substances. Also known as *MDMA.*

**ECT**
*See electroconvulsive shock therapy (ECT)/electroshock therapy (EST).*

**educable/educable mentally retarded**
In the older literature this is known as *mild mental retardation;* an IQ of 52 to 67.

**Educational Resources Information Center (ERIC)**
An electronic database available to assist students and professionals conduct a literature search (i.e., bibliography) for their class papers, journal article, research, thesis, or dissertation. Many public, college, and university libraries can secure ERIC searches for students and practitioners. Internet access is also an option.

**ego**
Sigmund Freud's psychoanalytic structural theory characterizes the mind or so-called psychic apparatus as being composed of three hypothetical entities: the id, the ego, and the superego. The ego—also known as the reality principle and analogous to the adult ego state in Eric Berne's transactional analysis—is the portion of the personality that regulates impulses from the id and the superego based on demands from the environment. The ego has also been termed the executive administrator of the personality. *See structural theory.*

**ego alien**
*See ego dystonic.*

**ego boundaries**
Refers to one's ability to separate reality from fantasy.

**egocentric**
A self-centered person and/or behavior.

**egocentrism**
Piaget's term to describe the fact that children younger than approximately seven years of age see the world only from their own vantage point or perception. If a human service worker stands facing a young child and asks the child to point to the worker's right hand, the child will point to her right hand, which of course would be the worker's left. Statements such as, "the snow is following me," also illustrate this phenomenon. The child behaves as if the universe exists only for him or her and is unable to comprehend another person's point of view. Egocentrism occurs in the preoperational stage.

**ego defense mechanism**
Unconscious distortions of reality that protect the individual from id or superego impulses. *See defense mechanisms.*

**ego dystonic**
An attribute that the client does not consider desirable. Thus, if a client viewed shyness as a negative trait then the shyness could be termed ego dystonic. Some of the literature uses the term *ego alien,* meaning the individual does not feel the symptom is consistent with the rest of his or her personality. *See ego syntonic.*

**ego ideal**
The Freudian notion of a perfect or ideal self housed in the superego. The conceptualization of the ego ideal comes from parental messages about right and wrong.

**ego strength**
(1) An individual's ability to cope and separate reality from fantasy. (2) In psychoanalysis, the ability to balance the id and the superego.

**ego syntonic**
An attribute that the client considers acceptable or consistent with his or her self-image. Often contrasted with *ego dystonic* or *ego alien,* ego syntonic traits are attributes that do not seem unacceptable. *See ego dystonic.*

**eidetic imagery**
The ability to remember precisely what was perceived such that it is as if the person is experiencing the perception in the present. Such vivid recall is seen in childhood but rarely occurs in adolescence or adulthood.

**e-journal**
A journal that is sent to you via e-mail or available over the Internet. The latter is sometimes referred to as an *online journal.* Some journals offer online versions; however, a subscription or membership to the organization producing the work is often required to view the entire publication. *See journal.*

**Elavil**
A popular antidepressant medicine.

**elder abuse and neglect**
Maltreatment of older people such as physically battering them, not feeding them, or psychologically harming them in any fashion.

**elderly**
Persons 65 and older.

**Electra complex**
Sigmund Freud's notion that daughters unconsciously want to have sexual relations with their father. This is the female counterpart of Freud's controversial Oedipus complex in males and occurs in the phallic stage, ages 3 to 5. *See Oedipus complex.*

**electroconvulsive shock therapy (ECT)/electroshock therapy (EST)**
A medical treatment for depression and mood disorders carried out by physicians and psychiatrists. The technique was created by Cerletti and Bini in 1938. Electrical current is passed through the brain, producing convulsions. The client is given a sedative and a muscle relaxant to reduce potentially harmful muscle contractions. Researchers are not certain why this procedure often works. Some degree of memory loss may be evident after the treatment. Most nonmedical therapists agree it should be used as a last resort, while others feel the procedure is inhumane under any circumstances.

**electroencephalograph (EEG)**
Used in conjunction with biofeedback, the term describes a device which monitors brain wave rhythms. *See alpha rhythm/alpha waves, beta rhythm/ beta waves, biofeedback, and delta rhythm/delta waves.*

**electromyograph (EMG)**
Used in conjunction with biofeedback, the term describes a device that monitors the degree of tension or relaxation in muscles.

**eligibility worker**
A human service worker who determines whether a client can receive a given service (e.g., Does the client meet the requirements to stay in a particular homeless shelter?). In most cases the term refers to whether a client can receive welfare services/benefits such as temporary assistance or food stamps. When a client is assessed to see if he or she is eligible for a service, the term *means test* is often used.

**Electronic Benefit Transfer (EBT).**
*See voucher.*

**Elizabethan Poor Law**
Refers to Queen Elizabeth's 1601 law to help poor unemployed citizens who might be disruptive to society. Increased taxes were used to create the social welfare programs administered by local governments, known as parishes, who provided assistance only for people in their specific jurisdiction. Historically, the Elizabethan Poor Law set the stage for later social welfare programs, including those in the United States, by distinguishing between the *deserving poor* (e.g., orphans, those who were blind or were not working due to no fault of their own) and the *nondeserving poor* (e.g., vagrants and drunkards). If the individual received services in the home the term *outdoor relief* was used. If the individual was unable to care for himself or herself *indoor relief* in the form of an institution called an *almshouse,* was provided. Nondeserving poor were sent to *workhouses* to perform menial tasks in order to receive the bare minimum necessary to survive.

**Ellis, Albert (1913–)**
The founding father of rational-emotive behavior therapy (REBT), a treatment approach that suggests that people have an inborn tendency to think in an illogical, irrational, and unscientific manner. Ellis feels that humans talk to themselves in irrational sentences or declarations (that Ellis calls self-talk or internal verbalizations) and this causes the bulk of most people's emotional disturbance. Ellis feels that the treatment for most unhappiness is learning to think in a rational manner. *See rational-emotive therapy (RET)/rational-emotive behavior therapy (REBT).*

**elopement**
Leaving a treatment facility against medical advice (often abbreviated as AMA in the client's chart or record) or simply leaving without telling anybody.

**emic approach to multicultural counseling**
Suggests that counseling must be targeted toward the cultural background of the person. Often contrasted with the *etic* approach, which asserts that clients of all cultures should be counseled in the same basic manner because we are more alike than different.

**emotional illness**
*See mental disorder/mental illness.*

**emotionally cut off**
Family therapy expert Murray Bowen's term that describes a family in which members avoid each other due to emotional problems.

**emotional deadness**
A condition in which an individual is not aware of his or her feelings or chooses to ignore them.

**emotion**
Feelings such as love, anger, happiness, or fear. Some of the literature uses the term *affect*.

**empathy**
The ability to understand another individual's situation. The human service worker who is empathic attempts to understand what life is like for the client. It is as if the worker is able to experience the client's thoughts, behaviors, feelings, and overall point of view. The worker then conveys this to the client. Carl R. Rogers, the father of person-centered counseling, felt that a helper must display accurate empathy along with unconditional positive regard and congruence (also known as *genuineness*) in order for the client to experience meaningful changes. These are considered the three core conditions of effective helping. Often contrasted with sympathy (or feeling sorry for the client), which is generally not viewed as therapeutic for the client.

**empiricism**
The notion that knowledge is acquired by experience. Usually attributed to the British philosopher John Locke (1632–1704).

**employee assistance program (EAP)**
A service offered by some employers so that employees can secure free counseling, therapy, or substance abuse treatment. Often the actual counseling is provided by an agency or hospital that provides EAP services rather than counselors hired by the firm the employee is working for. EAPs frequently limit the maximum number of sessions an employee may use. If more sessions are necessary, the EAP counselor will refer the employee for long-term outpatient or inpatient treatment.

**employment**
The act of working for money. Often contrasted with volunteering one's work for free.

### empower
Giving a client the knowledge, power, resources, and emotional strength to overcome a difficulty or reach a goal.

### empty chair technique
In Fritz Perl's gestalt therapy, a person role plays with an empty chair in front of him or her. Then the person moves to the empty chair to become the individual he or she is talking to or to play another part of his or her personality. Some of the literature refers to this as the *two chair technique. See Topdog and Underdog.*

### empty nest
Refers to the family structure after the children leave home (i.e., the husband and wife are alone).

### enabler
In addiction studies and mental health, a person who allows another individual to act in a dysfunctional manner. For example, a woman might buy beer for her husband, even though she knows he is alcoholic.

### encopresis
An inability to control the act of defecation.

### encounter group
Also called a *sensitivity group,* the encounter group (popularized by Carl R. Rogers) is intended to boost self-awareness, enhance human potential, and help the individual fine tune his or her interpersonal skills.

### endogenous *See exogenous.*

### endorphin
Assumed to be a natural chemical in one's brain that yields morphine-like properties to abate pain and produce elation in one's mood. Some researchers believe that aerobic exercise can incite its release.

### enmeshed/enmeshment
In family therapy, refers to family members who are too involved and overly protective of each other. Enmeshed family members suffer from a loss of autonomy.

### enrichment
Special advanced learning experiences for talented or gifted students. Generally used in regard to educational settings.

**entitlement**
The notion that a person should receive goods or services due to his or her status, such as a worker receiving unemployment benefits because he worked at a company for a designated period of time.

**entry-level worker**
A worker who is new or has little or no experience in the position.

**enuresis**
Bed wetting. An inability to control the discharge of urine.

**environment**
The parts of the client's world, including other people as well as the physical location and surroundings.

**epidemic**
A disease or problem that afflicts a high number of people.

**epigenetic principle**
A term from embryology used to describe Erik Erikson's theory that suggests that personality development unfolds in predetermined, orderly steps.

**epilepsy**
Seizures or convulsions. Types of epilepsy include: major epilepsy/ grand mal seizures that result in a loss of consciousness; minor epilepsy/ petit mal seizures, characterized by only a momentary lapse of consciousness; and Jacksonian epilepsy, occurring in only a portion of the body without loss of consciousness.

**epistemology**
The study of how we acquire knowledge.

**EPSEM**
In statistics and research, stands for the equal probability selection method in which every member of a population has the same chance of being selected for the sample.

**equifinality**
In family therapy, the tendency for families to behave in repetitive, redundant, habitual patterns of interaction (e.g., members will always argue or problem solve in a set pattern that will end in the same way, for example, not speaking to each other). The literal meaning of the term is "equal ending."

### equilibration/equilibrium
In Piaget's theory, the balance between assimilation and accommodation which results in a balance between the individual and the environment. *See assimilation and accommodation.*

### equipotentiality
The family therapy notion that different endings can be generated by the same initial situation (e.g., a clinician cannot make a prediction regarding the outcome of the situation based on an initial or precipitating event).

### ER
A hospital emergency room.

### ERIC
*See Educational Resources Information Center.*

### Erickson, Milton H. (1901–1980)
A psychiatrist, hypnotist and psychologist who is considered one of the greatest therapeutic geniuses of all time. His interventions paved the way for Jay Haley's work emphasis on paradox, Bandler and Grinder's NLP, numerous family therapy strategies, and a host of brief therapy techniques.

### Erikson, Erik (1902–1994)
One of the most famous analysts of all time, Erikson is primarily known for his eight-stage theory of psychosocial development over the life span as set forth in his 1963 book *Childhood and Society.* Each stage has a crisis/task that must be resolved in order for the individual to mature. He is also known for coining the term *identity crisis* and analyzing famous historical figures based on their biographies. *See autonomy versus shame and doubt, generativity versus stagnation, identity versus role confusion, industry versus inferiority, initiative versus guilt, integrity versus despair, intimacy versus isolation, and trust versus mistrust.*

### eros
The Greek god of love. In Freud's psychoanalytic theory it is the life/love instinct, often contrasted with *thanatos,* the death instinct.

### erotic
Refers to sexual thoughts and feelings; related to sexual pleasure or love.

**errogenous zone**
Any part of the body in which the person can feel sexual pleasure (e.g., in Freud's psychoanalytic theory the mouth, anus, phallus, and genital areas).

**Esalen Institute**
A famous psychotherapy and human potential training center in Big Sur, California.

**ESP**
*See extrasensory perception.*

**e-therapy**
Counseling or therapy that takes place over the Internet or e-mail. Also called *Internet Counseling* or *cybercounseling. See Internet counseling.*

**ethical dilemmas**
Refers to any situation in which ethical guidelines conflict or are not specific (e.g., one organization recommends one course of action while another has ethical guidelines that advocate something that is contradictory).

**ethics**
Rules, guidelines, conduct recommendations, codes of behavior, and standards of right and wrong for human service practitioners. Ethics protect workers as well as clients. All major professional organizations (e.g., the APA, NASW, NOHSE, and ACA) have ethical guidelines. These guidelines are often not identical and are frequently not as precise as professionals would like them to be.

**ethnic group**
A group of people who have a shared history that shapes their language, behavior, and religious customs.

**ethnocentrism**
(1) The belief that someone's culture is the best and that other cultures can be compared to that particular culture. (2) That your view of the situation is the same as the client's. This assumption may not be true.

**ethology**
The study of animal behavior, including man.

**etic approach to multicultural counseling**
*See emic approach to multicultural counseling.*

**etiology**
Refers to the cause of a disease, disability, or condition.

**euphoria**
An abnormally high degree of well-being that is not related to what is transpiring in the individual's life (e.g., something bad could be happening yet the person is still extremely happy). Often experienced in a manic state or induced by drug and alcohol abuse. *See mania/manic.*

**euthanasia**
The act of removing pain or distress caused via an incurable disease by inducing painless death. Has also been called *assisted suicide* or in older literature *mercy killing.*

**evaluation**
The process of assessing a person, program, or government policy. Many methods can be used to perform an evaluation, including site visits, focus groups, questionnaires, statistical tests, and psychoeducational tests.

**Examination for Professional Practice of Psychology (EPPP)**
This instrument is used to determine whether an individual has the knowledge to be licensed as a psychologist. The exam is composed of 200 multiple choice questions; each has four alternatives and there is no penalty for guessing. Only one question is correct. The test is necessary in every state in the US and all Canadian provinces. It is given twice each year, in April and October, and cut-off scores vary by the state or province. An oral exam may also be required. In most cases, practitioners who graduate from doctorate counselor education programs rather than doctorate-level psychology programs are not permitted to sit for the exam. This has been a source of tension between psychologists and counselors. The test has a reputation for being extremely difficult. Written materials and seminars intended to help psychologists pass the exam are readily available.

**exceptional child**
A child who is well above or below the norm and thus needs special educational experiences to make the most progress.

**excitatory personality**
In Andrew Salter's conditioned reflex therapy, the emotionally healthy personality. Such a person practices continual, direct, straightforward, honest emotional expression. Speech is seen as the primary means of expressing excitation. *See conditioned reflex therapy and inhibitory personality.*

**ex-con**
Slang for an individual who previously spent time in a prison, penitentiary or correctional facility.

**executive administrator of the personality**
In psychoanalysis, another term for the superego.

**executive director**
The top employee in an agency. On occasion, agencies use the term *president* to describe this individual. The executive director (except in very small agencies) deals primarily with administrative rather than clinical issues and has a board of directors to whom he or she reports.

**exhibitionist**
An individual who wishes to sexually expose himself or herself in public. Exhibitionists are generally males.

**existential therapy**
This form of treatment is associated primarily with the work of Viktor Frankl, known as *logotherapy,* which literally means "healing through meaning."

**exit interview**
A final interview with an individual before he or she leaves a job, treatment program, or educational institution. This interview can provide information for the institution (e.g., what the person found helpful or not helpful) and can be used to give the person future guidance (e.g., provide a list of colleges the student can attend to continue his or her education).

**exogenous**
In psychiatry and medicine, a disorder that is caused by factors outside of the individual's body. Thus, a clinical depression caused by events rather than a biochemical imbalance in the body is said to be an exogenous depression. Often contrasted with endogenous, which is a condition caused via factors within the body (e.g., thyroid or genetics).

**experiment**
*See true experiment.*

**experimental group**
A group of subjects in a research study who receive the independent or so-called experimental variable. An attempt is made to ensure that these subjects are nearly identical to those in a control group. *See control group.*

### expert witness
A helper who testifies in court regarding the cause of a certain behavior (e.g., she skips school because her mother abuses her) or makes recommendations (e.g., the child would be better off living with his father).

### express agreement when praised
This is the sixth technique, discipline, or rule of conduct suggested in Andrew Salter's conditioned reflex therapy for instilling healthy excitation into the personality.

### extended family
Includes the nuclear family (parents and kids) as well as aunts, uncles, grandparents, cousins, in-laws, etc.

### externalizing the problem
In narrative family therapy (created primarily by Michael White of Australia) the therapist discusses the difficulty as if it exists outside the family. Thus, instead of saying, "Let's work on the fact that you are a child abuser," the therapist might say, "Let's put an end to the this destructive monster that is tearing your family apart." This technique reduces the tendency for family members to blame each other for a given difficulty.

### external locus of control
*See locus of control.*

### external validity
Research and experimentation which can be generalized to the "real" world is said to have external validity.

### Exteropsyche
In transactional analysis, the Parent ego state. *See Parent ego state.*

### extinction
An operant conditioning behavior modification procedure in which a lack of reinforcement is used to reduce or eliminate an unwanted behavior. Thus, when a parent ignores a temper tantrum he or she is utilizing extinction. Human service workers recommending extinction procedures must be careful to take into account that a "response burst" or so-called "extinction burst" often occurs after implementation. That is to say, the behavior being modified sometimes increases before it begins to dissipate.

**extraneous variable**

An outside variable that is not being studied which could confound or falsify a study. If, for example, a counselor is attempting to research the impact reality therapy has on depression, the fact that several members of the experimental group are taking an antidepressant (the extraneous variable) could confound the experiment.

**extrasensory perception (ESP)**

Often called *telepathy* or *parapsychology,* ESP is the ability to perceive information without using our senses. Thus, an individual with ESP might know what another person is thinking or that a certain event will occur. Many experiments have shown that individuals who claim to have ESP were actually using tricks used by professional magicians. A well-known magician, James Randi, has offered a large sum of money to anyone who can produce a single act of ESP that he cannot prove was magic and thus far nobody has ever collected the money.

**extrovert**

In Jungian theory, a person who is outgoing. May be spelled *extravert* in older literature. Often contrasted with an introvert, who focuses more on his or her thinking and feelings than on the environment.

**eye contact**

The act of looking at someone else's eyes while interviewing them. Generally this nonverbal practice enhances the interview process.

**113**

**face validity**
Refers to whether a psychological or educational test looks like it measures, or appears to measure, what it is supposed to measure. Most experts feel that face validity is of minimal importance. *See validity, content validity, construct validity, and predictive validity.*

**facial talk**
In Andrew Salter's conditioned reflex therapy, the second of six disciplines (i.e., techniques) for increasing healthy excitation in the personality. To practice facial talk, the client is instructed to show true, natural, spontaneous emotion on his or her face. *See conditioned reflex therapy.*

**facilitator**
(1) A person who leads a group or workshop. When more than one facilitator is used, they are called *cofacilitators.* (2) Any human service worker who links clients to services is known as a *facilitator of services.* This is sometimes known as the *broker* role in human services.

**factor analysis**
Statistical procedures which attempt to summarize a lot of variables using the important or underlying factors. Hence, a researcher might try to ascertain which three factors out of hundreds make a human service worker effective.

**factorial analysis of variance**
An analysis of variance that measures the effects (factors) of two or more independent variables, each of which has a minimum of two levels (e.g., male or female; or a three-level variable such as associate level worker, 4 year degreed worker, or master's level worker). A factorial analysis of variance is often confused with a *factor analysis. See analysis of variance (ANOVA).*

**fact sheet**
Sometimes referred to as a *family face sheet* this document generally appears on the left inside cover of the client's chart or record and gives general information such as the client's address, phone number, number of children and birth dates, allergic reactions to drugs, and who is responsible for paying for the services rendered.

**fading**
In behavior modification, gradually introducing or removing/withdrawing a stimulus.

**Fair Labor Standards Act**
Legislation that governs minimum wage, overtime payment, and child labor issues.

**faith healing**
The use of prayer to help cure physical or emotional disorders.

**false consensus effect**
To overestimate the number of people who would make the same judgments and choices as we do.

**false memory syndrome**
Also known as *confabulation,* this occurs when an individual creates events to fill in memory lapses.

**false negative**
Occurs when a test indicates that a client does not have a condition (e.g., AIDS) when in reality he or she does.

**false positive**
Occurs when a test indicates that a client does have a condition (e.g., AIDS), but in reality he or she does not.

**family cap**
Any welfare policy that denies or limits benefits if a recipient exceeds a maximum number of children while she is receiving assistance. Thus, a state program might stipulate that a mother can only receive benefits for up to 3 children. This policy is also intended to curb the population growth.

**family counseling/therapy**
A modality of treatment that involves members of one's family in the therapeutic process. This process could include anyone in the extended family setting. Well-known family therapists include Nathan Ackerman (psychodynamic); Virginia Satir and Carl Whitaker (experiential); Murray Bowen (intergenerational); Salvador Minuchin (structural); and Jay Haley and Cloe Madaness (strategic/communications model).

**family court**
(1) A court that deals with legal issues related to the family such as divorce and domestic violence. (2) Some juvenile courts now call themselves family courts.

**Family Education Rights and Privacy Act (FERPA) of 1974**
Also referred to as the Buckley Amendment, this federal act dictates that schools receiving federal funding give parents of students under the age of 18 the right to access their children's educational records. The act also grants students 18 and older the right to view their own school records. Finally, student records may not be released to a third party without the written consent of a parent (if the child is under 18), or by the student, if he or she is over 18.

**family face sheet**
*See fact sheet.*

**fantasy**
Another name for a daydream or mental story that is played out in the imagination.

**farsightedness**
*See hyperopia.*

**FDA**
The U.S. Food and Drug Administration. One of the oldest consumer protection agencies, it regulates the safety of prescription medicines, medical devices, food, blood supply, and some nutritional supplements.

**featherbedding**
Hiring employees who are not required.

**federalism**
The division of power between the federal and state governments granted by the constitution.

**Federal Housing Administration**
A federal agency under the auspices of the U.S. Department of Housing and Urban Development (HUD intended to provide housing opportunities for low- to moderate-income families.

**feedback**
Giving a client or supervisee information about verbal or nonverbal behavior that might be relevant (e.g., "you seem upset every time we discuss your grandchildren").

**feeling-talk**
In Andrew Salter's conditioned reflex therapy, the first of six disciplines (i.e., techniques) for increasing healthy excitation in the personality. To practice feeling-talk, the client is instructed to deliberately say what he or she spontaneously feels. Salter says that feeling-talk occurs when the person is emotionally outspoken (e.g., "I like the food, I hate that picture, I love it when you say that, etc."). Fact-talk void of feeling (e.g., We are eating carrots tonight) is said to have no impact on improving one's mental health.

**fee splitting**
The result of an unethical practice that occurs when a provider receives a fee for making a referral. For example, if John refers a client to the Acme Counseling Center then he receives $5, or perhaps he receives $5 for each session the client attends. The problem with this practice is that it clouds John's objectivity and thus he may refer to the Acme Center even though better options (such as an agency that will not split the fee with him) exist. It should be mentioned, nevertheless, that this practice is indeed ethical in some professions not related to human services.

**feminism**
A movement that is intended to end prejudice toward women and help them advance.

**feminization of poverty**
Asserts that women are more likely than men to rely on public assistance and that the number of females who are poverty stricken is increasing.

**feral child**
A child raised in the wild by animals (e.g., wolves). Many behavioral scientists believe that feral children do not truly exist.

**fetal alcohol syndrome (FAS)**
Occurs when a pregnant mother's use of the drug alcohol causes problems for the fetus. Physical disabilities, mental retardation, and psychological difficulties can result from this condition.

**fetish**
Any inanimate object or body part that becomes sexually arousing to an individual. Use, contact, or thoughts related to the fetish are sources of sexual gratification and can become a controlling factor in one's life.

**FHA**
*See Federal Housing Administration.*

**fidelity**
In ethics, the notion that the helper will honor promises and commitments to clients.

**field work**
(1) Human service delivery provided outside of the office (e.g., counseling a client at his or her home or taking him or her to a doctor). (2) In research, an experiment or observation that is conducted in the real world rather than a laboratory.

**fight-or-flight response**
A response that may be triggered by physical or psychological stimuli, which prepares the body to take an action of fight or flight.

**fiscal year (FY)**
A twelve-month period used by an organization or government, which does not necessarily begin on January 1, in order to coincide with the institution's funding/accounting. For example, many agencies and schools begin their fiscal year on July 1, while the federal government begins theirs on October 1.

**119**

**fixation**
(1) A conflict in which a person is locked in an earlier psychosexual stage due to overgratification or undergratification during a specific stage. (2) The term is also used to describe an abnormally strong attachment to somebody else that hinders the person's mental health. For example, an adult may be so fixated on his mother that he cannot date women.

**fixed role therapy**
A therapeutic school created by psychologist George Kelly in which the individual role plays the person they would truly like to become.

**fixed schedule of reinforcement**
In behavior modification, always giving the client or animal the reinforcement in the same manner or pattern (e.g., after every two math problems). Often contrasted with a "variable schedule" in which the manner or pattern of the reinforcer changes (e.g., first it is given after two math problems, then after seven problems).

**flat affect**
No emotion or a distinct lack of emotion.

**flight to health/flight into health**
The notion that change often takes time and the helper is worried because the client improved too rapidly. Can be a sign of suicide. The person feels happy because they will soon be out of their mental pain.

**flight to illness/flight into illness**
A person rapidly develops symptoms to avoid something unpleasant in life.

**flooding**
A behavior therapy technique in which the client is exposed to a feared stimulus. For example, a client who is afraid of snakes because he feels they will bite him is exposed to the snake for an hour without the dreaded snake bite. Some of the literature refers to flooding as "deliberate exposure with response prevention."

**Flynn Effect**
J. R. Flynn made the observation that the average score on standardized IQ tests has been increasing worldwide. Experts are not certain why this is transpiring; however, one theory is that children's manual dexterity is

improving since they began playing video games on a regular basis and this boosts performance scores on the test.

### follow-up
Social service, mental health, or medical activity that occurs after formal treatment is terminated (e.g., a nurse might visit a patient at her home a week after she has left the hospital).

### Food and Drug Administration
*See FDA.*

### food stamps program
A social welfare policy program, which gives low-income individuals benefits to purchase nutrition items.

### forced-choice exam/test
A test that requires you to pick an answer such as "true or false" or "a, b, c, or d." Often contrasted with essay or projective tests in which the examinee can answer the question in any way he or she wishes.

### formal operations stage
*See Piaget, Jean.*

### forensic human service work
Deals with the legal aspects of human behavior and difficulties.

### foreplay
Sexual activity that occurs prior to intercourse.

### forward conditioning
In Pavlovian classical conditioning, the assumption that the conditioned stimulus (the CS, e.g., a bell) must come before the unconditioned stimulus (the UCS or US, e.g., the meat) for conditioning to be effective. Often contrasted with backward conditioning in which the UCS comes before the CS. This paradigm is usually very ineffective or won't work at all. *See Pavlov, Ivan.*

### foster care
A program that provides temporary housing to children who are abandoned, abused, neglected, or become wards of the state.

### free association
A Freudian psychoanalytic technique in which one talks about anything that may come to mind at a particular time.

### Freedmen's Bureau
Refers to the Bureau of Refugees, Freedmen, and Abandoned Lands, set up after the Civil War to help African Americans make the transition from slavery to freedom.

### free-floating anxiety
Anxiety that is not related to a given situation or event. The person may state that he or she is unaware of what is causing the nervous condition.

### frequency distribution
A description or a graph that indicates the number of times that a given behavior, attribute, or trait appears. Thus, the statement that 12 out of every 100 people in the sample were physically abused would connote frequency.

### Freud, Anna (1895–1982)
Daughter of Sigmund Freud (the father of psychoanalysis), and a well-known child analyst who is often remembered for her work related to defense mechanisms.

### Freudian slip
Also known as *parapraxis,* this principle asserts that accidental verbalizations reveal true unconscious feelings and thoughts. Many experts do not believe in this theory.

### Freud, Sigmund (1856–1939)
Famous Viennese psychoanalyst, physiologist, and neurologist. Founded the psychoanalytic school, and focused on the unconscious mind and psychosexual development. *See abreaction, ego, free association, id, psychoanalysis, superego, and transference.*

### frustration
Any response that occurs when a human or animal encounters a block that keeps them from achieving a goal. A student, for example, might be frustrated that he cannot get into the college of his choice.

### frustration-aggression hypothesis/theory
The theory that frustration leads to aggression, and aggression leads to frustration. Albert Ellis, the father of rational-emotive behavior therapy (REBT), feels that this hypothesis is untrue and leads individuals to irrational beliefs that lead to unhappiness.

**fugue/fugue amnesia**
From the Latin word meaning "flight," this term describes an individual who has severe memory loss (usually referred to as amnesia) and leaves home to start a new life.

**fulfillment**
To satisfy a need, want, or goal.

**functional disorder**
A difficulty that has no physical cause. Assumed to be caused by psychological factors.

**fundamental attribution error**
The tendency to emphasize internal causes and de-emphasize external causes when describing the behaviors of others.

**funding/funding source**
The manner in which an organization or program receives the money to perform its duties. Thus, an agency might get 50% of its funds from United Way (i.e., a funding source) and the other 50% from the fees clients pay.

**fund raiser**
(1) A person who attempts to raise money to help run an agency or a program. Often referred to as a "director of development," this person generally has other duties. (2) An activity such as a sports auction, bingo game, or golf tournament that would be intended to secure funding for the organization.

**GA**
*See general assistance (GA).*

**GAF Scale**
Also known as the *Global Assessment of Functioning Scale*, this scale is included in the *DSM IV-TR* on Axis 5 to evaluate the highest educational, social, and occupational level at which the client has functioned at for the last year prior to the interview. The scale goes from 0 (basically a highly suicidal individual or otherwise seriously impaired) to 100 (no symptoms whatsoever).

**GAL**
Abbreviation for guardian ad litem. *See guardian ad litem.*

**Galton, Sir Francis (1822–1911)**
A cousin of Charles Darwin, Galton is considered a pioneer in psychology for his creation of the notion of testing individual differences.

**Gambler's Anonymous (GA)**
A self-help group, similar to Alcoholics Anonymous (AA), for persons addicted to gambling.

**gambling addiction/compulsion**
An inability to control one's desire to gamble. Some experts believe that this problem will grow due to an increase in the number of legalized gambling facilities.

**games**
In Eric Berne's transactional analysis, an interaction between two people in which one of them gets hurt emotionally because the other is dishonest or has an ulterior motive to make him or her feel better (the good feeling is termed a *payoff*).

**gang-related crime**
The term merely indicates that the gang has broken the law. Often such acts include violence against a rival gang. Gang violence has also been called *wilding*.

**GATB**
*See General Aptitude Test Battery.*

**gatekeeper**
(1) A person who evaluates whether the client is eligible for services. (2) In group counseling, an individual who keeps the dynamics of the group moving. Although this is usually a positive role, gatekeepers who become too aggressive can compete with the leader for control of the group. (3) A primary care physician who oversees a patient's medical care. If a patient needs to see a specialist or be admitted to a hospital, the gatekeeper needs to authorize the intervention.

**gateway drugs**
Usually refers to the fact that alcohol or marijuana usage can lead the person to try other even more addictive and dangerous drugs such as cocaine or heroin.

**Gaussian curve/distribution**
*See bell-shaped curve.*

**gay**
Can apply to a male or a female who is homosexual; however, the term *lesbian* is generally used when the individual is a female.

**GED**
Stands for General Equivalency Diploma. This credential can be obtained by taking special training and then taking a test. Successful completion of the GED indicates that the individual has achieved an education that is equal to a high school diploma. This can help the individual secure a better job or enter higher education.

**geeker**
Slang for somebody who uses crack.

**gender bias**
An attitude that is held because of one's gender (e.g., men don't show feelings, or all women are overly sensitive).

**gender identity disorder**
Some individuals have an ongoing feeling that they would like to be the opposite sex. Cross dressing or transexual behavior is seen in many of these individuals.

**General Aptitude Test Battery (GATB)**
Aptitude tests measure potential. The GATB is a career appraisal instrument created by the U.S. Department of Labor, Employment, and Training Administration. The GATB uses twelve tests to measure a client's potential ability to perform job-related tasks.

**general assistance (GA)**
A state or local program that helps low-income individuals who are ineligible for federally funded public assistance programs (e.g., Temporary Assistance to Needy Families [TANF], social security, or Supplemental Security Income [SSI]).

**generalist preparation/generalist practitioner**
Most undergraduate social work programs emphasize that they are educating students to become generalists who work with a broad range of clients, policies, and problems in a variety of settings. The generalist often brings in helpers from a variety of disciplines to assist the client. The generalist is often contrasted with the specialist, who may focus a one special group of individuals, problems, work setting, or policies (e.g., gerontology, suicidology, agency administration, or school social work). Unlike social work programs, human services programs often offer specialties at the undergraduate level including disabilities, chemical dependency, criminal justice, and youth services, to name a few.

**generalizability**
Refers to whether a research finding can be applied or *generalized* to other people or settings. If, for example, a study shows that gestalt therapy helps those who suffer from panic attacks, counselors would want to know whether it would help others outside the study who have this problem.

**generalized amnesia**
An inability to remember anything that happened previously.

**generalized anxiety**
Also called *free-floating anxiety,* a condition characterized by excessive worry that is not tied to a given idea or fear. Generalized anxiety is often contrasted with a phobia in which the individual knows what is causing the anxiety (e.g., xenophobia, which is a fear of strangers).

**general practitioner**
A doctor who does not practice a specialty such as psychiatry or cardiology.

**general systems theory**
Built on the work of biologist Ludwig von Bertalanffy, this theory focuses on the interconnectedness/interrelationships of all living things. This theory is especially popular with family therapists who believe that one person's behavior in the family always impacts another. Thus, a mother and father's parenting will have an impact on their daughter. Many helpers forget, nevertheless, that the daughter's behavior will also have an impact on the parents' behavior.

**Generation X**
This term was derived from a book entitled *Generation X* written by Douglas Coupland in 1991. Coupland decided on the title after reading a book called *Class* by Paul Fussell who used the term to describe individuals who were not interested in money, status, or social class. Different sources define the term in different ways but it generally refers to persons born after the baby boomers (approximately 1961 to 1981). Generation X is often said to be raised on television and video games, and hence they are less prepared than the baby boomers for adulthood. The notion that they are underemployed, overeducated, frustrated people is a stereotype.

**generativity versus stagnation**
The 7th stage or middle age stage, in Erik Erikson's 8 stage psychosocial model. This stage—also known as generativity versus self-absorption—occurs at ages 35–60. Generativity, the opposite of stagnation, refers to the ability to create a career, a family, and to contribute to society. An individual who does not successfully master this stage will become self-centered and stagnate.

**generic drug/medicine**
A prescription or over-the-counter medication that is identical to the popular brand but is less costly due to the fact that the company selling it does not pay as much for advertising and marketing costs. A famous brand of aspirin, for example, is generally more expensive than the drug store's own brand despite the fact that from a chemical composition standpoint both pills are identical.

**genetic counseling**
Counseling that focuses on inherited disorders (e.g., Down's syndrome) resulting from a genetic abnormality.

**genital stage**
The final psychosexual stage in Freud's psychoanalytic model (i.e., oral, anal, phallic, latency, and genital). This stage manifests itself in puberty and allows the person to have a fulfilling, loving, emotional, and sexual relationship. Freud's stages have been criticized for being too focused on sex and not covering the entire life span.

**genogram**
A pictorial diagram of three family generations depicted by lines and geometric figures. This visual representation, which is very popular with family therapists, can indicate relationships such as marriage, divorce and death between family members. Created by family therapy pioneer Murray Bowen.

**gentrification**
Occurs when ghetto or run-down neighborhood homes and/or hotels are rebuilt or replaced (usually with plush condominiums) to attract wealthier individuals. The new dwellings will raise the city's income from taxes. Gentrified neighborhoods do not eliminate poor neighborhoods since this change will force the poor people who were living in the area to move, thus creating the probability of a new impoverished area.

**genuineness**
Also known as *authentic* or *congruent* genuineness occurs when someone's words and actions correspond. Being genuine is the opposite of being a phony. Carl R. Rogers helped popularize the notion that effective helpers must be genuine/congruent.

129

**genus**
A classification of species. Humans, for example, fall under the genus *homo* and the species *sapiens,* that is to say, *homo sapiens.*

**gerontology**
The study of aging. Most commonly refers to studies or work with the elderly.

**gerontophobia**
A morbid or exaggerated fear of elderly individuals.

**gestalt**
A German word with no precise translation that basically means form, figure, or configuration. The term *gestalt* implies that a whole is greater than the sum of its parts. Gestalt psychology was created by Max Wertheimer, Wofgang Koehler, and Kurt Koffka to help explain perceptual phenomena.

**gestalt therapy**
A form of therapy created by Fredrick (Fritz) Perls. This modality focuses on the here-and-now in an attempt to help the person become whole/complete again. The approach is experiential and relies on role playing, the empty chair technique, confrontation, and dream work. The client is urged to take responsibility for his or her life. *See empty chair technique.*

**gestational diabetes in pregnancy**
*See diabetes mellitus (DM).*

**getting down**
Slang for going to a place where an individual can gamble.

**getting even**
The act of gambling in an attempt to pay off debts or recoup gambling losses.

**ghetto**
The poor section of the city.

**GI Bill**
A program to help those who have been in the service secure education, training, housing, and medical care. This program was originally created out of necessity to help World War II veterans.

**gifted**
A person—usually a child—with extremely high intelligence or out-standing talent in one or more areas. Older literature used the term *genius* either literally or figuratively to describe such individuals.

**giving feedback**
Occurs when the human service worker tells the client his or her observa-tions and opinions about the client (e.g., "you may need to be more as-sertive" or your "nonverbal behavior tends to indicate you are very sad").

**glaucoma**
A disease of the eye where the interocular pressure becomes abnor-mally high, which can lead to significant vision loss and eventually blindness. The pressure of the eyeball is determined by an ocular com-ponent known as aqueous humor. When there is an overproduction or inadequate amount of outflow of aqueous humor, the pressure in the eye can become unusually high. This increase of interocular pressure can disrupt the visual information being sent to the brain by compress-ing the nerve fibers that are transmitting the signals. Most forms of glaucoma do not have distinctly obvious signs. However, subtle pe-ripheral vision loss is usually what individuals suffering from glau-coma notice first.

**Global Assessment of Functioning (GAF) Scale**
*See GAF Scale.*

**goal**
A target behavior a person wants or needs to reach by a certain date or by the end of treatment. The steps to accomplish the goal are generally called *objectives*. Hence, a client whose goal was to secure a job might have an objective of completing a GED program and then going to a course on job interview strategies.

**going home again**
A family therapy technique created by Murray Bowen in which the fam-ily members are told to go back to their respective homes to gain insight into their childhood so the person can become free of automatic emo-tional patterns.

**Goodwill Industries**
Short for Goodwill Industries International, Inc., a well-known nonprofit organization that trains the disabled, illiterate people, the homeless, and

those with a criminal history and then tries to help them secure gainful employment. Goodwill collects items that people no longer wish to keep and then sells them in their stores. Goodwill publicizes that "Goodwill bargains help people find jobs." In 1999 Goodwill served 373,205 people and placed 66,000 people in jobs.

### Graduate Record Examination (GRE)
A standardized test that is required for entrance to many graduate (i.e., masters and doctorate) programs. In our field, doctoral programs in clinical psychology are noted for requiring extremely high GRE scores from applicants in order to admit them to the program.

### grand mal seizure
The most powerful type of epileptic seizure characterized by loss of consciousness and convulsions. Can be induced by electroconvulsive shock therapy (ECT/EST).

### grant
A sum of money given by an individual, company, organization or the government to a provider such as an agency, hospital, individual, or school in order to give services or perform research. For example, Acme Corporation may have a $1000 grant to help children in foster care receive literacy services. Large organizations may employ trained grant writers or hire one for the specific grant in question; however, in small agencies any staff member could be asked to write a grant. At some organizations a director of development, who brings in money from a variety of sources including fund raisers and mailings, will be assigned this task. Often grants are graded precisely like a school paper, hence it is imperative that the writer follow the directions. *See hard money versus soft money.*

### GRE
*See Graduate Record Examination.*

### Great Depression
Refers to the decade following the stock market crash of October, 1929 that sparked the great economic depression in the 1930s. By 1933 the depression hit its low point and 16 million U.S. citizens (i.e., one-third of the labor force) were out of work. U.S. President Franklin Delano Roosevelt created a comprehensive program known as the *New Deal* to remedy the terrible state of economic turmoil. Some programs such as the Works Project

Administration (WPA) centered around manual labor (e.g., building or fixing bridges, parks, or highways), while others, such as one for unemployed artists and writers, helped those who were unemployed white-collar workers. New Deal programs put about 8.5 million people back to work. The Great Depression lasted about 10 years, and the nation saw a temporary increase in the suicide rate during those years.

**Great Society**
President Lyndon Baines Johnson declared an unconditional "War on Poverty" during his 1965 State of the Union address. The programs were later dubbed *Great Society* programs. Great Society programs were coordinated via the Office of Economic Opportunity (OEO). Great Society programs included: Head Start (preschool services), Job Corps (employment services for young adults), the Peace Corps (volunteers traveling worldwide to help the poor), Volunteers in Service to America (Vista); similar to the Peace Corps, but volunteers worked in the US in low income areas, Women Infants and Children (WIC) (services for mothers and their newborns), Medicaid (health care for the needy), and Medicare (health care for senior citizens). When Richard Nixon became President in 1968 many of these programs were scaled back or eliminated, as critics charged that the Great Society was extremely costly and did not provide a commensurate amount of benefits for the entire nation.

**Greek chorus**
A family therapy technique devised by Peggy Papp in which a treatment team which is observing the therapy sessions joins the therapy session to discuss their mixed feelings about what the family is saying and what the therapist is doing. This strategy is said to help the family with the ambivalence and uncertainty they often feel.

**grief**
Emotions and feelings in reaction to a loss (i.e., the death of an acquaintance or loved one). Also referred to as *bereavement*. Grief counseling and grief support groups are becoming very popular. *See bereavement.*

**group**
(1) Two or more individuals. (2) Two or more individuals with a common interest, shared purpose, or mutual goal. Some of the literature insists that a group must have a least three individuals since by definition two is a dyad rather than a group.

**group cohesion**
The bond formed between individuals when they are in a group together. Cohesiveness is seen as a therapeutic factor and can help the group achieve its goals.

**group counseling/psychotherapy/therapy**
Jacob Moreno coined the term group psychotherapy in the 1920s. The term refers to emotional and behavioral treatment that is performed with three or more clients at the same time (i.e., technically speaking, treatment with one client is individual while treatment with two clients is termed *couples counseling* or *counseling with a dyad*). Group work allows the practitioner to see more people during the same amount of time and thus it is said to be more cost effective than individual treatment. It also allows the client to receive feedback from more than one individual and it gives the helper the opportunity to see how the individual interacts with others in an actual social setting. Nevertheless, a group is not appropriate for everyone. Some individuals are uncomfortable speaking in a group, while others are too hostile or paranoid. Although the terms *counseling* and *therapy* are used interchangeably in individual treatment, some group practitioners only use the term *group psychotherapy/ therapy* to describe a longer-duration group that delves into one's personality deeply and that commonly focuses on childhood issues. *See universality.*

**group dynamics**
Refers to the interactions and transactions between group members. Can also be referred to as *group process.*

**group health/malpractice plan**
Health or malpractice insurance that is provided for employees of a business or members of an organization. Since the group is purchasing the policies in quantity the price per person is generally less than one would pay if he or she attempted to purchase the same policy as an individual. Group plans are not necessarily free. Employees or members may be required to pay a portion (e.g., an extra premium for their children). It is important to note that a malpractice plan covering an employee at work would rarely cover the same individual who was engaged in self-employed human service work outside of the organization (e.g., a person who had a private counseling practice).

**group home**
A residential facility for children and/or adults. The residents live at the facility, but may work or attend school elsewhere.

**group leader/facilitator**
The person who is in charge of running a group. In some cases more than one leader is used, and this is called *coleadership/facilitation.*

**group practice**
A number of providers who practice as a single entity for convenience and/or cost effectiveness. Income from all the providers comes into the practice as a whole. For example, five mental health counselors may share the same office, secretary, and even use the same practice name. This is the opposite of a solo practitioner, who is the only direct practice worker at his or her site.

**group pressure**
The act of allowing a number of individuals to influence someone to change his or her behavior. A group home leader might say, "It is up to all the members of this group home to make sure that Harry cleans his room. If he does not, we will not go to the movies." Although social psychology research indicates that this can indeed be a powerful technique, many agencies feel it is ethically wrong and have rules against using group pressure techniques.

**group tests**
A test that can be given to a group of people at the same time. Group tests are time and cost effective. In the case of intelligence tests, group tests are usually not as accurate as individual tests.

**group work**
Intervention that is performed with more than three or more clients at a time.

**guardian ad litem**
A person (in some cases, though not all cases, an attorney) appointed by a juvenile court/family court judge to help represent the child's interests. For example, in a custody dispute, a father may hire an attorney and the mother may have a attorney, but the child is in the middle. The guardian ad litem helps to insure that the child's best interests are taken into account.

### guardian consent
A type of informed consent which asserts that minors are not allowed to consent to treatment or services unless it is court ordered. Legal exceptions include a minor who wants counseling for dangerous drugs, narcotics, sexually transmitted diseases, pregnancy, birth control, or an examination after a sexual assault if he or she is over the age of 12. *See informed consent.*

### guardianship
Occurs when the court appoints an individual to manage and care for another person and/or property (e.g., guardianship of the child will be granted to the aunt and uncle).

### guidance counselor
An individual who works in an elementary or a secondary school and helps students with emotional problems, course scheduling, future educational decisions (e.g., which college to attend), and administers psychoeducational/vocational tests. If the school also has a school psychometrician, then some of the testing will be referred to the psychometrician, who often will not provide the other aforementioned counseling or guidance services. Most school counselors possess a master's degree in counseling or guidance and counseling (usually taught in the department of education, not psychology or social work) and must meet state certification guidelines. In some states it is necessary to be an elementary or secondary school teacher for a given period of time before becoming a school counselor.

### guilt
An emotion experienced when a person violates his or her own values or ethics concerning what is right or wrong. Some experts contrast guilt with shame, noting that shame occurs when another individual causes you to feel that your behavior is immoral or unethical.

### gustatory
In physiological psychology, having to do with taste.

### gynecomastia
A condition in males where the breasts grow in a female-like manner. Can be caused by antipsychotic medicines or the by increased usage of steroids among athletes and bodybuilders.

**habilitation**
To educate or train disabled clients to function better in the society.

**habit**
A pattern of behavior that occurs automatically without thought during a given situation. For example, an individual might bite his lip whenever he speaks to his boss. Some habit patterns are helpful while others cause problems for the individual.

**Habitat for Humanity**
An ecumenical Christian housing ministry founded in 1976 by Millard and Linda Fuller that helps people of all faiths. Their most famous supporter is former President Jimmy Carter. To date volunteers in this organization have built over 100,000 homes for needy individuals.

**habituation**
This term is typically used in behavior modification, psychopharmacology, and addictions studies to describe a situation in which a greater dosage of the substance must be used to secure the same result. A drug abuser, for example, might need more and more of a drug over time to get the same high he or she previously experienced using a lesser amount. A behavior modifier might discover that after giving a child candy in order to do his or her math, the child eventually receives so much candy that he or she no longer desires candy and thus it is no longer a reinforcer. Behavior modifiers use schedules of reinforcement to deal with this issue. Habituation is also known as *satiation* in some of the literature. *See schedule of reinforcement.*

**Haldol**
A psychiatric medicine intended to help clients who are psychotic.

**halfway house**
A transition center that helps a person readjust to society after being in a prison, hospital, or treatment facility.

**hallucination**
A person believes that he or she is experiencing something that is not happening in the real world. This is usually induced by a psychotic condition or a drug (e.g., LSD or mescaline).

**hallucinogen**
A drug which causes the person to hallucinate. *See hallucination.*

**halo effect**
The tendency to generalize about a person based on a single characteristic. Thus, a researcher might rate attractive persons as having a better personality even when this is not the case.

**handicap**
A physical or emotional impairment that puts the individual at a disadvantage when compared to others. Today the terms *disability* and *challenged* are preferred.

**handout**
(1) A negative term that describes any public assistance payment. (2) A document given out during a class, group, or educational seminar to clarify or enhance the participant's knowledge.

**hangover**
The impact, effects, and symptoms caused by drugs and/or alcohol after the person has used the substance. Thus, an individual who drinks too much the night before may experience an upset stomach, a headache, or even tremors the next morning.

**hang up**
Slang for a psychological problem that a person has.

**hate crime**
A violent act against a person or group of persons because of their race, ethnicity, beliefs, etc. Thus, a hate crime perpetrator might burn down a store because it was owned by African Americans or Jews.

**Hawthorne effect**
The term gets its name from a famous study conducted at the Hawthorne works of the Western Electric plant in Chicago, Illinois from 1927 to 1932. The researchers (of whom Elton Mayo was one), who were experimenting with lighting conditions on work production, discovered that work output increased with improved or impaired lighting. The finding indicated that the experimenter's presence or attention had an impact on the individuals being studied. Thus, the mere fact that someone is part of an experiment could change his or her behavior even in cases where the independent/experimental variable is not responsible for that particular change.

**HD**
*See Huntington's chorea/Huntington's Disease (HD).*

**headshrinker**
Slang for a psychiatrist or other mental health professional who performs counseling, therapy, or psychoanalysis.

**Head Start Program**
Created as a result of the Economic Opportunity Act of 1964, which was part of President Johnson's "War on Poverty," this preschool program was intended to help disadvantaged children. The program was created to address the fact that poor children were seemingly unprepared to enter school.

**health care access**
Refers to the client's ability to secure health care. This is dictated by factors such as the location of the health care center, services provided by the center, transportation, the client's ability to pay for the service, and the client's insurance.

**health insurance**
An insurance plan that pays the cost (or a portion of the cost) of medical or mental health services. Plans differ radically in what they will or will not pay for, and in general the cost of the plan increases with one's age.

**health maintenance organization (HMO)**
An organization that provides health care for its members. The members pay a fee and then receive free or low-cost health care services. Since the members are often told what doctors they must see, what medical procedures are covered, how often they can go, etc., HMOs are often referred to as *managed care.*

**hedonist**
(1) A person who seeks pleasure at any cost. (2) The notion that humans seek pleasure and avoid pain.

**helpee**
Another name for the client or the individual receiving treatment or services.

**helpline**
*See hotline.*

**herbal remedy**
The use of a plants to treat physical or emotional difficulties, such as the use of St. John's Wort for mild depression. In the US this practice is used primarily by alternative medical practitioners and is generally not covered by insurance companies or HMOs; however, the practice is very common in other countries (e.g., Germany).

**here-and-now**
(1) Describes any school of counseling or technique that focuses on the present moment rather than the past. Also known as *ahistoric counseling*. (2) The tendency of a client to work on thoughts, feelings, and perceptions of the present moment. Modalities such as behavior therapy, brief therapy, solution-focused therapy, T-groups, and gestalt emphasize the here-and-now.

**heredity**
All characteristics genetically passed from parents to a child.

**heredity versus environment**
*See nature versus nuture debate.*

**hermaphrodite**
A person with male and female sex organs.

**heroin**
A powerful, expensive, and highly addictive opiate narcotic which produces horrendous withdrawal symptoms. Interestingly enough, heroin withdrawal, while extremely painful, is much less dangerous and life threatening than alcohol or other sedative withdrawal. Clients treated for heroin addiction are often given a synthetic heroin known as "methadone" in addition to counseling. Detractors claim this is a pernicious process, since methadone itself is highly addictive and does indeed produce withdrawal symptoms. Hence, the client is merely trading one addiction for another.

**Hertz (Hz)**
In biofeedback, rehabilitation, and physiological psychology, a unit of sound equal to cycles per second (cps).

**heterogeneous**
(1) This term can be used in group counseling or in research to describe clients or subjects who have little in common and do not have the same problems, attributes, or traits. (2) In statistics, it can refer to the fact that experimental groups do not have similar variance. *See homogeneous.*

**heteronomous morality**
According to Piaget, the first stage of moral development (the second is autonomous morality), beginning around age 4 and ending at approximately age 8. Rules are viewed as absolute and the child believes that infractions will always lead to punishment. *See autonomous morality.*

**heterosexual**
Sexual attraction to persons of the opposite sex.

**hidden job market**
This concept suggests that most jobs (perhaps up to 80%) are not advertised.

**high**
(1) Under the influence of drugs (especially hallucinogens such as LSD). (2) A win in gambling.

**high blood pressure**
*See hypertension.*

**hippocampus**
A part of the brain that seemingly controls smell and short-term memory functions.

**histogram**
In statistics, a pictorial bar graph.

**histrionic personality**
A person who is usually dramatic, dependent, immature, and overreacts to situations. The individual may also be seductive.

**HIV**
The human immunodeficiency virus that some researchers believe causes or helps to cause AIDS.

**HMS**
Abbreviation for human services.

**holistic treatment**
A type of intervention that treats the whole person rather than just one aspect of the individual. Hence, a holistic practitioner might have the client see a medical doctor, a chiropracter, a nutritionist, a financial planner, and a physical therapist to assist all of the person's needs.

**Holocaust**
Nazi actions before and during World War II intended to wipe out the Jewish population. Over six million Jews were killed.

**homebound**
A sick or disabled individual who cannot leave his or her home or institution.

**home economist**
A professional who visits the client's house to help with meal planning and budgeting. The home economist is usually referred by the human service worker when he or she sees a need for this service.

**home health care**
Describes medical services, counseling, physical therapy, or other social services that are provided in the home of the client.

**homeless person**
An individual who does not have a permanent place to live and thus may live on the street.

**homeless shelter**
A facility intended to help homeless persons who have no permanent place of residence.

**homemaker**
An individual who goes to the client's home to help them cook meals, do housework, and other chores to run the home. Homemakers are generally referred by the human service worker who has visited the home and sees a need for homemaker services.

**homeostasis**
A state of balance or equilibrium.

**home starts**
A statistic that describes the number of new homes that began construction for a given period of time.

**home visit (HV)**
The act of interviewing or performing a human service intervention in the client's home rather than the office. Human service workers who perform this task have traditionally been referred to as *caseworkers.*

**homework assignment**
A helper gives the client an assignment between counseling sessions. Homework assignments allow clients to test new thoughts, feelings, and/or behaviors learned during the treatment process. A client receiving assertiveness training, for example, might be asked to assert himself or herself in a situation where he or she would typically behave in a nonassertive manner. A client with a phobia could be asked by the counselor to engage in the phobic-producing behavior. Generally, homework assignments are more popular with active-directive and behavioristic counselors than with nondirective or psychoanalytic practitioners.

**homicide**
The act of killing another individual. About 12 out of every 100,000 people in the US are victims of homicide. There are about 21,000 homicides each year. In 4 out of 100 cases a suicidal individual will kill somebody else before killing himself or herself, making the act a suicide/homicide.

**homicide assessment**
The use of an interview and/or evaluation system to determine how likely it is that an individual will commit a homicide. A homicide assessment, for example, would be utilized if a client came to an agency and stated that he had thoughts related to murdering his boss.

**homogeneous**
(1) The term can be used in group counseling or research to describe clients or subjects who have similar problems, attributes, or traits. A group made up of unwed teen mothers, for example, could be referred to as a homogeneous group. (2) In statistics, it can refer to the fact that experimental groups have similar variance. *See heterogeneous.*

## homophobia

Literally means "a fear of men." In human services, it implies a fear of homosexuals or homosexuality. Psychodynamic theory holds that the fear could be abetted by one's own latent fear of being homosexual.

## homosexuality

Professionals use this term in a number of different ways. (1) Having sexual contact with an individual of the same sex. (2) Sexual attraction between members of the same gender. (3) An individual whose primary outlet for sexual gratification is a person of the same sex. The term *gay* often refers to homosexual males but can also depict homosexual women. The term, *lesbian,* however, is specifically used to describe women. In the literature, homosexuality is sometimes specified as ego dystonic (the desire to eliminate homosexual desires) or ego syntonic (the individual accepts his or her sexual orientation with no desire to change it). The current edition of the *Diagnositic and Statistical Manual* of the American Psychiatric Association does not list homosexuality as a disorder. Homosexuality had been listed for 23 years as a diagnostic category until 1974 when American Psychiatric Association members voted to delete it based on the fact that homosexuality did not cause emotional distress or impair social functioning on a regular basis. Ethical standards for helpers generally stipulate that discrimination against client due to their sexual orientation is an ethics violation.

## homosexual panic

An extreme fear or panic reaction in a heterosexual who is experiencing homosexual thoughts.

## hospice

A program for terminally ill patients that allows them to receive medical and/or mental health services in the home rather than a hospital, nursing home, or residential facility.

## hotline

A telephone service generally providing crisis counseling, information, guidance, and/or referrals to callers. Many hotlines provide twenty-four-hour service and rely on trained volunteers. Hotlines can offer general services (whatever the caller wants to talk about), or intervention geared toward specific populations (e.g., suicidal teens, unwed mothers, or abused women). The term "helpline" is preferred by some professionals.

**hot seat**
A role-playing technique popularized by gestalt therapy in which the counselor focuses on one individual in the group. It is as if the counselor is doing individual therapy with a person in a group setting. Other group members, nevertheless, can respond to the client in the hot seat if the counselor feels it is appropriate.

**house arrest**
When an individual has violated the law he or she may be required to stay in his or her house in place of incarceration in a prison or corrections facility. The house arrest is enforced via calls and/or visits to the individual's place of residence. Video equipment is also utilized to ensure compliance.

**household**
According to the Census Bureau this term describes an individual or group of individuals who are living in the same dwelling. Such individuals need not be related.

**Hull House**
The first settlement house for the poor cofounded by Jane Addams and Ellen Gates Starr in Chicago in 1889. By 1915 there were 300 settlement houses in the US. Most settlement houses were set up by wealthy individuals who moved into the slums and helped the poor. Hull House has been referred to as the birthplace of contemporary social work. It served as a training facility for social service workers.

**humanistic counseling/psychotherapy/psychology**
Often called *third force psychology* (i.e., psychoanalysis was the first great force and behaviorism was the second major force), this approach believes that men and women are more than just their unconscious instincts (analytic) or conditioned/learned responses (behaviorism). This approach frowns on the practices of labeling the individual and asserts that the practice of using animal research to create psychotherapeutic modalities (as behavior modifiers often do) is dehumanizing. This school is primarily associated with the work of Abraham Maslow, Viktor Frankl, Sidney Jourard, and Carl R. Rogers. The ultimate goal is not merely to help the person with his or her problems but rather to move them to a higher level of functioning known as *self-actualization*. Uniqueness of personal reality, the here and now, the conscious rather than the unconscious, and freedom of choice are emphasized in this model. Humans are

not a finished product but rather they continue to define themselves and make choices throughout the life span. Humanism is often cited as an esoteric approach that cannot be defined via a single definition but has been heavily influenced by existential philosophy.

**human resources department**
The division of an organization that computes payroll, hires, discharges, and trains employees, as well as managing retirement plans and benefit packages.

**human services/human services worker**
There are a number of definitions of human services: (1) According to the National Organization for Human Service Education (NOHSE), human services is a profession that provides interdisciplinary education and services to clients. The help is not limited to the remediation of difficulties but also to helping individuals meet basic human needs. In addition, the profession advocates for change in the systems that affect the lives of clients. (2) Organizes activities that help people with healthcare issues, mental health problems (including those who are mentally challenged and/or disabled), social welfare, childcare, criminal justice, housing and the homeless, addiction, those who need crisis intervention, recreation services, and education. *See the definition of human services written by Dr. Harold McPheeters (at the introduction of the book) and human service assistants.*

**Human services honor society**
*See National Human Services Honor Society Alpha Delta Omega.*

**human service assistants**
Also referred to in the *Occupational Outlook Handbook (OOH)* as "social and human service assistants" this refers to generic helpers with a job title of human service worker, case management aide, community support worker, social worker assistant, mental health aide, community outreach worker, life skill counselor, or gerontology aide. The *OOH* states that these workers work under the direction of professionals from a variety of fields, including nursing, psychology, psychiatry, physical or rehabilitative therapy, or social work, and that the responsibility and supervision varies greatly. The human service assistant provides direct and indirect client services and they often help clients establish their eligibility for benefits and services such as Food Stamps, Medicaid, or Temporary Assistance. They also keep case records on clients that they will

often transport or accompany to service sites. The *OOH* further indicates that workers of this ilk may organize and lead groups, assist clients who need counseling or crisis intervention, and administer a food bank or emergency fuel program. If they work in a half-way house, group home, or government-supported housing program they assist clients with personal hygiene and daily living skills. They confer with medical personnel and provide emotional support. When working with clients in psychiatric hospitals, rehabilitation programs, and outpatient clinics they work with other mental health professionals to help clients master everyday living skills, teach them better communication, and teach them how to get along with others. They support the client's participation in the treatment process. Job opportunities for those without a bachelor's degree are excellent; however, pay is low.

### human service worker categories/levels

The Southern Regional Education Board (SREB) delineated four levels of competence in the 1979 publication of *Staff Roles for Mental Health Personnel: A History and a Rationale*. Level 1 is considered an entry-level category for workers with a few weeks or months of training as well as some in-service education. Such individuals possess little actual job experience. Level 2 is the technical/apprentice level, which includes workers with one to two years of formal training or experience. These workers often possess an associate's degree. Level 3 is termed the associate professional level and includes workers with experience and training that includes a bachelor's degree. Level 4 has been dubbed the professional/specialist level and includes helpers with master's and doctoral degrees.

### human service worker roles

In 1969 the Southern Regional Board (SRB) identified 13 specific roles for human service workers. Human service workers perform one or more of these functions: (1) *Outreach worker,* who might visit clients in their homes or in the community. (2) *Broker,* who helps find services for clients and makes referrals. (3) *Advocate,* who champions clients' rights and causes. (4) *Evaluator,* who assesses programs to ensure accountability. (5) *Teacher/educator,* who is didactic and acts as a mentor, tutor, or models behavior for the client. (6) *Behavior changer,* who uses behavior modification, counseling, or psychotherapy to assist clients. (7) *Mobilizer,* who organizes client and community support in order to provide needed services. (8) *Consultant,* who provides guidance and imparts knowledge to

**147**

other professionals, agencies, or community groups to solve problems. (9) *Community planner,* who designs and implements new services for clients and works with community boards and committees. (10) *Caregiver,* who provides direct support, encouragement, and hope to clients. (11) *Data manager,* who gathers facts and statistics, and uses them to create an agency or program plan or to evaluate a program. (12) *Administrator,* who supervises community services programs. (13) *Assistant to specialist,* who works as an aide or a helper to a professional.

### human service worker salaries
Salaries are often based on geographical location, agency size and wealth, and job title. Nevertheless, the *Occupational Outlook Handbook (OOH)* lists the median annual salary of social and human service assistants without a bachelor's degree at $22,300 for the year 2000. The middle 50 percent had salaries between $17,820 and $27,930. The lowest 10% earned less than $14,660, while the top 10% earned more than $35,220.

### hunger strike
Refusing to eat in order to change an undesirable situation. A homeless person, for example, might go on a hunger strike until a homeless shelter that has been unfairly shut down reopens.

### hung up
Slang for not paying a bookie for a bet. Also called "stiffed."

### Huntington's chorea/Huntington's Disease (HD)
First described by George Huntington in 1872, this is a hereditary disorder that is caused by degeneration to an area of the brain known as the basal ganglia, more specifically the striatum. The most visible symptoms of this disorder are the involuntary twitchlike movements of the muscles and cognitive decline. This usually occurs between the ages of 30 to 50. The rate for the general population is from 5 to 10 people per 100,000.

### hustler
Slang for *prostitute.*

### HV
*See home visit (HV).*

### hydrocephalus
A condition where the head is enlarged due to spinal fluid in the cranial cavity. Can cause brain dysfunction including retardation.

**hyperactivity/hyperkenesis**
Extreme or excessive motor activity and restlessness. *See attention deficit disorder (ADD) and attention deficit hyperactivity disorder (ADHD).*

**hyperopia**
Also known as "farsightedness," this is a vision problem where people can see distant objects very well but have difficulty seeing objects that are up close. Hyperopia occurs when light rays entering the eye focus behind the retina. The eye of a farsighted person is shorter than normal. This condition affects approximately one-fourth of the population. *See myopia.*

**hypersomnia**
Excessive sleeping.

**hypertension**
Best known as *high blood pressure,* meaning that blood pressure readings are above average during three or more separate screenings. Hypertension can be described as a systolic pressure (the amount of force against the walls of arteries after the heart has contracted to push the blood out) over 140 mm of Hg and a diastolic pressure (the amount of force against the walls of the arteries when the heart is filling with blood) over 90 mm of Hg. Hypertension is one of the main contributors to heart-related problems.

**hyperventilation**
Breathing very hard and fast. This can cause the heart to beat fast and a feeling of lightheadedness as well as tingling in the extremities. Often occurs when an individual is having an anxiety or panic attack.

**hypervigilance**
A term commonly used in psychological reports to indicate that the client continually studies his or her surroundings for threatening stimuli. This is a common symptom experienced by people who suffer from post-traumatic stress disorder (PTSD).

**hypnogogic imagery**
A semiconscious state of mind characterized by dreamlike thoughts and mental pictures which occur just before an individual falls asleep. *See hypnopompic imagery.*

**hypnopompic imagery**
A semiconscious state of mind characterized by dreamlike thoughts and mental pictures which occur immediately after a person wakes up. *See hypnogogic imagery.*

**149**

### hypnosis
From the Greek word "hypnos" meaning sleep. Originally called "animal magnetism" by Franz Anton Mesmer. A procedure in which the counselor places the client in a state of heightened suggestibility. Direct suggestion can be employed to abate unwanted behaviors (e.g., a desire to smoke or anxiety related to dental work), accentuate the positive, or allow the client to remember a repressed memory (e.g., a childhood trauma). Since some states do not have credentialing requirements for persons performing hypnosis, human service workers should make certain that the practitioner has a license (e.g., counseling or psychology) before making a referral for this service.

### hypochondriac/hypochondriasis
A person who is obsessed with his or her health and generally has numerous complaints and symptoms without any medical basis.

### hypodermic needle injection
Injecting a prescription or street drug under the skin or into the blood stream.

### hypoglycemia
Also known as *low blood sugar,* this condition is thought to be responsible for a myriad of physical and psychological disorders (e.g., depression and attention deficit hyperactivity disorder). Ironically enough, this condition is often brought on by eating too much sugar. Human service workers who suspect hypoglycemia should refer the client to a medical practitioner for a glucose tolerance test (GTT). Today researchers believe that a deficiency of the trace minerals chromium and vanadium may at least be partially responsible for this condition. The theory of hypoglycemia in emotional disorders is not universally accepted; however, orthomolecular psychiatrists and alternative health practitioners claim the evidence is overwhelming.

### hypomania
A very mild manic condition. *See mania/manic.*

### hypothermia
A condition in which the body temperature is below normal. Poor people without heating sometimes die from this malady.

**hypothesis**
A hunch or assumption that serves as an explanation and can be tested using a scientific experiment (e.g., reality therapy groups are beneficial to people experiencing panic attacks).

**hypothesis testing**
The use of the scientific experimental model to ascertain whether a hunch, assumption, or best guess is correct.

**hysteria**
Used primarily in Freudian and psychoanalytic literature to describe a condition in which the person has a symptom for which there is no physical difficulty that is causing the problem. Thus, a client might say that he or she cannot see or cannot move his or her hand, yet an examination reveals nothing is wrong with him or her. The analysts believe that the symptom is caused by an unconscious conflict. Also called a *conversion reaction*.

### iatrogenic disorder/illness

Any disorder resulting from the treatment process itself. Originally known as a *doctor-induced illness,* the term is now used in the mental health field to describe emotional and psychological problems abetted via the counseling, therapy, or helping process. That is to say, the intervention actually causes a difficulty that was not present prior to treatment. If, for example, a client was incorrectly diagnosed as schizophrenic and then began acting in a schizophrenic manner for the first time, the condition could be considered an iatrogenic disorder.

### ICD

*See International Classification of Diseases.*

### ice

The street name for methamphetimine that can be smoked or injected. Ice is generally a low-cost, highly addictive drug that produces euphoria followed by extreme depression and/or psychotic reaction. When injected, it is often referred to as "crank." Ice is produced in illicit laboratories.

### ice breaker

Any technique or exercise that helps individuals in a group to know each other better. In order to be effective, ice breakers must be nonthreatening and must not embarrass anybody since one of their purposes is to make the members in the group feel more comfortable. For example, a leader might put participants in smaller groups of two or three people and say:

"If you could talk to anybody who ever lived for an hour who would it be?" There are literally scores of effective ice breakers and entire books devoted to describing tested activities for this purpose.

### id

According to Freud's structural hypothesis in psychoanalysis, the psyche has three components: the id, the ego, and the superego. In Latin, the word means "it." The id houses the animalistic instincts and the libido, and seeks bodily gratification. The id is in the unconscious and has no contact with the outside world. The id is governed by the so-called *pleasure principle* (i.e., it attempts to achieve immediate reduction of tension) and is present at birth. The id is said to be chaotic, wants immediate gratification, and has no sense of time. The id houses eros, the life instinct, and thanatos, the death instinct. The id is analogous to what is known as the Child ego state in Eric Berne's transactional analysis. *See ego, structural theory, and superego.*

### ideal self

The person who the client really wants to be. This term is used extensively in Rogerian person-centered, nondirective client-centered therapy.

### ideation

A thought or belief. Generally used to describe thoughts of suicide (i.e., she has suicidal ideation).

### identical twins

*See monozygotic twins.*

### identified client/patient

Refers to the person who is viewed as having the problem and thus in need of treatment. Often human service workers working with families and/or organizations discover that the identified client is not always the individual who needs treatment the most. Ironically enough, often the person in the family who really needs treatment is the one who insists that the identified client needs treatment. Hence, a mother may bring her daughter for counseling because she feels her daughter is "sick" and needs help. The counselor could discern that it is mom—not her daughter—who could benefit most from the counseling process. Family therapists generally do not adhere to either of the aforementioned definitions, positing that the entire family is the identified client.

**identity crisis**
Not being certain exactly what your role is as a person. Very common during the adolescent years.

**identity versus role confusion**
In Erik Erikson's eight-stage psychosocial model of development, each stage represents a social challenge or crisis. This is the fifth stage and occurs between ages 12 and 18 years.

**idiopathic**
A condition caused by internal difficulties rather than external effects.

**idiot**
Derived from the Greek word *idiotes,* meaning "a person without knowledge." In older literature, the term was used to describe persons with an IQ of 20 or below. Also intended to describe an adult who has the mentality of a child two years old or younger. Today the term *profound mental retardation* is the accepted label.

**idiot savant**
French for "scholarly idiot." The term *savant* is generally preferred. A mentally retarded person who seems to be a genius in a few areas of his or her life. A savant, for example, might memorize every street on a map or be able to perform amazing feats of mathematical calculation. About 10% of all autistic children are savants.

**ignoring**
A form of extinction used in behavior modification, ignoring is the act of purposefully not responding to a behavior in order to eliminate it. The theory states that when a behavior is not acknowledged it is not reinforced and thus will become less frequent or in time go away. Often, however, the behavior will be worse before it gets better. This phenomenon is known as an *extinction burst* or a *response burst* and should be explained to clients and human service workers alike before allowing them to use ignoring.

**illegal**
Against the law.

**illegitimate child**
A child born out of wedlock/marriage. Also known as a *nonmarital birth.*

**illicit drug**
Any drug that is against the law to use. Some addictive drugs can be legally prescribed by a physician for a medical condition, and the term "illicit" would not apply in such cases.

**illiterate**
Inability to read or write that is not due to mental retardation. Literacy programs are intended to teach people with this condition.

**imbecile**
A term that is no longer used to describe a mentally retarded person with a mental age of 3–7 years old.

**imitation**
To copy another person's behavior. A popular strategy in behaviorism. *See modeling.*

**immediacy**
Occurs when a helper can effectively deal with something significant that just transpired during the interview or therapy session.

**immigrant**
An individual who moves to a different country and decides to live there.

**immunization**
A medical procedure (e.g., a vaccination) that lowers the likelihood that the individual will contract a certain disease. Also known as *inoculation.*

**impaired helper/professional**
Refers to a helper who is not able to function in an effective or ethical manner due to a personal problem (e.g., alcoholism) or condition (e.g., brain damage). Most ethical guidelines suggest that competent professionals should report an impaired practitioner to their ethical or state licensing board.

**impersonal illustration**
A counseling or therapy technique in which the helper relates a story about an anonymous client or person in order to teach the client or provide additional insight.

**implementation plan**
The precise steps and methodology that will he taken to help the client or create a program.

**implosive therapy**
A behavior therapy technique performed by having the client close his or her eyes and then describe fearful stimuli. The procedure continues until the anxiety is gone. The fearful stimuli are often chosen for psychoanalytic reasons.

**impotence**
The inability for a male to achieve an erection. Can be due to physical (e.g., circulatory difficulties) or psychological (e.g., performance anxiety) factors. Often referred to as a *sexual disorder*. Antidepressant medicinals and other prescription drugs can cause this problem. In recent literature, the term *erectile disorder* or *erectile dsyfunction* is preferred.

**improvisation**
In Andrew Salter's conditioned reflex therapy, the sixth and final discipline (i.e., technique) to help the person acquire an excitatory/healthy personality. The client is instructed to live in the now, be spontaneous, and not daydream about the future.

**impulse**
An urge.

**impulse control disorder**
A *DSM* category that refers to one's inability to resist an urge that could prove harmful to one's self or others such as excessive gambling or kleptomania (compulsive stealing).

**incarceration**
Placing an individual in a corrections facility or a mental hospital, usually because his or her behavior could be detrimental to other members of society.

**incest**
Sexual acts between close blood relatives (e.g., a natural father and his daughter). Incest is considered a form of sexual abuse and therefore human service workers are mandated to report it to their state child abuse hotline.

**incidence**
In statistics and research, the magnitude of a given condition, situation, or behavior during a specified period of time. Incidence statistics answer the question: How common is this problem or trait? A suicide researcher,

157

for example, might say that the incidence of suicide in this country is 12/100,000, meaning that for every 100,000 people 12 will take their own lives in a year. Most incidence rates are quoted per 1000 or per 100,000 people.

**inclusion**
Sometimes referred to as "mainstreaming," this policy allows disabled students to stay in a regular classroom unless special services are required for a portion of the day.

**incoherent**
A person is said to be incoherent if his or her communication is so confusing that you can't understand what he or she is trying to say. When it occurs in schizophrenics it is termed *word salad.*

**incomplete sentence exercise/test**
The client is given a partial sentence and then is asked to finish it. For example: When I think of my mother I feel _____ . Although there are formal incomplete sentence tests, many agencies create informal incomplete sentence tests or exercises to elicit information that meets the needs of their organization.

**incongruent**
A term popularized by Carl R. Roger's person-centered theory to describe an individual who is not acting in accordance with his or her true beliefs and feelings.

**incorrigible**
A term used in the older literature to describe a juvenile delinquent who was out of control and/or engaging in criminal behavior.

**incrementalism**
Making small changes rather than giant leaps. This term can refer to work with clients or policies (e.g., the legal blood alcohol level will be reduced by .01 per year).

**independent living programs**
Centers where disabled individuals can live and that have services such as mental health counseling, career guidance, and financial advice.

**independent variable (IV)**
An independent variable is said to cause and/or determine the dependent variable. In an experiment, the independent variable is said to be

the experimental variable. The independent variable is the variable that the researcher varies such as type of treatment, dosage of medicine, number of months in the program, etc. Thus, if you believe that therapeutic homework lowers depression then therapeutic homework would be the independent variable and a measure of depression would be the dependent/outcome variable if an experiment were conducted.

### Indian American
A multicultural diversity term used in older literature to describe American Indians. Currently, the term *Native Americans* is preferred.

### individual counseling/therapy/intervention/treatment
A counseling or therapy situation consisting of one or more helpers and a single individual client. The procedure is often contrasted to marriage, family, couples, or group counseling in which more than one client receives intervention. When the helping relationship consists of one client and one counselor it is often termed *one-on-one counseling/therapy*.

### individuality
The qualities that make each person unique and different from all other people.

### individualized education plan (IEP)
Since 1975 schools have a legal requirement to assess students with disabilities and to create a specific plan for that child to meet his or her unique educational needs.

### individual psychology
A theory of behavior and treatment espoused by Alfred Adler based on the notion that feelings of inferiority cause individuals to overcompensate. A person who feels intellectually inferior might exercise excessively to build his or her body.

### individuation
Carl Jung's term for becoming a separate unique individual from others.

### inductive reasoning
A model of thinking or logic in which general principles are developed after noting a specific or single situation. Thus, a student who had an unfair statistics professor would conclude that all statistics professors will be unfair. *See deductive reasoning.*

**industrial human service worker/psychiatrist/psychologist/social worker**
A helper who deals with problems of work, job training, employee selection and virtually anything related to the work setting. Sometimes called an *I/O* or *industrial/organizational helper.*

**industry versus inferiority**
In Erik Erikson's eight-stage model of psychosocial development this is the fourth stage, ages 6–12 years. In each stage the individual must confront a social crisis. In this stage the child must master social and academic tasks to feel a sense of self-worth or he or she will end up feeling inferior.

**infancy**
The first year of life.

**infantile sexuality**
(1) Freud's psychoanalytic notion that infants experience sexual pleasures. (2) Freud's oral and anal stages or Freud's oral, anal, and phallic stages. *See anal stage, oral stage, and phallic stage.*

**infant mortality rate**
A measure of the number of new-borns who die each year. The infant mortality rate is often viewed as a barometer of a country's health care system.

**infant whiplash syndrome**
The notion that shaking a baby too hard can cause brain damage or death.

**inferential statistics**
An inference occurs when one makes a conclusion based on a previous conclusion. Thus, any statistical procedure that investigates a sample and then infers that the principle will apply to the population at large is said to be inferential. Hence, a study that works with a sample of depressed individuals and finds that family therapy relieved their depression would infer that the probability is high that family therapy could help others in the population who are depressed. Inferential statistics are often contrasted with descriptive statistics, which merely describe a sample.

**inferiority complex**
The term was created by Alfred Adler, who believed that an individual's feelings of physical and mental inadequacies determine how the person will mold his or her life.

**inflation**
An economic term which suggests that the cost of living is higher than normal, thus reducing one's ability to make purchases.

**informal admission**
Allowing a client to enter a facility (usually a hospital) with the understanding that he or she is free to leave at any time even if that decision conflicts with a doctor or human service worker's recommendation.

**informal test**
Roughly the opposite of a standardized test that is always scored, administered, and normed in the same manner regardless of where or when it is given. Tests that are purchased through psychoeducational testing companies are almost always standardized. Informal tests are created by teachers, agencies, and hospital employees to meet the needs of their specific population. They are not normed against the general population. A final exam, for example, created by an Introduction to Human Services professor, would be informal since the results could not be compared (i.e., they are not standardized) to other Introduction to Human Services courses that rely on a totally different instrument of evaluation.

**information giving**
The act of giving the client knowledge or information. A human service worker, for example, might give the client facts about dealing with a parent suffering from Alzheimers.

**informed consent**
Giving the client the necessary information so he or she can consent to or reject treatment, testing, or interventions. Informed consent procedures are recommended by all major ethical guidelines. Informed consent is roughly the opposite of being vague or mystical with clients. If a client asks, "Why are you recommending such and such?" the ethical human service worker would need to give the client a satisfactory verbal or written explanation. Hence, relying on informed consent, a human service worker might inform a client that certain things he says in the interview could be revealed in a court of law. Many agencies now require all clients to sign an informed consent statement that describes the agency's services, limits of confidentiality, qualifications of the staff, access to records, alternative services, and risks prior to rendering the actual services. Medical doctors also adhere to this principle.

**inhalant abuse**
A form of substance abuse in which a compound is inhaled (i.e., the person breathes it in) such as glue, gasoline, or spray paint. Inhalant abuse can cause brain damage or even death.

**inhibitory personality**
In Andrew Salter's conditioned reflex therapy, an individual who suffers from constipation of emotions. Such persons do not express genuine feelings and routinely conceal them. According to this theory, this practice of not continually venting feelings is responsible for a myriad of mental and emotional problems. The goal is to create an excitatory personality in which emotional expression is the rule. *See conditioned reflex therapy and excitatory personality.*

**initial interview**
The first interview with a client.

**initial stage**
In group work, the first stage. The beginning stage has also been called the *forming* stage, where people get to know each other and the ground rules for behavior in the group are delineated.

**initiative versus guilt**
The third stage in Erik Erikson's eight-stage psychosocial development model. Each stage presents a challenge or crisis between the individual and society. In this stage (ages 3–6), the child attempts to accept responsibility and become independent without feeling guilty.

**ink blot test**
*See Rorschach Inkblot Test and projective test.*

**in kind contribution/donation**
A contribution to an organization that is not cash (or is in addition to cash) and that is a good (e.g., a computer) or a service (e.g., training the staff). Sometimes referred to as *gifts in kind.*

**inmate**
An individual who lives in a prison or a hospital.

**innate**
A trait that is present at birth, although it may not be evident until later in life.

**162**

**inpatient treatment**
Refers to a client who resides at a given facility during the treatment process (i.e., the inpatient client actually sleeps overnight at the treatment center). This form of intervention is often contrasted with *outpatient* or *day treatment* in which the client is not living and sleeping at the treatment center.

**insane/insanity**
A legal term for someone who has a mental disorder so severe that he or she is unable to function in a normal psychological manner. This term is controversial inasmuch as some individuals who have committed serious crimes were deemed insane and thus were not responsible for their actions. It is important to note that the term *insane* is not used at agencies or hospitals as a psychiatric diagnosis.

**inservice education/training**
Any educatory program for individuals who are currently working in the counseling field.

**insight/insight-oriented treatment**
(1) Also called the *a-ha experience*, it is where one finally understands the meaning behind a behavior, emotion, or symptom. (2) Traditional psychoanalysts contend that true insight takes place when a client consciously understands the unconscious reason for the problem, although most human service workers use the term to describe the notion that the client now understands something that can be used to change his or her feelings and behavior. Insight-oriented treatment suggests that understanding is necessary for change and is often called *psychodynamic therapy*. Other schools (e.g., brief strategic therapy or behavior therapy) do not support this notion.

**insomnia**
An inability to sleep.

**instincts**
Any behavior with which all members of a species are born. An instinct is present at birth and does not need to be learned. Since most human behaviors must be learned they are not considered innate or instinctual. Freud postulated life (eros) and death (thanatos) instincts, but this notion is controversial.

**institutional barrier**
Any factor or policy of an organization that makes it more difficult to receive services (e.g., no access to the agency by bus, very high fees, a policy that makes it difficult to be accepted as a client, etc.).

**institutionalization**
Refers to placing somebody in a long-term care facility, usually a mental hospital.

**intake interview/intake worker**
The first interview with a client. This interview usually focuses on whether the agency can help the client and if so what services or referrals can be provided. The worker who performs this service is sometimes called the *intake worker.* The interview is used to gather information to diagnose or assess the client's needs.

**integration**
Bringing together different racial, ethnic, or social groups to promote better relations and equality.

**integrationalism**
*See eclectic.*

**integrative counseling/therapy**
*See eclectic.*

**integrity versus despair**
In Erik Erikson's eight-stage psychosocial model of development each stage represents a challenge or crisis with the social environment. This is the final stage that occurs after approximately age 65. The person must contend with whether his or her life was seemingly productive or filled with regrets and/or missed opportunities.

**intellectualization**
An ego defense mechanism in which the person only looks at situations in a logical, intellectual manner to avoid dealing with threatening emotions.

**intelligence**
Experts cannot seem to agree on precisely what this term means, however, it is used to describe how bright or intelligent someone is and how well the person can grasp abstract concepts. *See intelligence quotient/IQ.*

**intelligence quotient/IQ**
A formula created by the mathematician Wilhelm Stern to score IQ tests. The mental age (from the test) is divided by an individual's chronological age (the actual age) and multiplied by 100 to secure the IQ score. Although this formula has not been used to score such tests for over 30 years now, the term *IQ* is still used to convey one's numerical score on an intelligence test. An average IQ is 100, with the average range from 90–110. 0 to 20 is considered profound retardation; 21–35 severe retardation; 36–50 moderate retardation; 51–70 mild retardation; 70–90 dull or slow learner; 110–120 is superior; 120–140 is very superior; and 140 and above is gifted. The average IQ score is increasing throughout the world. This phenomenon has been dubbed the Flynn Effect. *See Flynn Effect.*

**intelligence test/IQ test**
A test that is intended to measure one's intelligence. The Wechsler and the Stanford Binet are two of the most popular intelligence tests. Tests that are administered to a single individual at a time are generally more accurate than those administered to a group of people. *See Resources section of the text for a description of Popular IQ tests.*

**intensity**
A family therapy technique where the therapist puts a lot of pressure (sometimes for an extended period of time) on the family to change. The therapist may keep telling the family the same thing again and again to get them to give up their dysfunctional behaviors.

**intentional**
Implies that an individual did something on purpose. For example, he purposely drove off the road in an attempt to hurt himself. Often contrasted with *unintentional*, which implies that the act was not implemented on purpose.

**interdisciplinary approach/team**
A team of experts from different professions working together to help solve a problem. For example, a depressed mother might see a psychiatrist for antidepressants; a clinical psychologist for psychological testing; a social worker for psychotherapy; a caseworker for advice about food stamps; and a physical therapist for an injury that is healing.

**interest inventory**
A test or appraisal instrument that measures vocational interest. Used frequently by school guidance counselors and others who provide vocational counseling.

**intergenerational**
Any connections between past generations and the current generation.

**interindividual difference**
Refers to the differences between two or more individuals on one or more traits, tasks, abilities, skills, or tests. Often contrasted with intraindividual difference. *See intraindividual difference.*

**interlocking pathology**
Family therapy pioneer Nathan Ackerman's term for dysfunctional family members who unconsciously remain psychologically connected.

**intermittent reinforcement**
In behavior modification, a schedule of reinforcement where every desirable behavior is not reinforced. Say, for example, that a child is being reinforced for completing math problems. Instead of reinforcing him for every problem he might be reinforced on an average of every 3 problems he completes.

**internal locus of control**
A person who follows his own thoughts and feelings rather than depending on what others think (i.e., what is known as an external locus of control that is not as healthy).

**International Classification of Diseases (ICD)**
A guide of taxonomy (i.e., classification) created by the World Health Organization (WHO) which includes all physical and mental diseases and disorders. An insurance company or third-party payer generally requires counselors to give the client an *ICD* or *DSM* (*Diagnostic and Statistical Manual* written by the American Psychiatric Association) diagnostic code in order to receive payment.

**Internet counseling**
Also known as *web counseling* or *cybercounseling,* where the helper treats the client via e-mail or related electronic means. The major professional organizations are beginning to create special guidelines for this growing yet controversial practice. Often the helper does not have access to the

client's vocal inflections and nonverbal behaviors. Some problems, such as sexual abuse, do not lend themselves to Internet counseling.

**interpersonal**
Refers to what is transpiring between two or more people. Often contrasted with intrapersonal which refers to what is occurring within a single individual.

**interpersonal group leader**
Conveys the message that a group leader favors stategies which promote interaction between group members. If the technique includes the group as a whole it is often known as a *horizontal intervention* and is contrasted with a *vertical intervention* where the group leader focuses on a single individual. *See intrapersonal group leader.*

**interpretation**
Occurs when a helper explains to a client the real meaning of his or her behavior. A popular technique with analytically trained therapists but shunned by some schools of thought such as person-centered counseling and behaviorism.

**interval scale of measurement**
A scale of measurement that has numbers scaled at equal distances but no absolute zero point. Using this scale, distances between each number are equal yet it is unclear how far each number is from zero. Division is not permissible inasmuch as division assumes an absolute zero. (If you had an absolute zero you could assert that a person with an IQ of 140 would be twice as smart as someone with an IQ of 70.) The Fahrenheit and Celsius scales of temperature are common examples of interval scales. Most tests given in school fall into this measurement category. *See nominal scale of measurement, ordinal scale of measurement and ratio scale of measurement.*

**intervention**
Counseling or other help provided to the client.

**interview**
A meeting with one or more clients and a human service worker in order to gather information, assess the client's needs (sometimes known as a *diagnostic interview*), or help the client with his or her difficulties (sometimes referred to as *the helping interview*). Often the term is loosely used to refer to a counseling or psychotherapy session.

**intimacy versus isolation**
In Erik Erikson's eight-stage model of psychosocial development, each stage presents a social challenge or crisis. This is the sixth stage and takes place between the ages of 18 and 35. The young man or woman must give up a degree of independence to create a love relationship or remain lonely and isolated.

**intoxicated**
Used to describe a psychological/physiological state induced by ingesting alcohol and/or other drugs.

**intraindividual differences**
Differences within a single individual. Usually refers to differences revealed via tests or assessments. A human services worker, for example, might note that a client has high verbal skills but below-average performance skills. Often contrasted with interindividual differences. *See interindividual difference.*

**intrapersonal**
Refers to what is happening within a single person. Often contrasted with *interpersonal,* which refers to what is transpiring between two or more individuals.

**intrapersonal group leader**
Conveys the message that a group leader favors strategies which focus on a single member of the group rather than interaction between members. This is often known as a *vertical intervention* and is contrasted with a *horizontal intervention* where the group leader performs group-as-a-whole work. *See interpersonal group leader.*

**intrapsychic**
That which occurs in the individual's mind.

**introjection**
An ego defense mechanism in which ideas of others are uncritically accepted as part of one's self.

**introspection**
To look into or analyze one's own mind with the goal of achieving insight. *See insight/insight-oriented treatment.*

**introvert/introversion**
Carl Jung's term for an individual who is withdrawn, passive, and stays to oneself. Often contrasted with his term *extrovert/extroversion,* which implies that the individual is outgoing.

**inverse correlation**
In statistics, a negative correlation (e.g., $-.75$) in which one variable goes up while another goes down. Thus, a correlation examining the behavior of alcoholics would most likely show that the more they attend treatment groups the less they drink. An inverse/negative correlation is often contrasted with a positive correlation. In a positive correlation (e.g., .75), when one variable goes up the other variable also increases. Hence, the more one studies the higher his or her grade point average. *See correlation and correlation coefficient.*

**inversion**
Sigmund Freud's psychoanalytic term for homosexuality.

**investigation worker**
A human service worker who tries to determine whether a client has abused, neglected, or exploited a child. Often known as a *child abuse worker* or a *protective service worker.*

**invisible loyalties**
An unconscious decision made by grown children to help their parents, caretakers, and families of origin.

**in vivo**
In behavior therapy, and more specifically systematic desensitization, the act of actually attempting a fearful behavior in real life, such as riding an elevator when a fear of elevators is the presenting complaint. *See systematic desensitization.*

**involuntary discharge**
Terminating a patient or client from a hospital or agency program even though he or she does not wish to leave.

**involuntary hospitalization**
Occurs when a client who may be dangerous to himself and others is kept in a psychiatric hospital against his will for observation and further assessment.

### involuntary treatment
Providing services to somebody who does not willingly ask for or want the services. For example, a mother who has her children taken away may be told that she must participate in a therapy program in order to get the children back. A person who does not want treatment but is actively threatening to hurt himself may be placed in a psychiatric ward.

### ipsative scale
Any appraisal measure or test that gives information about a single person but cannot be utilized to compare the individual to others. Often contrasted with a *normative scale* that does allow the person to be compared to others who have taken the test. Most psychoeducational tests are normative rather than ipsative.

### irrational beliefs (IB)/thinking
In rational-emotive behavior therapy (REBT), an illogical thought resulting in emotional disturbance. Albert Ellis—the father of this school of thought—lists a number of prime examples in his writings The major irrational ideas include: (1) The notion that one must be loved and/or approved of by almost everyone. (2) Some people are bad and wicked and thus should be punished for their behavior. (3) One must be thoroughly competent and adequate to be worthwhile. (4) Human unhappiness is externally caused. (5) It is catastrophic when life is not the way one would like it to be. (6) An individual should repeatedly dwell on dangerous or anxiety provoking situations. (7) One must have somebody stronger on whom to rely. (8) It is easier to avoid life's difficulties than to face them. (9) When a perfect solution to a problem is not evident it is awful. (10) One should be quite upset when others are experiencing difficulties. (11) The thought that the past is all-important and determines your behavior and mood in the present. Counseling and therapy are aimed at replacing the aforementioned ideas with rational, logical, and healthy beliefs. Ellis believes that humans have a propensity to think in an irrational, illogical, and unscientific manner. *See A-B-C/A-B-C-D-E theory of personality and rational-emotive therapy (RET)/rational-emotive behavior therapy (REBT).*

### irrelevant response
Occurs when a client gives an answer to an interview question that has nothing to do with the question.

**irreversible condition**
A medical condition that cannot be cured via treatment. For example, certain drugs may cause permanent brain damage in children that cannot be changed by treatment or the passage of time.

**isophilic**
A term coined by psychiatrist Harry Stack Sullivan to describe feelings of affection toward someone of the same gender without sexual feelings or homosexual desire.

**I statement**
(1) The act of taking responsibility for one's own feelings by using the word *I* at the beginning of a declaration. I statements are viewed as healthier than *you statements.* Hence, a client who says "You make me feel terrible when you criticize me" might be instructed to rephrase the sentence to, "I feel terrible when you criticize me." (2) In Andrew Salter's conditioned reflex therapy, the fourth technique, discipline, or rule of conduct for increasing healthy excitation in the personality. The client is asked to deliberately use the word *I* as much as possible when conversing with others.

**item weighting**
In psychoeducational testing, the act of making some questions worth more points or less points than others when calculating the total score. For example, one question on a 100-point test might be worth 5 points, while another question might be worth 25 points.

**IV drug user**
A drug user who uses a needle to inject the drug into his or her bloodstream. Often referred to as an *intravenous drug user.*

**James, William (1842–1910)**
Founded the first psychology laboratory in America in 1875 and created the school of psychology known as *functionalism* that popularized the notion of *stream-of-consciousness.* James believed in studying the process of the consciousness rather than breaking it up into fragments like the rival psychological school at the time which was known as *structuralism.*

**jargon**
Refers to terminology used in a profession that would not be understood by individuals not trained or working in the field.

**JCAHO**
*See Joint Commission on Accreditation of Healthcare Organizations.*

**Jellinek's model of alcoholism**
A description of the stages of alcohol dependence according to Jellinek. Early, middle, and late stages are described with signs and symptoms associated with each stage. According to Jellinek and many addiction professionals, alcohol dependence progresses from one stage to the next in a rather predictable fashion. There are several types of alcoholism and each will progressively worsen without treatment.

## jelly bean group
Slang for a treatment group that has participants with a wide range of problems (e.g., one member is depressed, another has anger management issues, another has panic attacks, etc.). A group where everybody's problem was gambling addiction would therefore not fit into this category.

## Jim Crow laws
Prior to 1964 segregated facilities such as restaurants and restrooms posted signs that said "White Only" or "Colored Only." Since 1964 this practice has been deemed unconstitutional because it deprived African Americans of their basic civil rights.

## JINS
Short for "juveniles in need of supervision."

## job analysis
An industrial psychology term suggesting that the job is analyzed in order to determine the abilities needed to perform the work. The process can help select an appropriate employee for the tasks at hand.

## job
In career and vocational counseling the term refers to work settings that are comparable (e.g., jobs in hospital social work).

## Job Corps
Legislation known as the Economic Opportunity Act of 1964 during the so-called War on Poverty that provided disadvantaged youth ages 16 to 21 with job training at neighborhood centers.

## job description
A written document that gives the precise tasks, assignments, and responsibilities for a worker in a given position. A human service worker should request a job description prior to beginning a new job.

## Job Training and Partnership Act (JTPA)
A program instituted by President Ronald Reagan in 1982—after the Comprehensive Employment and Training Act (CETA) was terminated—that was designed to help disadvantaged individuals secure jobs. Contracts were given to job-placement centers which received a fee for each person placed in a private business setting.

**Jocasta complex**
Occurs when a mother has a pathological attachment to her own son.

**Johari Window**
A popular technique to enhance awareness that has been popular especially in transactional analysis and growth groups. The window analogy asserts that there are four parts to the personality: the public self (known to the self and others); the blind self (known to others but not to the self); the private self (known to self but not others); and the unknown self (unknown to self or others).

**John Henry effect**
In research, the notion that subjects in a control group put out extra effort that is not typical, thus undermining the validity of an experiment. A line worker who believes he or she will be replaced by a machine may work extremely hard to prove that the machine is not superior. The phenomenon is also called *compensatory rivalry of the comparison group.*

**joining**
In structural family therapy, the notion that a counselor can symbolically become a part of the family system and thus can interact like a family member to abet change.

**joint**
Slang for marijuana that is wrapped in cigarette paper. Also known as *pot* or *weed*. Smoking a joint is a common way for people to ingest marijuana. *See marijuana.*

**Joint Commission on Accreditation of Healthcare Organizations (JCAHO)**
An organization—formerly known as the Joint Commission on Accreditation of Hospitals (JCAH)—that evaluates hospitals and other health-care facilities every two years to see if they meet certain standards for accreditation. A hospital must be accredited to secure Medicaid and Medicare payments.

**joint custody**
This is a legal term used in divorce decrees to describe a situation in which both parents retain responsibility for raising a child. In most cases, the child would live with each parent for an equal amount of time, while in other situations the child may physically live primarily with one parent but the other has just as much input. Joint custody allows each parent to have a say in important matters such as medical and educational decisions. In some cases, both parents have joint legal custody while one parent has primary physical custody. The parent who does not have primary physical custody typically has designated times with the child such as one night a week and every other weekend.

**joint funding**
Occurs when two or more agencies combine financial resources to fund a program.

**Jones, Ernest (1879–1958)**
A British psychoanalyst who wrote the official three-volume biography of Sigmund Freud. He helped create the American Psychoanalytic Association in 1911 and the British Psychoanalytic Association in 1913 and is accredited as being the first person to bring analytic concepts to the English-speaking countries.

**journal**
A professional publication usually produced by an organization (e.g., the National Organization for Human Service Education or the American Psychological Association) related to the organization's field of study. Many organizations publish a journal for every division (e.g., one for clinical psychology and another for experimental psychology) and many journals include a high number of statistical/experimental articles. A journal may periodically offer special editions such as "ethics in social welfare." Journals have articles written by professionals in the field who are not paid. Journals have specific author guidelines that stipulate the length, topic, and other relevant factors. The articles are screened by a review board composed of other professionals before they are accepted. In many cases, even if the article is accepted the author or authors will be required to make changes recommended by the review board members. Most journals require that the article begin with a brief abstract that summarizes what the article covers and that the article uses documentation and references that follow American Psychological Association (APA)

Style. This can create problems for beginning students since most composition classes teach a different style known as MLA. A recent criticism of journals is that they are intended to illuminate cutting-edge research and thought in a field, but by the time the article is published it might be a year or two later.

**journaling**
The client keeps a log of his or her thoughts, feelings, and behavior. This process is beneficial to the helper and the client in terms of illuminating progress, areas of concern, and repetitive patterns.

**judgment**
The act of picking a course of action based on the facts and previous experience. For example, "the client used poor judgment when she left her newborn home alone."

**Jung, Carl Gustav (1875–1961)**
A Swiss psychoanalyst who studied with Freud. They were very close and Freud assumed that Jung would be heir to the psychoanalytic throne. Jung broke away from Freud in 1914 and founded his own approach known as *analytic psychology.* Jung—unlike Freud—was interested in mystic phenomenon and felt Freud emphasized sex too heavily.

**justice**
In ethics, the notion that a helper is fair and provides equal treatment to all clients regardless of race, ethnicity, gender, disability, or economic status.

**just noticable difference**
In psychology, the minimum amount of difference between two stimuli one can perceive. A subject who was blind-folded, for example, might be able to feel the difference between one piece of chalk in her hand and two pieces of chalk in her hand only 50% of the time.

**"Just Say No"**
A campaign in the war against drugs that was created during the Reagan administration.

**just-world hypothesis**
In social psychology, the notion that people get what they deserve.

**juvenile**
Refers to individuals 18 years of age and under who are not considered adults.

**juvenile court**
Sometimes known as the *family court,* this institution deals with legal matters of individuals 18 and younger (e.g., child neglect and truancy).

**juvenile delinquent**
Refers to an individual under 18 who behaves in a manner which would be considered criminal if he or she were an adult.

**K**
Abbreviation for potassium. Low levels of potassium can cause dangerous heart and circulatory problems.

**Karpman's triangle**
Stephen B. Karpman's notion in transactional analysis that an individual who is dysfunctional engages in the so-called *drama triangle* by switching and playing three roles: a helpless person known as a "Victim"; a "Persecutor" who enforces rules with extreme, excessive, or sadistic brutality; and the "Rescuer" who helps others in order to foster dependency. This paradigm is used to analyze the drama. According to this explanation, an individual may play more than one role concurrently. In transactional analysis, a drama is often contrasted with a *game* in which an individual makes one major role switch. In a drama, there are more switches and events.

**Knight Dunlap's Beta hypothesis**
*See beta hypothesis.*

**Kibbutz**
A collective community in Israel in which everyone pitches in to provide goods, services, education, and child care. Parenting is a communal activity.

**kinesthetic sense**
Information from sensory modalities (e.g., the inner ear) and organs which tells us the position and/or movements of our body.

**Kinetic family drawing (KFD)**
This instrument is used as a supplement to the Draw-A-Person test (DAP) in which the client is asked to draw everyone in his or her family engaged in an activity. It is then used as a projective measure of the personality.

**Kinsey study**
Alfred Charles Kinsey (1894–1956), the director of the Indiana University's Institute for Sex Research, conducted the first major study of sexual behavior in the US. Data were based on interviews during the 1940s and 1950s. Since interview procedures varied, and the sample size was small and not particularly representative of the population at large, generalizations based on his data have been criticized.

**kleptoagnia**
J. C. Kierman's term for sexual excitement resulting from the act of stealing.

**kleptomania**
An impulse control disorder characterized via a compulsion to steal.

**Kohlberg, Lawrence (1927–)**
Kohlberg's theory of moral development is well-known in the social sciences. Working as a student at the University of Chicago, Kohlberg set out to expand on Jean Piaget's theory of moral development. Kohlberg currently suggests six general stages of morality. In the first or preconventional level, behavior is governed by consequences. Stage 1 is the Punishment and Obedience Orientation, in which the child obeys in order to ward off punishment. The severity of a violation is determined by the severity of the punishment administered. Stage 2 is referred to as Naive Hedonism, and the child conforms to rules in order to receive rewards. The second level, conventional morality, is characterized by a desire to conform to socially accepted rules and roles. Stage 3, is the Good Boy/Good Girl Orientation, where the individual wants approval and acceptance for his or her behavior. Stage 4 is the Authority and Social Order Maintaining Morality, where rules are followed with the thought that authority and rules are for the good of the entire society. The highest level is termed Postconventional Morality, in which self-accepted moral principles dictate behavior. Stage 5 is Morality of Contract, Individual Rights, and Democratically Accepted Law, in which the individual accepts that contradictory values exist. Stage 6 is Morality of Individual Principles of Conscience, where morality is based on self-imposed ethical standards. Some individuals never reach the final stage.

**Kohler, Wolfgang (1887–1967)**
A psychoanalyst who helped found gestalt psychology along with Max Wertheimer and Kurt Koffka. (Note: gestalt psychology is not synonymous with gestalt therapy created by Fritz Perls.) He is also remembered for his work during World War I with the great apes at the Germanj primate station located on the Canary Islands, which led to the discovery of insight learning, sometimes loosely referred to as the *a-ha experience.*

**Korsakoff's syndrome**
Can also be spelled Korsakov or Korsakow. Named after the Russian doctor S.S. Korsakoff who first noted short-term memory loss in alcoholics. Can also be referred to as *alcohol dementia,* or *alcohol amnestic disorder.* The alcoholic who has amnesia of this nature often makes up things (i.e., engages in confabulation) to account for this condition.

**Kruskal-Wallis test**
A nonparametric one-way analysis of variance sometimes called the *H-test. See analysis of variance.*

**Kubler-Ross theory of grief**
Elisabeth Kubler-Ross analyzed terminally ill individuals and discovered that most persons experience five basic stages as they face their own death: (1) denial, (2) anger, (3) bargaining, (4) depression, and (5) acceptance.

**Kuder Occupational Interest Survey (KOIS)**
An interest inventory that makes the assumption that a person will find satisfaction in an occupation where workers have similar interest patterns. This is a 100-triad inventory in which the respondent must choose between three activities, stating the one activity preferred the most and the activity preferred the least. It takes approximately 30 minutes to complete and must be scored by computer. Primarily suited to those in the tenth grade and beyond.

**Kuder-Richardson formulas/KR-20, KR-21**
Methods for securing a correlation to estimate internal consistency reliability of a test utilizing data yielded by a single administration of that particular test.

**Ku Klux Klan (KKK)**
A group that is against African Americans, Jews, and persons who reside in the US from other countries. Members often wear robes, hoods, burn crosses, and commit violent acts against the aforementioned groups.

**kurtosis**
A statistical term that refers to the peakedness or flatness evident when a distribution of scores is plotted. The normal curve is said to be *mesokurtic,* while flat curves are deemed *platykurtic,* and those which are tall and pointed are said to be *leptokurtic.*

**kwashiorkor**
A form of malnutrition seen primarily in Third World countries that results from inadequate protein intake. This affliction impacts physical and mental development.

**label**
The process of naming a client's condition. The label generally comes from the *DSM* and is called a *diagnosis*. Labeling is a controversial subject. On one hand a label is generally positive since it helps professionals know within reason what symptoms go along with a certain label or diagnostic category, so that two helpers talking about the same label will mean roughly the same thing. Moreover, some clients feel better just knowing that their condition is not that unusual; that it has a name and others also suffer from the affliction. The negative, however, is that the label can become an excuse for a behavior (e.g., "what do you expect from me, I have attention deficit hyperactivity disorder") or the label becomes a self-fulfilling prophecy. Insurance companies and other third party payers require a diagnostic label in order for the helper to receive payments.

**la belle indifference**
The term literally means "beautiful indifference" and is used to describe a situation in which a client shows a distinct lack of concern regarding his or her symptoms.

**labile**
Implies that a client's emotional state changes rapidly and is highly unstable.

**laissez-faire leadership style**
(1) In group counseling, a "hands off" leadership style where the facilitator interferes very little with the group process. (2) Can also refer to the idea that the government should not try to control or dictate specific social policies. (3) An administrator who does not interfere with decisions and actions of the staff.

**lame**
Slang for a person who does not use drugs.

**lanugo**
Hair growth that resembles what is normal in a new-born child that appears on the body of an individual with anorexia nervosa.

**lapsus linguae**
In psychiatry or psychoanalysis, a slip of the tongue, assumed to be triggered via unconscious processes.

**larceny**
The act of stealing something that belongs to another person.

**latchkey children**
Refers to children who supervise themselves after school as their parents or caretakers work. Often called *home-alone children.*

**latency period/stage**
Freudian psychosexual developmental theory postulates the oral, anal, phallic, latency, and genital stages. In the latency stage, from age three to approximately five years of age, until approximately age twelve the individual has little interest in sex. Instead, the person is focused on socialization skills.

**late-entry worker**
An individual (typically female) who enters the work place after spending a long period of time at home (e.g., raising children).

**latent**
Something that exists but is not visible (i.e., dormant or hidden).

**latent content**
In psychoanalysis the dream is said to have manifest content (i.e., what the dreamer is dreaming about) and latent content. The latent content is the hidden unconscious meaning. The term has also been applied to fantasies.

**latent homosexual**
Refers to an individual who unconsciously wants to engage in homosexuality. If the conflict is strong enough, the individual may engage in an ego defense mechanism known as *reaction formation* and show hatred, such as anger or gay bashing, towards homosexuals. Persons who fit this profile are sometimes designated as *homophobic,* meaning they have a dire fear of homosexuals and homosexuality. *See reaction formation.*

**latent schizophrenia**
A schizophrenic condition that is not as severe as full-blown schizophrenia. Usually referred to as *schizotypal personality disorder* or *borderline schizophrenia.* Some of the older literature uses the term *prepsychotic.*

**Latino**
An individual from Latin America, Central America, Spain or the Caribbean. As of late, the term *Hispanic* is preferred.

**law**
(1) A collection of rules created by a society or a government. A system of negative consequences or punishments is usually set up for those who violate the rules. (2) Something that is always true in science and nature (e.g., the law of gravity).

**law of association**
Edward Thorndike's studies demonstrated that learning can occur when two things are paired.

**law of effect**
Edward Thorndike's studies demonstrated that a response followed by a pleasant consequence is strengthened or repeated. This model was later expanded upon and became the basis for B. F. Skinner's operant conditioning and the behavior modification movement.

**lay analyst**
A trained psychoanalyst who does not have a medical degree. Thus, a Ph.D., Psy.D., DSW, or Ed.D. analyst would be a lay analyst.

**LCSW**
*See Licensed Clinical Social Worker.*

## lead
In interviewing, counseling, and therapy, any verbal or nonverbal behavior that encourages the client to talk (e.g., shaking one's head up and down to implicitly say, "yes, it is okay to talk").

## leadership styles
The way a leader or facilitator runs a group. *See authoritarian leadership style, democratic leadership style, and laissez-faire leadership style.*

## lead poisoning
Generally occurs when children ingest lead-based paint, which is found in older buildings. High lead levels can cause physical and emotional damage. Often lead-painted surfaces are sealed and repainted, or better still the lead paint is removed and the surface is repainted. Some experts believe that the affliction is higher in the summer since vitamin D from the sun increases lead absorption. Can also occur in adults who work around lead (e.g., plumbers who work around lead pipes), and some of the older literature may refer to the condition as *plumbism.*

## learned helplessness syndrome
In the late 1960s psychologist Martin E. P. Seligman and his colleagues gave dogs mild electric shocks. These dogs found that they could jump or run away to escape the shock and could even be classically conditioned to avoid the shock altogether. Dogs, however, that were initially held down and thus could not avoid the shocks seemingly became helpless and did not attempt to escape them when they were unrestrained. Often this experimental paradigm is used as an analogy to explain depression in which the person feels helpless, hopeless, and gives up. The person, like the dog, has somehow learned that struggling doesn't help or will seemingly makes things worse.

## learned optimism
Refers to psychologist Martin E. P. Seligman's position that individuals who practice cautious optimism in terms of their thinking process are less likely to become depressed, ill, or a victim of the learned helplessness syndrome, even when exposed to adverse circumstances. *See learned helplessness syndrome.*

## learned pessimism
Martin E. P. Seligman's research that pessimistic individuals do not fare as well in life as cautiously optimistic people. They are more depressed and have more health problems. Seligman believes that cognitive ther-

apy can teach the individual to think in a more productive, optimistic ways. *See learned helplessness syndrome.*

## learning
The acquisition of a new behavior or information.

## learning curve
The curve obtained when a pictorial diagram or graph is created to show changes in learning over a period of time. In most cases the amount of information acquired or performance will be graphed on the vertical axis (also known as the $y$ axis or the ordinate) and the time needed to acquire the information or skill will be plotted on the horizontal axis (also known as the $x$ axis or the abscissa).

## learning disability
Refers to afflictions that hinder the learning process in children who sport average or above-average intelligence. Typical learning disabilities include: dyslexia, characterized by problems learning to read; dyscalculia, difficulty mastering operations of calculation; and dysgraphia, in which learning to write is the obstacle.

## learning theory
Any theory that attempts to explain how we learn or acquire knowledge. When the term is used in the literature it nearly always applies to several major theories: behavior modification/operant conditioning, behavior therapy/classical conditioning, and/or social learning theory. All of the aforementioned theories believe that the environment, not unconscious impulses, provides the key to understanding learning.

## least restrictive environment (LRE)
This term, which comes from Public Law 94-142, stipulates that a disabled child should be educated in a setting which is as similar as possible to the regular classroom. Often used in special education and facilities that work with the disabled. LRE is also called *mainstreaming.*

## left wing
Slang for someone who is extremely liberal, especially in terms of political and social issues. Often contrasted with *right wing*, which describes an individual who is very conservative.

## legal
(1) Pertaining to the law. (2) Obeying the laws.

**legal aid**
Legal services provided free (i.e., pro bono) or at a reduced rate to clients who cannot afford the legal fees of private attorneys. The service could be funded via a government program, a law school, or even a bar association.

**legal separation**
A legal process that allows a husband and wife to live apart without securing an actual divorce.

**leisure**
Time spent away from work doing something the person wishes to engage in.

**leisure class**
Refers to wealthy people who make enough money to have an abundance of leisure time.

**leptokurtic**
In statistics, a graph that has a very high or steep peak. Often contrasted with a normal curve, which is bell shaped, and a platykurtic curve, which is flat. The degree of peakedness or flatness in a frequency distribution curve is known as *kurtosis.*

**lesbian**
A female homosexual. Older literature may use the term *sapphism.*

**lethal**
Anything that can be deadly. For example, an overdose of some drugs can be lethal. The term *fatal* is also commonly used.

**lethality scale**
Any standardized or informal measure that attempts to assess how likely it is that an individual will commit suicide or homicide. Lethality scales are routinely used by workers on suicide help-lines.

**leukemia**
*See acute leukemia and chronic leukemia.*

**level of confidence**
*See alpha level and type I error.*

**liability insurance**
Also known as *malpractice insurance,* a policy of this nature is intended to protect a human service worker in the event of a malpractice suit. Liabil-

ity insurance is often available at a reduced rate from professional organizations (e.g., the American Counseling Association).

## libel
The act of writing something about another person that is harmful and inaccurate.

## liberal
Someone who champions the rights of the poor, elderly, disadvantaged, minorities, and anybody else who can benefit from social programs. Often contrasted with *conservative* individuals, who do not support programs that help the aforementioned individuals.

## libertarian
A political party that recommends as little government as possible. Libertarians generally believe that private citizens and industry can do virtually anything better and more efficient than local, state, or national government.

## libido
In psychoanalytic theory, the sexual drive, energy, or instinct. Human service workers often use the term in a broader fashion such that it refers to love, pleasure, and erotic desires.

## Licensed Clinical Social Worker (LCSW)
A social worker licensed by the state to practice clinical social work. In most cases, an MSW from an accredited school, supervised experience, and passing a state social work exam are required. A continuing education requirement may also be stipulated for those who have achieved licensure.

## Licensed Independent Clinical Social Worker (LICSW)
In some states, this licensing designation would allow the social work practitioner to engage in private practice and receive third-party reimbursement and insurance payments without a referral or supervision from another mental health provider (e.g., a psychiatrist).

## Licensed Professional Counselor (LPC)
A counselor licensed by the state to practice counseling. In most cases a master's degree with course work in specific areas, supervised experience, and passing a state exam are required. In some states, a doctorate would lower the supervision requirement (e.g., a doctorate-level person would need 1500 hours while a master's-level practitioner would need 3000 hours). Since some states use an exam that is identical to a certification exam (e.g.,

the National Counselor Examination [NCE] or the Certified Clinical Mental Health Counselor's Examination), a state may accept a score from that particular exam, assuming that the score was high enough to meet the state board's requirements. A continuing education requirement can also be stipulated for individuals who have achieved licensure.

## Licensed Psychologist
An individual who graduates from an approved program in psychology accredited by the American Psychological Association (APA). After postgraduate experience/supervision, the person will need to pass the Examination for Professional Practice in Psychology (EPPP).

## licensing board
A state board related to a given profession (e.g., the committee for licensed professional counselors or the committee for licensed clinical social workers) that reviews applications for licensure, supervision, licensure exams, reciprocity, in some cases continuing education, and ethical violations.

## licensure
Occurs when a government agency (e.g., the state board of counseling or healing arts) authorizes an individual to engage in a given occupation (e.g., counseling or psychology). It also determines who can use a given professional designation. Hence, a person who is not a licensed counselor or psychologist cannot use the title. Licensing helps assure that the public will receive competent services and thus persons must meet the required standards before being licensed. Licensing is not the same as certification. Hence, a counselor who is certified but not licensed cannot practice in a state that requires practitioners to be licensed. *See certification.*

## LICSW
*See Licensed Independent Clinical Social Worker.*

## life expentancy
An educated or statistical guess of how long someone will live (e.g., the average female in such and such country lives to age 76).

## life script
*See script/script analysis.*

## life span theories
Any developmental theory that attempts to explain the typical stressors, transitions, tasks, and crises experienced by an individual when he or she

ages. Popular theories include Freud's psychosexual theory, Erik Erikson's eight-stage psychosocial theory, Jean Piaget's four stages of cognitive development model, Lawrence Kolberg's six-stage theory of moral development, Daniel Levinson's three major transitions model, and Gail Sheehy's passages paradigm.

**lifestyle**
This term is generally used in the field of career counseling, vocational guidance, and Adlerian Individual Psychology. It describes an individual's total style and mode of living including work, leisure, social, and family activities.

**light therapy**
One theory is that depression is abetted by a lack of sunlight. This affliction is called *Seasonal Affective Disorder (SAD)*. If the person cannot secure actual sunlight full spectrum lights can be substituted. Special high-priced devices with very strong lights are available to treat this condition; however, full-spectrum bulbs that are weaker and designed for household fixtures are now readily available.

**Likert scale**
Created by Rensis Likert, an attitude measurement scale where the client indicates agreement or disagreement (e.g., strongly agree, uncertain, strongly disagree) with a given statement. Generally, between three and seven choices are provided.

**limbic system**
The area of the brain that regulates thirst, emotions, motivation, eating, and sexual feelings.

**limited term psychotherapy/treatment**
A therapeutic model in which the date of the final session is set during the first interview.

**linear causality**
The notion that one event causes another (a bad childhood caused the person to be disturbed as an adult). Often contrasted with circular causality, which most family therapists put more stock in and which assumes reciprocity (e.g., that a person in the family affects every other per-

son in the family system and every other person in the family affects that person). *See circular causality.*

### linguistics
The study of language and words.

### linking
In group counseling, the counselor looks for common themes and concerns discussed by group members and then attempts to connect members by attempting to foster group interaction between them. The technique serves to promote member-to-member interaction while sometimes lowering interaction between the counselor and the group members. This technique is popular with group leaders who favor an interactional model.

### listserve
An e-mail network made up of people who have a common interest (e.g., counseling) or belong to a given organization. A message and the responses to it can be viewed by the entire listserve population so others can respond if they would like.

### literacy programs
Any program that teaches children and/or adults how to read and/or write.

### lithium carbonate
A trace mineral, available in therapeutic doses only by prescription and very small dosages without a prescription, which helps to control the manic tendencies experienced by those suffering from manic-depressive illness (also known as *bipolar disorder*). In some instances, it is sometimes prescribed for clinical depression. Scientists are not certain how lithium (trade name Eskalith and Lithane) works, and currently its purpose in human physiology is unknown. Large dosages can cause irreversible kidney damage, nausea, tremors, pulmonary difficulties, or death. Clients on lithium should be closely monitored by a physician.

### Little Albert
The name of a five year old that John B. Watson and Rosalie Rayner (1920) used to prove that fears could be learned or conditioned. Little Albert was literally taught to fear furry animals. This notion suggested that

there was no need for theories about the unconscious mind, abnormality, or psychopathology in such clients. The affliction was merely learned. This experiment is often quoted as being indicative of the behaviorist model or paradigm. Controversy surrounded this experiment inasmuch as Watson did not cure the boy once the experimental fear was induced. In a later experiment, Mary Cover Jones did indeed prove that a learned fear such as Little Albert's could be eliminated via a special type of learning called *counterconditioning*. The case of Little Albert is often contrasted with the case of Little Hans, which seems to support the Freudian psychoanalytic model. *See Watson, John Broadus.*

### Little Hans
A famous case of Freud's depicted in his 1909 paper "Analysis of a Phobia in a Five Year-Old Boy," that is often quoted as being indicative of the psychoanalytic model. Hans was afraid of horses, but in reality Freud discovered it was his father he was afraid of, because Hans felt his dad was his rival in terms of his mother's affection. The youngster was analyzed by mail with Freud corresponding with the young man's father. The case of Little Hans is often contrasted with the case of Little Albert, which seems to support the behavioristic model.

### Little Professor
In transactional analysis, the Child ego state is seen as having three parts: the Natural Child, the Adapted Child, and the Little Professor. The Little Professor houses the unschooled wisdom of the child. The Little Professor is creative, intuitive, inventive, imaginative, manipulative, and acts on hunches.

### living will
A legal document that specifies what to do if the patient becomes very sick and thus is unable to communicate his or her wishes. Generally a "Do Not Resuscitate" (DNR) order to withhold life support measures that could keep the person alive.

### Lloyd Morgan's Canon
In 1894, comparative psychologist Lloyd Morgan suggested that the simplest explanation of an animal's observed behavior should be utilized. In human services the term merely implies that the simplest possible explanation of a phenomenon or behavior is preferred. Also known as *parsimony* and *Occam's Razor*.

193

**load**
Short for *caseload,* the term applies to the number of clients or type of clients a human service worker is helping (e.g., she has 32 homeless families in her caseload).

**locus of control**
Julian B. Rotter's notion that an individual believes he or she is in control of life circumstances (i.e., an internal locus of control) or that an individual believes the outside world controls his or her behavior (i.e., an external locus of control). A personality emphasizing an internal locus of control is considered healthier.

**logotherapy**
A form of existential therapy created by psychiatrist Viktor Frankl, who was imprisoned in Nazi concentration camps. *Logotherapy* literally means healing through meaning. Logotherapy attempts to remove the sense of meaninglessness and emptiness in one's life. Existential therapies espouse that each person creates his or her destiny via actions.

**longevity**
(1) Refers to the total length of life. (2) *Longevity strategies* refers to any technique or substance (e.g., a hormone) that can make someone live longer.

**longitudinal research/study**
Occurs when a researcher follows one or more persons (i.e., the same subject or subjects) for an ongoing period of time. Often contrasted with a cross-sectional study / research. *See cross-sectional research/study.*

**long-term memory**
The ability to remember information that was acquired a long time ago. Some long-term memories are never forgotten. Often contrasted with short-term memory, which is not permanent. *See short-term memory.*

**long-term therapy/treatment**
An imprecise term that implies that the intervention will last very long (e.g., over 15 sessions or over 6 months) and that the client could require several sessions per week. Often contrasted with *brief therapy* or *brief strategic therapy/treatment. See brief counseling/therapy and brief strategic counseling/therapy.*

**looking glass self**
A sociological theory that postulates that a portion of one's self-image is acquired via feedback, criticism, etc. from other people.

**loosening of associations**
A pattern of communication seen primarily in schizophrenia in which the individual goes from one topic to another unrelated topic. Also known as *schizophrenic thinking* or *tangentiality.*

**lost child**
The theory that in an alcoholic family one child is likely to separate himself or herself from the family system.

**low class/lower class**
Refers to people who have very low incomes, low paying jobs, and little education.

***LPC***
*See Licensed Professional Counselor.*

**LRE**
*See least restrictive environment.*

**LSD/Lysergic Acid Diethylamide**
A strong hallucinogenic drug discovered in 1942 which can abet psychotic symptoms. Some users report flashbacks to the hallucinations that are very disturbing. The drug's street name is *acid,* and a negative experience with the drug is known as a *bad trip.*

**lucid**
Refers to the fact that an individual is in touch with reality and can accurately convey what he or she is experiencing.

**lumbago**
Lower back problems.

**lunacy**
An unscientific term in older literature for a person who is crazy, psychotic, or insane, based on the belief that the earth's relationship to the moon caused mental health difficulties.

**lying**
Technically speaking, lying is the act of consciously not telling the truth. Often contrasted with *confabulation* in which the person is unaware that he or she is lying but merely filling in memory gaps.

**lymphoma**
A type of cancer. *See cancer.*

**MAC**
*See Master Addiction Counselor (MAC).*

**macro practice**
A somewhat imprecise social work term that varies from source to source. Generally the term signifies the practice of social work with organizations and communities and includes policy development, analysis, and research. *See mezzo practice/system and micro practice.*

**macular degeneration**
This disease is the leading cause of blindness. The disease breaks down the macula, the part of the retina that is responsible for the distinct vision we use for driving and reading. The specific causes of macular degeneration are still unknown. However, in most cases aging is a factor. The disease is hereditary and can also occur as a result of a side effect of certain drugs.

**magical thinking**
The dysfunctional belief that thinking influences the environment and thus is equivalent to behavior. Magical thinking distorts the notion of cause and effect and is often observed in very young children and psychotics.

**mainstreaming**
*See least restrictive environment (LRE).*

**maintenance**
Counseling or other intervention aimed at maintaining a given level of progress rather than attempting to instill additional changes.

**maintenance-oriented roles**
*See task-oriented roles.*

**major affective disorders**
A somewhat obsolete term from the *DSM-III*. Today the term *mood disorder* is preferred and connotes depressive disorders or bipolar disorders.

**maladaptive/maladjustment**
Refers to an individual's unsuccessful attempts to cope within a given environment. The term is often used to describe any person that has unresolved emotional problems or a mental disorder.

**malignant**
*See cancer.*

**malingering**
The act of exaggerating a condition or disability in order to avoid a situation or reap personal gains. A client, for example, could act more depressed than he really is in order to escape an undesirable work situation.

**malpractice**
(1) Bad, unethical, or illegal practice that could harm a client. (2) Practice that violates ethical guidelines for the profession.

**malpractice insurance**
Also known as liability insurance, this term refers to any policy that helps protect the human service worker in the event of a lawsuit.

**malpractice suit**
Occurs when a client (i.e., a plaintiff) asks for money because he or she feels that the helper has caused some sort of damages.

**managed care firm**
An organization that oversees health and mental health care to be certain the care is appropriate and cost effective. A managed care firm may dictate who the client or patient can see, what diagnoses (i.e., conditions) will be paid for, how often he or she can be seen, the beginning and end date of treatment, the amount the provider will be paid, and the type of treatment (e.g., individual outpatient therapy is acceptable but group therapy is not). Managed care is a very controversial issue. Some believe that it has gone too far and has denied individuals the best treatment in favor of cost containment.

**mandated reporter**
Refers to the fact that human services professionals must report child abuse, neglect, exploitation, sexual abuse, and elderly abuse to the appropriate state hotline. There are legal consequences if the practitioner does not make the report in a timely manner. Often contrasted with permissive reporters (e.g., a friend or neighbor of the person in question) who are not required by law to make a report but can initiate one.

**mania/manic**
(1) A mood disorder characterized by rapid thought, speech, and behavior as well as an elevated mood. Often refers to the hyperactive phase of manic-depressive (i.e., bipolar disorder) illness. (2) The word *mania* can also be utilized as a suffix to indicate compulsive behavior indicative of an impulse disorder. Kleptomania, for example, is a compulsion to steal.

**maniac**
Slang for a disturbed person who is prone to violence.

**manic depressive illness**
An old term for bipolar disorder. *See bipolar disorder.*

**manifest content**
In psychoanalysis, the belief that dreams contain manifest content (i.e., the actual content of the dream), as well as latent content (i.e., the unconscious meaning of the dream).

**man in the house rules**
The notion that if a welfare worker discovered that a man was in the home (regardless of his relationship to the client), then the client was able to support herself and thus was not in need of welfare payments. This practice became illegal after the Supreme Court case King v. Smith, in 1968.

**manipulation**
Dysfunctional behavior that attempts to exploit others.

**mantra**
A word or phrase one repeats over and over to induce meditation.

**MAO/MAOI**
Monamine oxidase inhibitor. These antidepressants (e.g., Nardil, Marplan, or Parnate) theoretically inhibit the enzyme monamine oxidase in the brain and raise biogenic amines to reduce depression. Some of the literature refers to this process as the "the theory of biogenic amines." *See antidepressant.*

**marasmus**
(1) Food deprivation that results in poor physical and mental development of a child, generally an infant. (2) An infant who has signs of malnutrition that actually resulted because the child was not properly mothered (i.e., touched, cuddled, etc.). Also known as *anaclitic depression.*

**marathon**
A very long psychotherapeutic encounter, usually in a group counseling or therapy setting.

**marijuana**
Also known as *pot, weed, grass, reefer,* or a *joint,* it refers to the leaves of the hemp plant Cannabis sativa. A compound known as THC or delta-9-tetrahydrocannabinol, isolated in 1964, is responsible for the intoxicating properties of marijuana. When smoked, marijuana causes behavioral changes including euphoria, higher pulse rate, red eyes, increased hunger and sex drive, and the feeling that time is moving slowly. It impairs memory and interferes with visual-motor skills such as driving a vehicle. Addiction to marijuana is thought to be more psychological than physical.

**marital skewness**
The term is used to describe a marital relationship in which one partner dominates or controls the other.

**marriage counseling/therapy**
Intervention intended to ameliorate difficulties and enhance the relationship of married couples. When the pair is seen together the term *conjoint marriage counseling/therapy* is permissible. When the man and woman are not married the procedure is called *couples counseling/therapy* or *premarital counseling/therapy.*

**masculine**
Male traits or characteristics.

**masculine protest**
Alfred Adler's concept that applies to women who wish to escape the feminine gender role and become a male. In men, the wish to dominate and become superior is said to be evident of masculine protest.

**Maslow's Hierarchy of Needs**
Abraham Maslow (1908–1970) postulated that survival needs must be met prior to focusing on higher or more emotionally based needs. Maslow's hi-

erarchy (from the bottom to the top): *Physiological Needs* such as food, water, air, and shelter; *Safety Needs* including security, stability, and the need for structure and order; *Belonging and Love Needs* such as affection, love, belonging, and family and friends; *Esteem Needs*, for example, self-esteem, recognition, achievement, and dignity; and the highest rung on the hierarchy, the *Need for Self-Actualization,* characterized by one's own ability to have a sense of meaning and life fulfillment. Maslow is considered one of the pioneers of humanistic or so-called third-force psychology.

**masochism**
The act of feeling gratification when one is abused by himself/herself or another individual. Can refer to self-punishment and/or self-destructive tendencies. When the pain is associated with the sexual act it is considered a *paraphilia*. Often contrasted with *sadism* in which the individual receives pleasure by hurting others. Paradoxically, both of these traits often occur in the same individual.

**massed practice**
The notion that learning without a break or a rest period is generally not as effective as learning with breaks (known as distributed practice).

**Master Addiction Counselor (MAC)**
A special certification given by NBCC (National Board for Certified Counselors) to individuals who have the National Certified Counselor (NCC) status with special experience and training in addiction treatment. This is a national certification. Some states have their own certification in this area that can be received with considerably less education. All MACs, however, must have at least a master's degree and the NCC credential.

**masturbation**
Self stimulation of one's sex organs.

**maternal deprivation**
Lack of attention from one's mother. Can occur due to poor parenting or a loss situation (e.g., death or divorce).

**matriarchy**
When a society, group, or organization is run via females.

**maturation**
The process of growth and development.

**201**

**maturational crisis**
A typical crisis that occurs due to maturation.

**maze-bright**
In experimental psychology, a rat or other animal that can run through a maze very rapidly.

**maze-dull**
In experimental psychology, a rat or other animal that is not able to run through a maze at a very rapid rate.

**McNaughten rules**
Suggests that an individual is not responsible for his actions if he didn't know right from wrong due to a defect, disease, or insanity.

**McPheeters, Harold L. (1923–)**
A psychiatrist who has been dubbed the father of Human Services. Dr. McPheeters was born in 1923 in New York City and grew up in Garden City, NY, where he attended local public schools. He graduated from Lafayette College in Easton, PA, and then from Medical School at the University of Louisville. He was in the Army Specialized Training Program during World War II and then served as a medical officer in the U.S. Navy during the Korean conflict. His residency training in psychiatry was also at the University of Louisville. He is board certified in Psychiatry and is a Fellow of the American Psychiatric Association. He served as Assistant Commissioner and then as Commissioner of the Kentucky Department of Mental Health from 1955 to 1964 and as Deputy Commissioner for Program Administration of the New York Department of Mental Hygiene, 1964–1965. He then moved to Atlanta, Georgia, where he served for 22 years as Director of the Education Board, an interstate compact organization of the 15 southern states dedicated to improving higher education and services to the people of the region. Dr. McPheeter's work with the Southern Regional Board helped create community college mental health programs. He retired from the board in 1987. Dr. McPheeters defines human services as "The occupation/profession that uses a blend of primarily psychological and sociological theories and skills in preventing, detecting, and ameliorating psychosocially dysfunctioning people and in helping them attain the highest level of psychological functioning of which they are capable." *See Dr. McPheeter's contributions at the beginning of the book.*

**meals on wheels**
Occurs when a social service agency delivers meals to clients' homes because the clients are unable to meet their own nutritional/food needs because of physical or emotional difficulties. The original meals on wheels program started in 1972 through the Federal Elderly Nutrition Program via an amendment to the Older Americans Act of 1965 and was intended to improve nutrition for the elderly.

**mean**
In statistics, the arithmetic average. The mean—also called a *measure of central tendency*—is computed by taking the sum or total of all the scores and then dividing by the number of scores. Thus if the scores are 50, 100 and 150 the scores are first added together. This yields are figure of 300. 300 divided by 3 (i.e., three scores) equals 100, which is the mean. Often contrasted with the *median* and the *mode*. *See average, median and mode.*

**means test**
Checking individual, family, or household income and assets in order to ascertain whether they meet the economic criteria to receive assistance from a program or an agency. Thus, an agency might stipulate that to receive a given service the household must have an income of under $10,000 per year and less than $500 in the bank. Often contrasted with social insurance programs that do not utilize a means test. *See social insurance.*

**measure of central tendency**
Another term for the word *average*. *See mean, median, and mode.*

**median**
In statistics, the middle score or hypothetical middle score when the distribution of data are rank ordered. In the distribution of scores 1, 3, 5, 7, and 9, 5 is the median because it has two scores above it and two scores below it. The memory device that "the median is the middle of the highway" is often useful. Often contrasted with two other measures of central tendency, the *mean* and the *mode*. *See average, mean, and mode.*

**mediation**
When an objective third party is brought in to help with a dispute. *See divorce mediation.*

**Medicaid**
A medical program in which the federal and state government shares the cost (i.e., jointly-funded) to pay for health care services for low income

and/or "medically needy" people. Each state has its own Medicaid program with its own set of rules, eligibility requirements, and services. Over 36 million Americans receive Medicaid. The program was created by the Title XIX of the Social Security Act, which became a law in 1965. Medicaid should not be confused with Medicare, a federal insurance program for individuals who are age 65 or older or disabled. *See Medicare.*

### medical human services worker/medical social worker
A practitioner who works in a health care setting such as a hospital.

### medical model
The notion that the person seeking help has a sickness or mental disease rather then problems of everyday living and coping. Treatment would generally consist of prescription medicinals and electroconvulsive shock therapy (ECT).

### Medicare
The federal health insurance program for the elderly and disabled. Medicare consists of Hospital Insurance, commonly called Part A, and Medical Insurance or Part B. (Medicaid is a different program.) Medicare is administered by the U.S. Department of Health & Human Services, Centers for Medicare and Medicaid Services. Most of the funds for Part A come from earmarked earnings taxes levied on employees, employers, and the self-employed. Part A helps pay for inpatient hospital care, hospice, skilled services for homebound patients, and short-term inpatient care in skilled nursing facilities if the patient is there primarily for rehabilitation. Funds for Part B come from monthly premiums ($54 per month in 2002) and a subsidy of general revenues of the federal government. Part B covers doctor bills, outpatient care, medical equipment, and supplies. Generally, the minimum age for Medicare eligibility is 65. However, three groups can have Medicare before 65: people who receive Social Security disability benefits because they have amyotrophic lateral sclerosis (also known as Lou Gehrig's disease), other disabled people who have received Social Security disability insurance benefits for at least two years, and kidney patients of all ages who need dialysis or a kidney transplant because of end-stage renal failure. Medicare began July 1, 1966 as a result of the 1966 Amendments to the Social Security Act. *See Medicaid.*

### medication
Any prescribed or over-the-counter drug intended to help a person with an illness.

**medigap**
Refers to any private health insurance plan that supplements Medicare benefits by helping to cover costs that Medicare will not.

**meditation**
A relaxation procedure for physical, emotional health, and increased self-awareness that centers around repeating a word or phrase (called a mantra) or focusing on one's breath or a mental picture.

**megalomaniac**
A person who is obsessed with having power and control over others. Often referred to as a "power hungry" individual.

**mega-vitamin therapy**
Slang for orthomolecular psychiatry. *See orthomolecular psychiatry.*

**melanoma**
*See cancer.*

**meloncholia**
An intense depression or sadness accompanied by a distinct lack of activity.

**melting pot**
An analogy in multicultural and diversity studies indicating that different cultures assimilate or melt into the larger or dominant culture. Most experts currently reject this model, and believe that the *salad* analogy (i.e., lots of different cultures continuing to exist in the larger culture) is much more accurate.

**memory**
The act of recall or ability to remember that which has been learned and/or perceived.

**menarche**
The first menstrual period.

**mendacity**
A pathological need to lie. Constantly trying to deceive others.

**meningitis**
An inflammation of the lining that surrounds the brain and the spinal cord. The cause of this disease is usually bacterial or viral in origin. This type of disease is uncommon but very contagious, which can result in

widespread epidemics. Commonly spread via the air, symptoms are fever, headache, nausea and vomiting, and a stiff neck.

**menopause**
A condition that occurs in middle-age when a woman stops menstruating.

**mensch**
Yiddish term for a wonderful individual with high ethical and moral standards who treats others well.

**mental age**
In IQ testing, the age level where 50% of the children answer the test question correctly.

**mental disorder/mental illness**
Any emotional illness which impairs one's ability to function or relate to others. The illness includes symptoms and may be caused by psychological or biological factors. In most cases, when this term is utilized it is assumed that professional assistance would be desirable. Mental disorders are described in the *Diagnostic and Statistical Manual (DSM)* of the American Psychiatric Association.

**mental health**
A state of well-being and adjustment. The ability to cope effectively with problems of everyday life (e.g., work, love, and relationships).

**mental health counselor**
(1) A counselor who works in a mental health setting. (2) A counselor licensed as a mental health counselor by the state. (3) A counselor who has secured certification as a Certified Mental Health Counselor (CCMHC) conferred by the National Board of Certified Counselors (NBCC) after securing National Certified Counselor (NCC) status.

**mental retardation**
(1) Below normal intelligence. Often categorized by IQ scores: 50–75, mild; 35–55, moderate; 20–35, severe; and below 20, profoundly retarded. The figures in each category can vary by 5 or 10 IQ points depending on the literature one examines. (2) Any person with an IQ score that falls at least 2 standard deviations below the mean or an IQ score of 68 or lower.

**mental status examination**
The term is primarily used in psychiatric settings and simply refers to the clinician's assessment of the client's overall mental state. The exam often yields a diagnosis, severity of the condition, and prognosis for treatment.

**mescaline**
An hallucinogenic alkloid drug from the peyote cactus used to induce altered states of consciousness that are similar to those experienced on LSD.

**mesmerize**
The term is named after Franz Anton Mesmer (1733–1815) whose work later became known as *hypnosis*. At times, the word is used in place of the term *hypnosis. See hypnosis.*

**mesomorph**
An individual with an inherited physically muscular constitution (i.e., body type).

**metacommunication**
The nonverbal portion of the message that is often seen as more accurate than the verbal portion of the communication.

**methadone**
A controversial synthetic narcotic drug utilized to treat those addicted to heroin. Methadone minimizes or eliminates the horrendous symptoms associated with heroin withdrawal. The treatment is highly controversial inasmuch as methadone is highly addictive and detractors claim that methadone clinics have merely served as breeding grounds for a legal addiction to methadone.

**Meyer, Adolf (1866–1960)**
American psychiatrist from Johns Hopkins who coined the term *psychobiology.*

**mezzo practice/system**
(1) Social work practice with a family or a small group. (2) A system that works to connect micro- and macrosystems. *See micro practice and macro practice.*

**microcephalus**
A condition in which the skull is unusually small and mental retardation and/or brain damage are evident.

### microcounseling
(1) Utilizing video feedback to train counselors. (2) A training paradigm set forth by Robert Carkhuff and Allen E. Ivey that focuses on specific behaviors a counselor can learn to improve his or her interviewing skills.

### microcounseling skills
Behaviors that facilitate the helping process such as open body posture, good eye contact, listening and attending, paraphrasing, and open-ended questions. The term has been popularized by literature and training materials created primarily by Robert Carkhuff and Allen E. Ivey.

### micromanagement
A term with negative connotations that refers to upper level supervisors or board members who are overly involved with minor details of the organization.

### micro practice
An imprecise social work term that varies from source to source and usually implies clinical work with individual clients, although some sources can include work with families, couples, or groups. Often contrasted with macro practice (e.g., political action) that focuses on change for the entire social system or community. *See mezzo practice/system and macro practice.*

### microsystem problem
A problem experienced by an individual client, couple, or family.

### middle age
Generally refers to individuals in the 40- to 60-year-old age range.

### milieu therapy
Environmental therapy such as activity or recreational therapy. Can refer to any therapeutic intervention based on stimulating environment.

### Miller Analogies Test (MAT)
A test that is used to screen applicants for graduate school (especially doctoral programs). Sometimes it is used as an adjunct to the more popular Graduate Record Examination (GRE).

### minimal brain damage (MBD)
A term found in some of the older literature to describe a child with a learning disability but no medical evidence of brain damage.

**Minnesota Multiphasic Personality Inventory (MMPI/MMPI-2)**
A pencil and paper personality test for adolescents and adults.

**miracle question**
Popular with brief strategic therapists, the client is asked to ponder how he or she would act if the person woke up the next day and a miracle occurred.

**mode**
In statistics, a measure of central tendency described as the most frequently occurring score or category. Thus in the distribution of scores 10, 15, 15, 20, 30, and 40, 15 is the mode since it occurs more than any other number. *See average, median, and mean.*

**model**
A theoretical explanation of a problem and/or the treatment of that problem. A model is also known as a paradigm. For example, rational emotive behavior therapy asserts that most human disturbance is fostered via irrational thinking and can be eliminated by thinking in a more rational manner.

**modeling**
A behavior modification term which asserts that learning can occur by imitation or by watching someone else who is reinforced for behaving in a given manner. Hence, a child who watches another child receive a treat for saying "please" is much more likely to say "please" as well.

**Mongolism**
A form of mental retardation that is now referred to as *Down's Syndrome* caused by the fact that the individual has 47 rather than 46 chromosomes. *See Down's Syndrome.*

**monoamine oxidase inhibitors**
*See MAO/MAOI and antidepressant.*

**monopolizer**
In group work, a client or student who talks incessantly and does not give others a chance to talk.

**monozygotic twins**
Identical twins from a single fertilized ovum. Often contrasted with *dizygotic twins,* who are no more alike than siblings (i.e., they are from different ova).

**209**

**mood**
An emotional state (sometimes called an affective state) such as depression or happiness.

**mood disorders**
A clinical depression, a dysthymic low-level depressive state, cyclothymic disorder, or bipolar manic-depressive state.

**mood swings**
Refers to changes in one's mood or affective state. Implies the mood varies or is not stable. The person may be very happy and then a short time later be extremely sad and depressed.

**morals**
(1) The behavioral guidelines and manners set by society. (2) The ability to discern right from wrong.

**morbid**
An unhealthy state of mind or diseased condition.

**mores**
Habits, folkways, and customs in a society that are viewed as beneficial for the welfare of the people, thus they are often enforced via laws.

**morphogenesis**
Occurs when a client or a family is able to improve or change.

**morphostasis**
Occurs when a client or family resists change in order to remain the same.

**motivated client**
A client who wants to change and does what he or she is told in order to make progress. For example, a motivated client who is given an assignment or task after a counseling session is much more apt to attempt it than a client who is unmotivated.

**mourning**
A reaction to a loss such as a death or a break-up of a relationship.

**MS**
*See multiple sclerosis (MS).*

**M.S.W.**
Master of social work degree from an accredited Council on Social Work Education (CSWE) program. Most programs require approximately 60 graduate credit hours; however, this number may be reduced for students who already have an accredited Bachelor of Social Work degree (B.S.W. or B.S.S.W). M.S.W. students must complete at least 900 hours of field placement in an approved social work setting.

**multiaxial classification system**
The *DSM-IV-TR* classifies mental disorders by using axes: Axis I, Clinical disorders, the primary problem; Axis II, personality and mental retardation; Axis III, medical conditions; Axis IV, psychosocial and environmental difficulties; and Axis V, the global assessment of functioning. *See DSM-IV-TR and GAF.*

**multicultural counseling**
The act of counseling somebody who has a culture different than your own. The terms *cross-cultural* and *inter-cultural* counseling are also permissible.

**multiple personality disorder (MPD)**
Morton Prince's term for a dissociative state in which a person develops two or more personalities. The term schizophrenia is often inappropriately used to describe MPDs. A high percentage of MPDs have been sexually abused. Recently, the term *dissociative identity disorder* has been used in place of MPD.

**multimodal distribution**
In statistics, a distribution with several modes (high scores or categories). Graphically this distribution appears to have hills or mountains running through it.

**multimodal therapy**
Created by the well-known psychologist Arnold Lazarus, this approach is routinely described via the acronym BASIC ID. The therapist focuses on 7 key areas: B = behaviors; A = affect or emotions; S = sensations such as sight, sound, or touch; I = images, such as self-perception, memories, or even dreams; C = cognitions; I = interpersonal relationships; and D = drugs, such as nutrition, biology, addictive substances, etc.

**multiple baseline research**
This type of research (which was popularized by behavior modification experts) looks at more than one dependent variable (DV) at a time. For

**211**

example, an initial baseline might be taken to see how many beers a client drinks daily and how much he smokes. After treatment both variables (i.e., drinking and smoking) will be investigated to see what influence, if any, the treatment had on these two baseline measures.

### multiple sclerosis (MS)
A type of autoimmune disease that leads to the deterioration of the protective sheath covering the nerve fibers in the central nervous system. This produces a problem with nerve impulses being sent, which causes difficulty with motor output (muscle movements) and can even lead to paralysis. This condition afflicts 1 out of 1,000 people and the cause is unknown. Women are approximately twice as likely to suffer from MS than men, and although it can strike at any age it usually begins between 20 and 40 years of age. Common symptoms of the disease include weakness of the muscles and double vision. No cure is available at this time.

### Munchhausen syndrome
A condition wherein a client desires surgery and may repeatedly hospitalize himself/herself without any evidence of sickness or pathology. Helpers often use the *DSM* diagnosis *factitious disorder* to describe such clients.

### muscular dystrophy (MD)
A condition, thought to be inherited, in which the skeletal muscles become progressively weaker. At this point in time the condition is irreversible.

### mutism
An inability to speak.

### Myers-Briggs Type Indicator (MBTI)
A widely used measure of personality disposition and preferences. It is based on Carl Jung's theory of perception and judgment. Four bipolar scales are used, resulting in 16 individual personality types, each of which are given a four-letter code used for interpreting personality type. It is suitable for use with upper elementary-aged children as well as adults.

### myopia
A vision problem also known as "nearsightedness" where people have difficulty seeing objects at a distance. Most are able to see up-close tasks (e.g., reading). Myopia occurs when the eyeball is somewhat longer than normal from front to back, which causes the light rays to focus in front of the retina, rather than directly on it. Myopia affects approximately one-third of the population. *See hyperopia.*

**NA**
*See Narcotics Anonymous.*

**NAACP**
*See National Association for the Advancement of Colored People.*

**naive subject**
A subject who is purposely misled as to the purpose of an experiment.

**NAMI**
*See National Alliance for the Mentally Ill.*

**narcissistic personality**
Narcissism is a condition in which the person has a high degree of self-love yet displays a distinct lack of caring or concern for others. The individual exaggerates his or her self-importance. The person has an unusually high need for attention and is preoccupied with a need for tremendous success. Individuals with this disorder have difficulty maintaining relationships.

**narcolepsy**
A sleep disorder that causes the individual to fall asleep even when the person is not attempting to do so.

**narcotics**
Opiate-derived and opiate related drugs that induce a dreamlike state or sleep. Narcotics have the ability to greatly reduce pain and are thus sometimes referred to as *analgesic*. Morphine, codeine, methadone, and heroin fall into this category. Narcotics are extremely addictive substances and often produce terrible withdrawal symptoms.

**Narcotics Anonymous (NA)**
A self-help group based on the twelve-step philosophy of Alcoholics Anonymous (AA) for anyone who is addicted to mood-altering drugs.

**NASW**
*See National Association of Social Workers (NASW).*

**National Alliance for the Mentally Ill (NAMI)**
A self-help advocacy group comprised of family members of those who suffer from schizophrenia.

**National Association for the Advancement of Colored People (NAACP)**
This organization, formed in 1909 in New York City by a group of Black and White citizens interested in social justice, is the oldest and strongest civil rights organization in the US. It began as a an aggressive watchdog of Negro liberties. Today the NAACP states that its main purpose is to ensure economic, political, educational, and social equality for all minority groups in the US.

**National Association of Social Workers (NASW)**
The largest umbrella organization for social workers, which was formed in 1955 and which currently has nearly 160,000 members. The organization helps to enhance social workers' status, develop relevant professional policies, and has a Code of Ethics.

**National Board for Certified Counselors (NBCC)/National Certified Counselor (NCC)/National Counselor Examination (NCE)**
The National Board for Certified Counselors (NBCC) was incorporated in 1982. The organization confers the generic certification of National Certified Counselor (NCC) to counselors who meet the educational, fieldwork, and supervision requirements and pass the National Counselor Examination (NCE). The test has 200 multiple choice questions; however, only 160 questions are graded. Forty questions are being field tested for suitability on future exams. After securing NCC status the

counselor may specialize as a Certified Clinical mental health counselor (CCMHC); a National Certified Career Counselor (NCCC); a National Certified School Counselor (NCSC); a National Certified Gerontological Counselor (NCGC); or a Master Addiction Counselor (MAC). NCCs can specialize in one or more of the aforementioned areas.

**national health insurance**
A health insurance policy that would cover everyone living in the nation.

**National Human Services Honor Society Alpha Delta Omega**
Founded in 1988 at the University of Wisconsin, Oshkosh, the organization is open to any Human Services major if the school has a chapter. A GPA of 3.0 is required as well as an essay describing the student's commitment to excellence and philosophy of working in the field. *See contact information in resources section of this text.*

**National Institute of Mental Health (NIMH)**
On July 3, 1946 President Truman signed the National Mental Health Act which designated the formation of a National Institute of Mental Health. The organization currently states that their mission is "to diminish the burden of mental illness through research." The NIMH asserts that research into neuroscience, behavioral science, and genetics can give us the scientific tools to understand, treat, and ultimately prevent mental illness. The organization maintains a web site for practitioners, researchers, and the general public.

**National Institutes of Health (NIH)**
This organization, founded in 1887, is one of the world's largest research centers and is considered a focal point for medical research in the US. The NIH is actually composed of twenty-five separate institutes and centers that are part of the U.S. Department of Health and Human Services. NIH's mission is to secure new knowledge that will provide better health for everyone. It should be noted that the organization only sees patients who are enrolled in their research studies.

**National Organization for Human Service Education (NOHSE)**
An umbrella organization intended to unite educators, students, clients, and practitioners, which was established in 1975 at the fifth Annual Faculty Development Conference of the Southern Regional Education Board (SREB). NOHSE also initially received support from the National Institute of Mental Health. The organization views human service education

215

as interdisciplinary and takes the position that human service workers need to be concerned with remediation of problems, helping clients meet basic needs and advocating for change in the systems that impact clients' lives. NOHSE states its purposes as: (1) To provide a medium for cooperation among Human Service Organizations and faculty, practitioners, and students. (2) To foster excellence in teaching, research, and curriculum for improving the education of those who provide human services. (3) To encourage, support, and assist local, state, and national human services organizations. (4) To sponsor conferences, institutes, and publications that offer creative approaches to human service education and delivery. According to NOHSE, members have diverse educational and professional backgrounds including mental health, corrections, addictions, developmental disabilities, child care, social services, human services resource management, recreation, and gerontology. *See Dr. McPheeter's article at the beginning of this book, human services/human service worker, and human service worker roles.*

### National Training Laboratory (NTL)
An organization founded in 1947 in Bethel, Maine, by Kurt Lewin to train individuals to facilitate groups. NTL is often cited as the pioneer in the sensitivity and encounter group movements.

### National Vocational Guidance Association (NVGA)
The first professional organization for counselors, formed in 1913. The formation of this organization is often said to be the result of seminal work by Frank Parsons, the so-called "father of guidance," who wrote a landmark book *Choosing a Vocation* in 1909 that led to the first vocational guidance conference in 1910.

### Native American
A racial, cultural, ethnic group, referred to in the past as "American Indian" or "Indian American." It describes those whose ancestors originally inhabited North America prior to European settlement.

### nativism
A viewpoint that asserts that personality characteristics are genetically transmitted rather than learned.

### Natural Child
In transactional analysis the child ego state is further divided into the Adapted Child, the Little Professor, and the Natural Child. The Natural

Child is what the child would become if no outside influences existed to alter the personality. The Natural Child is curious, affectionate, playful, impulsive, sensuous, spontaneous, and uncensored. *See Child ego state.*

**naturalistic observation**
The act of researching a phenomenon by observing what occurs in a natural setting (not a laboratory) without interfering with the process. No variables are controlled and there is no experimental manipulation in the data collection process. This is the oldest-known method of research methodology, and it is popular when studying children.

**naturalization**
Securing status as an official citizen of a country.

**nature of man**
Most theories of counseling or psychotherapy make the assumption that man has certain predispositions. Popular examples include a tendency to be motivated by instinctual sex and aggression (e.g., in psychoanalytic theory), an inclination to be irrational (e.g., in the case of rational-emotive therapy), man is basically good (e.g., humanistic approaches), or behavior is learned (e.g., behaviorism).

**nature versus nurture debate**
Nature stands for heredity and nurture refers to the environment. An ongoing controversy in the social sciences has been whether inherited traits (nature) are more important than learning and upbringing (nurture), or vice versa. Most human service workers today believe that both factors are extremely important. Strict behaviorists, of course, stress the environment/nurture more than nature.

**NBCC/NCC/NCE**
*See National Board for Certified Counselors (NBCC)/National Certified Counselor (NCC)/National Counselor Examination (NCE).*

**nearsightedness**
*See myopia.*

**NEC**
Literally means "Not Elsewhere Classified;" in the *International Classification of Diseases*, a guide sometimes used to diagnose clients.

**necrophilia**
Sexual contact or sexual attraction to dead bodies.

### necrophobia
An extreme fear of death or dead people.

### need
(1) Something that is necessary. A child, for example, needs nutrients to grow at a normal rate. (2) A tenet of rational-emotive behavior therapy (REBT) is that many people are disturbed because they view things they merely want as needs. A client might believe that he or she needs a good job in order to feel happy. REBT would assert that it would be nice if the individual had a wonderful job but that it is not necessary in order for the person to feel content.

### negative cooperation tasks
A paradoxical technique for working with resistant families in which the therapist gives family members a task that they agree to complete; however, the helper expects that the family will not complete the assignment.

### negative practice
The act of intentionally practicing a maladaptive behavior, error, or unwanted act to gain conscious control over it so it can be eliminated. A typist who frequently typed the letter "q" when she meant to type the letter "a" would be asked to deliberately and repeatedly type the letter "q."

### negative reinforcement
This is an operant conditioning behavior modification term. When the removal of a stimulus raises the probability that an antecedent/past behavior will occur or strengthens the behavior, then the stimulus is defined as a negative reinforcer. If, for example, you remove loud music from a work room and the worker's output increases then the music is a negative reinforcer. Negative reinforcement is not punishment. All reinforcers raise or strengthen behavior. Punishment decreases or weakens the strength of a behavior.

### negative transference
According to psychoanalytic theory, transference occurs when a client relates to a helper as if he or she is a significant other from the past. When the client is negative or hostile it is labelled *negative transference.* Psychoanalysts believe that transference always occurs during psychotherapeutic encounters.

**neglect**
A duty that is not acted upon which could result in harm, such as not taking a child for medical attention. Human service workers are mandated to report neglect and abuse to state abuse and neglect hotlines.

**negotiation**
To discuss or bargain to reach a mutual agreement. A human service worker, for example, might negotiate for a higher salary. In many cases, both parties will need to compromise.

**neoconservatism**
Although traditionally conservatives did not believe in welfare waste, the neoconservative position recognizes that that some welfare programs are necessary.

**neo-Freudian**
Can refer to any therapist who modifies or makes additions to Freudian psychoanalysis. Most neo-Freudians place more emphasis on psychosocial factors than Freud. Eric Fromm, Karen Horney, and Harry Stack Sullivan are the most notable examples. Some literature lists Alfred Adler and Carl Jung as neo-Freudians, although purists take exception with this since these particular theorists created their own theories. This minor distinction makes it very difficult to handle exam questions on this issue.

**neoliberalism**
Usually refers to a more conservative position on welfare programs than that espoused by liberals. Thus smaller programs with less benefits are stressed.

**neologism**
Refers to words that are made up generally by those who suffer from schizophrenia.

**neonate**
The term literally means a "newborn child" and is used in the area of human growth and development.

**neophyte worker**
A new or inexperienced worker.

**neopsyche**
In transactional analysis, the Adult ego state. *See Adult ego state.*

**nepotism**
Occurs when a relative is given a position even if he or she is not the best-qualified person for the job or position. To combat nepotism many agencies have rules against hiring or supervising relatives.

**nervous breakdown**
A lay term used to describe an individual who requires hospitalization or is immobilized in everyday life due to his or her emotional difficulties.

**nervous habit**
Repetitive actions such as smoking, nail biting, rocking (mainly in young children) or tics that help to calm a nervous person.

**network counseling/therapy**
A family counseling/therapy procedure used with an individual client in the family; a portion of the family; or the entire nuclear family. The counselor brings in extended family, friends, individuals from the client's place of employment or school, etc. into sessions to assist in the treatment process.

**networking**
The act of meeting and communicating with other agencies and/or professionals in person, by mail, or by telephone to enhance one's skills and/or referral source base.

**neurolinguistic programming (NLP)**
A system of treatment that blends psychology, linguistics, and communications. NLP was created by Richard Bandler, a California linguistics professor, and John Grinder, a mathematician and computer scientist, after investigating what strategies unusually successful therapists (primarily Milton H. Erickson, Virginia Satir, and Fritz Perls) used during the course of therapy. Using techniques such as anchoring and reframing, NLP claims that difficult problems such as learning disabilities and phobias can be cured in less than an hour. *See reframing.*

**neurologist**
A doctor who specializes in the treatment of disorders of the nervous system. If a client has actual physical damage to the brain or nervous system then a neurologist should generally be consulted rather than a psychiatrist. *See psychiatrist.*

**neuron**
A single nerve cell in the nervous system. The neuron is composed of a cell body, the axon that sends electrical impulses away from the cell, and the dendrite or dendrites that send the electrical impulse to the cell (i.e., generally the axon sends the message to a dendrite).

**neurosis**
Refers to persons who are psychologically disturbed. Anxiety caused by emotional rather than physical causes is generally the major symptom.

**New Deal**
Refers to the economic and social policies set forth by President Franklin Delano Roosevelt in the 1930s to help the country bounce back from the great economic depression, which began on October 29, 1929. The most important program was the Social Security Act of 1935. Job programs such as the Works Progress Administration (WPA) and the Civilian Conservation Corps (CCC) were also created by the New Deal. Roosevelt believed that the government needed to act in a humane manner at a time when one out of every four Americans was unemployed and one of every six was on welfare.

**new poor**
Refers to those individuals who have only recently become poverty stricken. Often the term is used to describe middle-class individuals who lost their job or have experienced a severe reduction in income.

**nicotine dependence**
A psychoactive substance abuse disorder listed in the *DSM* that is characterized by the inability to control one's use of tobacco (i.e., cigarettes, chewing tobacco, or cigars).

**night-terror**
A dream that is often more terrifying than a nightmare in which the person wakes up screaming or in a panic. Generally the individual is unable to remember all the specifics of the dream. Also known as *sleep-terror disorder* or *pavor nocturnus*.

**NIH**
*See National Institutes of Health.*

**nihilist**
(1) An individual who believes life is meaningless, purposeless. Nihilists often believe in nothing and have no philosophy of life. A person who says "no" to everything. (2) An individual who believes political and economic institutions must be taken away to make way for new institutions.

**NIMH**
*See National Institute of Mental Health.*

**NLP**
*See neurolinguistic programming.*

**nocebo effect**
*See placebo effect.*

**no excuses**
In the practice of William Glasser's reality therapy there are eight steps. Step six suggests that a counselor must accept no excuses after a client has committed himself or herself to a plan of action. The counselor could, nevertheless, change the plan if necessary.

**nominal scale of measurement**
A qualitative scale of measurement that is used to categorize logically separated groups such as a *DSM* or *ICD* diagnostic category. The nominal scale merely classifies, labels, or names something. Since a nominal scale does not provide qualitative (i.e., measurable) information, adding, subtracting, multiplying, or dividing a nominal category would prove meaningless. The nominal scale is considered the most elementary scale of measurement. *See ordinal scale of measurement, interval scale of measurement, and ratio scale of measurement.*

**nonaddictive**
Refers to substances, such as drugs and medicines, that do not cause the person to crave the substance. Nonaddictive substances do not cause dependency. Often contrasted with addictive substances, which the person craves more of after usage (e.g., cocaine).

**nondirective counseling/therapy**
(1) The original name for the helping approach created by Carl Ransom Rogers. The school was later called *client-centered counseling,* and most recently *person-centered counseling.* (2) Any technique or approach in which the counselor does not steer or direct the client to talk about a given topic

or issue. The counselor makes no attempt to direct the nature of the interview. Nondirective interviews are sometimes referred to as *unstructured interviews.*

### nondogmatic
The notion that effective human service workers are tolerant of clients who have values and beliefs that are different from their own.

### nonevent
In family therapy the notion that something does not occur that the family expects will occur (e.g., a couple does not have the number of children they planned). Often contrasted with an active event that causes a crisis.

### nonprofit
*See not-for-profit organization.*

### no punishment
In the practice of William Glasser's reality therapy there are eight steps. Step seven suggests that a counselor will not punish a client for failing to follow a plan of action. This policy is in contrast to other therapeutic modalities, such as behavior modification or rational-emotive therapy, which do at times utilize punishment.

### nonmaleficence
In ethics, the notion that the helper will not engage in acts that could harm others. The term literally means "to do no harm."

### nonparametric tests
A classification of statistical tests that can be utilized when the researcher cannot assume a normal population (i.e., the distribution of data is not normal curve). The chi-square, Mann-Whitney U, the Spearman Rank-Order correlation, and the Wilcoxon fall into this category. The terms *distribution-free tests* or *assumption-free tests* are also permissible.

### nontraditional family
Any family that does not match the normal or so-called traditional family composed of a husband, wife, and children. Hence, a gay family or a blended family would be considered nontraditional.

### nonverbal behavior
Any method of communication between two or more individuals that does not involve words (e.g., body language, tone of voice, eye contact, gestures of the hands or legs). Many experts believe that nonverbal com-

munication conveys the actual message more accurately than the actual statements the person has made.

### nonwhite
Refers to individuals who are not Caucasians, such as Asian Americans, Native Americans, or African Americans.

### normal
(1) average or typical (2) A person who has no diseases or disturbances.

### normal curve/distribution
*See bell-shaped curve.*

### norm group
A group used to establish a standard, typical, or representative behavior. Others will be compared to the norm group. Hence, once a new test is normed (using a norm group), everyone who takes the test will be statistically compared to the norm group.

### norms
(1) In group counseling and sociology, the written or unwritten rules of conduct or acceptable behavior. (2) An established standard for behavior and/or performance often expressed by statistical averages. (3) The typical, representative, or expected behavior from an individual, organization, or group. A researcher, for example, could compare a group of children who received advanced education to a norm group that is composed of typical or average students.

### NOS
Literally means "Not Otherwise Specified" in the *Diagnostic and Statistical Manual (DSM)* of the American Psychiatric Association.

### no-show
Slang for a client who misses his or her appointment.

### nosology
The branch of medicine that specifically studies the classification of disease. In human services, the *Diagnostic and Statistical Manual (DSM)* and the *International Classification of Diseases (ICD)* serve as nosological resources.

### no-suicide contract
A verbal or written contract with a suicidal person in which the person agrees he or she will not kill himself or herself. If the person is feeling like

hurting himself or herself then he or she is instructed to call the human services worker. A crisis helpline or hotline number is also included in case the worker is not available or does not receive the message. Written contracts are preferred as a copy can be signed by the worker and the client, and the client receives a copy. If a client will not sign or verbally agree to a contract then his or her will to live is waning and hospitalization (though it is not a panacea) is recommended.

### not-for-profit organization
Also referred to as a *voluntary agency* or *nonprofit*, in some of the literature this term describes an organization that has a board of directors/trustees and that may receive funds, endowments, grants, and donations from individuals, and businesses organizations such as United Way. Not-for-profit organizations are generally tax exempt. They are often contrasted with *proprietary* or *for-profit agencies* or *public agencies* which are established by laws and are operated by state, local, or federal governments.

### Now I've Got You, You S.O.B.
In transactional analysis, a game played from a persecutor role to get even and prove that another individual is not okay. A boss playing this game, for example, might purposefully leave a confidential document in the lunch room and then accuse his secretary of stealing or reading confidential papers when he walks in the lunch room and sees it in her hands. The individual who is the recipient of the persecution is "set up" by the person who initiated the game.

### NTL
*See National Training Laboratory.*

### nuclear family
Includes the father, mother, and the biological or adopted children. Also called the "traditional family," or the "traditional nuclear family."

### null hypothesis
The word *null* means "no thing" or "no difference" and is used in regard to experimental research. The null hypothesis states that any differences/relationships found between groups are the result of chance factors and thus are not significant. When the null hypothesis is accepted, the experimental/alternative hypothesis is rejected. Say, for example, that a control group and an experimental group that received assertiveness training are examined using an inferential statistical test. The null

hypothesis would assert that the research will find no significant difference in the control group who received the assertiveness training on the dependent/outcome variable.

### NVGA
*See National Vocational Guidance Association.*

### nyctophobia
A morbid or exaggerated fear of darkness.

### nymphomania
An excessive, insatiable sexual desire in females. Often contrasted with *satyriasis,* which refers to the same condition in males. The term *sexual addiction* can apply to either condition.

**OA**
*See Overeaters Anonymous (OA).*

**OASDHI**
*See Old Age, Survivors, Disability, and Health Insurance.*

**obedience**
The act of conforming to authority. This is a popular term in social psychology.

**obesity**
(1) An extremely high level of fat in the body. (2) An individual who weighs 20% or more over his or her normal weight. (3) An unscientific description of an individual who is severely overweight.

**object**
In psychoanalytic and object relations theory, a significant other that a child bonds with.

**objective account**
An oral or written description of a client's behavior or the helper's interaction with the client that is not distorted by feelings or prejudices. The human service worker must emotionally detach from the situation in order to be objective. Hence, a statement in a record such as "the house was very dirty," could be considered subjective or biased. A more objective statement might be "there were four plates of food on the floor in the kitchen."

**objective test/objective response**
A test or a response that is unbiased and not the result of prejudice. Something that is fact or reality and not dependent on the observer. For example, a true/false or a multiple choice test is objective since only a specific response is correct regardless of who is grading the test. An objective test/response is often contrasted with a *subjective test/response* such as an essay or a short answer on a test. On a subjective test there could be many appropriate or correct answers. Moreover, on a subjective measure, two persons scoring the same material could disagree on the appropriateness of an answer.

**object permanence**
Piaget's description of a child's ability to understand that an object exists even when it is out of the child's view. According to Piaget, this ability develops during the first year of life in the sensorimotor stage.

**observational learning**
*See modeling, vicarious, vicarious conditioning/learning, and vicarious reinforcement.*

**obsession**
A recurring, persistent or constant idea or thought. The person often has a compulsion (i.e., urge) to act on the thought.

**obsessive-compulsive disorder (OCD)**
This is an anxiety disorder in which an individual is plagued with repetitive, often irrational thoughts and feels an overwhelming desire (i.e., compulsion) to carry out a behavior or ritualistic act. Carrying out the compulsive act (e.g., hand washing) serves to rapidly remove tension.

**obtained score**
In statistics, a raw score that is not altered. *See raw score.*

**Occam's Razor**
Named after the mediaeval philosopher and theologian William of Occam (or Ockham), who proposed that the simplest scientific explanation is always preferred when several explanations exist. Can also be called the *principle of economy, Lloyd Morgan's Canon,* and *parsimony.*

**occupation**
Describes a class of jobs. For example, a psychologist could secure a job as a clinical psychologist, a school psychologist, an experimental psychologist, or an industrial/organizational psychologist.

## Occupational Outlook Handbook (OOH)
The most common resource used by career counselors, this book, published by the U.S. Department of Labor, is updated every two years. The text is replete with information on the training needed for an occupation; the job outlook for the field; salaries; and working conditions. This book was first published in 1946 to provide World War II veterans with accurate career information and now provides information on over 800 careers.

## occupational therapy
The use of activities in the helping process.

## occurrence-based liability/malpractice insurance
A policy that continues to insure the policy holder for the time he or she was insured even if he or she is no longer carrying the policy. If, for example, a policy holder had an occurrence policy in 2002 and a client took legal action against him or her during 2005 for something that took place in 2002 the policy would still cover him or her. This type of policy is often contrasted with lower cost claims-based policies, which will only cover the policy holder while he or she has the coverage. Occurrence-based policies are recommended for all human services professionals.

## ocular
Refers to the eye or one's vision.

## Oedipus complex
The most controversial part of Freud's psychoanalytic theory, which stipulates that male children in the phallic stage (i.e., ages 3 to 7 years) have an unconscious sexual attraction to their mothers. They are also worried about retaliation for these feelings from their fathers. Freud—who was fascinated by Greek mythology—borrowed the idea from a tragedy in which Oedipus killed his father and married his mother. In females the child wants her father's affection, and this is known as the *Electra complex. See Electra complex.*

## offender
A person who broke the law.

## Old Age Assistance (OAA)
A public assistance program for the elderly that was replaced by the federal Supplemental Security Income (SSI) program administered by the Social Security Administration.

### Old Age, Survivors, Disability, and Health Insurance (OASDHI)
On August 14, 1935, legislation created a government program to set up a permanent national pension plan for the aged. Congress enacted the Social Security Act in 1935. The program now provides benefits from payroll taxes and those from employers for retirees, children with disabilities, surviving relatives, and Medicare.

### old brain
An evolutionary theory that the part of the brain that handles automatic reflexes is still part of our body. From an evolutionary standpoint this was the first part of the brain.

### old epistemology
Ideas from the past that do not apply to the present.

### oldest old
Refers to individuals ages 85 and above.

### olfactory
In physiological psychology and rehabilitation, the sense of smell.

### omission
In professional ethics, a situation where a human service worker did not do something that should have been done (e.g., informing a teen's parents that the child stated he would commit suicide that night).

### oncology
The study of cancer.

### one-way mirror therapy/supervision
A popular technique with family therapists and brief strategic therapists, a team of experts sits behind what appears to be a mirror to the client or clients. The team behind the mirror can see and hear the entire therapeutic transaction. The team can then make suggestions by contacting the therapist via a phone or actually entering the therapy room. The clients are introduced to the team prior to the session. The strategy is also useful in terms of supervising helpers.

### online treatment
Using a computer system such as the internet or e-mail to treat a client. Sometimes known as *Web counseling* or *cybercounseling,* this practice has special ethical guidelines beyond face-to-face practice. *See Internet counseling.*

**ontology**
A view or way one perceives the world.

**open-door policy**
(1) Generally refers to an administrator who allows employees to come in without an appointment to discuss ideas or concerns. (2) A facility that allows clients to leave whenever they want.

**open-ended question**
A question which does not require a "yes," "no," or specific answer and thus the client can elaborate on a given issue. Since open-ended questions do not restrict the client's response as much as close-ended questions, they are generally preferred in most counseling situations. An open-ended question such as "Can you describe your panic attacks?" will generally elicit more information than a close-ended question such as: "Did you have a panic attack this week?" *See closed-ended question.*

**open group**
A group that allows new members to join and/or attend after the group is running. Open groups are positive in the sense that new members can bring new information and interaction to the group. Moreover, they can replace members who have dropped out. On the negative side, however, a new member has not had the same background as the other members and has not had as much time to bond with others. Often contrasted with a *closed group* in which new members are not permitted to join after the first or initial session. *See closed group.*

**open hospital**
A psychiatric hospital that does not used locked wards or otherwise restrain the patients.

**operant conditioning**
A learning theory proposed by Burrhus Fredrick Skinner (i.e., B. F. Skinner) (1904–1990) that became the basis of the behavior modification movement. The theory asserts that the probability of a behavior or the strength of it is determined by the consequences after the behavior. Often contrasted with classical or respondent conditioning, which is based on reflexive responses that became the basis of the behavior therapy movement. *See Pavlov, Ivan, reinforcement, positive reinforcement/reinforcer, negative reinforcement, punishment, and extinction.*

**operational definition**
A definition or set of instructions which is so clear and precise that any-one can duplicate the procedure. A very popular term in research and be-havior modification. For example, "We rewarded the child for good school work behavior" is not specific and thus would not qualify as an operational definition. On the other hand, "We gave the child a stick of gum for every three math problems he completed correctly on page 6 of the text book" would qualify since someone else could duplicate the procedure.

**ophidiphobia**
A morbid or exaggerated fear of snakes.

**opiate**
A drug derived from opium (the poppy plant) such as morphine.

**oral stage**
In Freud's psychosexual model of development the oral stage is the first of five stages (i.e., oral, anal, phallic, latency, and genital) that occurs dur-ing the first year of life. The libido and conflicts tend to focus on the mouth (e.g., biting or sucking). The mouth is viewed as an erogenous zone and chewing, eating, etc. help reduce the sexual tension. According to this theory, excessive drinking, smoking, eating, and even sarcasm serve the same purpose during adulthood.

**ordinal scale of measurement**
In statistics, data that represent the magnitude or order of the vari-able. For example, you could rank the scores students made on a final exam. Often contrasted with *nominal measurement* where the data merely represents the qualities or categories of a variable, for exam-ple, whether a client is Caucasian, African American, or Asian Ameri-can. *See nominal scale of measurement, interval scale of measurement, and ratio scale of measurement.*

**ordinate**
The vertical reference line on a graph often used to plot the dependent variable. Also known as the *y axis.*

**Oriental Exclusion Law of 1924**
A law that restricted the number of Asian immigrants who could enter the US.

232

**orientation**
(1) A helper's preferred mode of treatment. A counselor who favors person-centered Rogerian counseling, for example, may be described as having a humanistic or nondirective orientation. Can also refer to the helper's training or educational background (e.g., she was trained in behavior modification). (2) Can also be used to define one's sexual preference (e.g., he has a homosexual orientation).

**organic disorder**
An illness that is caused by an actual physical or chemical problem in the body. Often contrasted with *functional disorders*, which are caused by one's mind.

**organizational chart**
A pictoral diagram that shows who is in what position and who reports to whom in an agency, hospital, practice, etc. Most boards of directors require that the agency has an organizational chart and the charts are often required when an organization applies for a grant or for funding.

**orphanage**
A facility that cares for children whose parents or caretakers are unable to do so. Currently, the foster care system deals with this dilemma.

**orthomolecular psychiatry**
The treatment of mental disorders by providing the client with an optimal molecular environment. In the popular press this approach has been dubbed as *megavitamin therapy* since large doses of vitamins, minerals, amino acids, and other nutrients may be prescribed. Natural substances rather than unnatural drugs are used to regulate behavior. This approach emphasizes biochemical individuality such that one client may need one hundred times more of a given nutrient than another client in order to ward off schizophrenic thought patterns or other undesirable behavior. Many orthomolecular psychiatrists also use standard prescription medicines. Because of the fact that most insurance companies will not pay for this type of alternative treatment and possible ethical concerns, many psychiatrists try to avoid calling themselves orthomolecular practitioners.

**orthopsychiatry**
The prevention and/or early treatment of mental, emotional, and psychiatric disorders. In some of the literature this discipline is known as *mental hygiene.*

## osteopath
A physician who has a D.O. or Doctor of Osteopathy rather than an M.D. or Doctor of Medicine. Osteopaths are licensed physicians who put more emphasis on the bones and skeletal structure than do M.D.s. A psychiatrist can have a D.O. degree.

## outcome data/variable
Usually known as the *DV* or *dependent variable*, this data gives you the results of an experiment. *See dependent variable/DV, true experiment, and independent variable/IV.*

## outpatient services
Medical or mental health care that does not require the patient to be hospitalized. For example, a doctor might say: "The patient's surgery can be performed in my office on an outpatient basis." Often contrasted with "inpatient services" in which the patient must be hospitalized to receive the care that he or she needs.

## outreach counseling/services
The practice of counseling or providing other human services to a client in a setting which is outside the agency's office, such as the client's home, work, church, park, etc.

## overachiever
Used to describe a person who stresses himself or herself out by trying too hard or an individual who does more than what is expected. Often contrasted with an *underachiever,* who does not try as hard as he or she could or who does less than what is expected.

## overactive
Another word for *hyperactivity.* A person who cannot sit still and focus on a given task is often called *overactive* or *hyperactive.*

## overcompensation
Ongoing behavior that is intended to offset a perceived inferiority.

## overdetermination
A psychoanalytic term that implies that all behavior is caused by more than one thing. Also called *multiple causation.*

## overdose
The act of taking too much of a drug or a medicine. The result can be serious psychological and physical side effects or even death.

**Overeaters Anonymous (OA)**
A twelve-step self-help group based on Alcoholics Anonymous (AA) for individuals who can't control their eating.

**overt**
Any behavior that can be observed. Often contrasted with *covert* behaviors such as thoughts, feelings, and mental images that cannot be directly observed. The terms *overt* and *covert* are very popular in behavior therapy.

**Pacific Islanders**
*See Asian American.*

**panacea**
A cure-all.

**pandemic**
A condition that is very prevalent and seems to appear everywhere.

**panhandling**
The act of begging for food, money, or other goods on the street.

**panic attack/disorder**
Anxiety that is so severe that the individual may feel that he or she is dying. Sometimes occurs with *agoraphobia,* which refers to a fear of leaving home or a fear of open places.

**panphobia**
A morbid or exaggerated fear of everything.

**paper and pencil measure**
Any test or exam that requires written answers.

**paradigm**
A model. For example, the Freudian paradigm explains human behavior in terms of the unconscious mind, while the behaviorist paradigm espouses that behavior is molded by the environment.

## paradigm shift
A whole new way of thinking about or conceptualizing a situation.

## paradoxical strategy/intention
A technique that can be implemented when common sense strategies fail. Often called *prescribing the symptom*. The therapist tells the client to exaggerate the behavior he or she wants to ameliorate. Hence, a client who fears he will shake in front of an audience is instructed to shake as much as possible while giving the speech. The technique is contraindicated for clients with suicidal, homicidal, abusive, or self-abusive tendencies. The strategy has been popularized by Viktor Frankl, Milton H. Erickson, and Jay Haley.

## paralysis
Loss of feelings or movement in a portion of the body. Hence, a person who suffers a stroke may not be able to move some of his or her facial muscles.

## parametric statistical tests
Statistical tests such as the *t* test or analysis of variance (ANOVA) that make assumptions about the variance of the population (i.e., that the variables have a distribution that is normal in the population). Often contrasted with *nonparametric statistical tests* in which the data are nominal or ordinal and the assumption of a normal distribution cannot be assumed.

## paranoia/paranoid
Extreme suspicion of others. Feelings that others are after you or are trying to persecute you.

## paraphilia
Sexual disorders that involve sexual gratification without orgasm or with a partner who does not consent to sex. Examples include exhibitionism (exposing ones self); voyeurism (watching a person or persons in a sexual situation); pedophilia (a sexual desire for children); masochism (sexual pleasure resulting from pain or humiliation); sadism (sexual pleasure resulting from hurting or humiliating others); transvestic fetishism (dressing like the opposite sex); fetishes (sexual pleasure attained from a nonhuman object such as an article of clothing); and frottage (the act of receiving sexual gratification by rubbing against someone else in public).

**paraphrasing**
The act of restating what the client has said in your own words to help the client know that the helper has understood what has been said. The practice also allows the client to better understand his or her own feelings. Paraphrasing is very popular with person-centered, nondirective practitioners.

**paraplegic**
Refers to an individual who suffers from paralysis of both legs or the lower body caused by spinal cord injury.

**paraprofessional**
A helper who does not possess the credentials of a professional.

**parapsychology**
The study of phenomena that cannot be explained via traditional scientific research such as ESP or telepathy.

**Parent ego state**
In Eric Berne's transactional analysis, the portion of the personality that houses the conscience as well as other attitudes, thoughts, and feelings that are learned from one's parents or caretakers. Somewhat analogous to Freud's super-ego. *See Child ego state, Adult ego state, and Transactional Analysis (TA).*

**Parkinson's disease**
A neurological disease that is distinguished by damage to a portion of the brain known as the pars compacta region of the substantia nigra. The area, in healthy individuals, produces a neurotransmitter known as dopamine. Dopamine is needed to generate smooth and accurate muscle contractions. Individuals with Parkinson's lack this neurotransmitter and this causes them to have resting tremors and muscle rigidity. This disease is more common in men and individuals over 60 years of age.

**parsimony**
The notion that the simplest explanation of a phenomenon is preferred. Also called *Morgan's Canon, Occam's Razor,* or the *principle of economy.*

**partial reinforcement**
In operant conditioning and behavior modification, the act of not reinforcing on a continuous basis. For example, a child who receives a piece of candy for doing her math may be reinforced for every third problem rather than every problem. Also known as *intermittent reinforcement.*

**participant observer**
Occurs when a researcher participates in the group he or she is studying.

**passive-aggressive**
Occurs when an individual is angry but expresses the anger in an unhealthy indirect manner. A man who is angry at his boss after a meeting may smile and say he feels fine about the decision and then slam the door on the way out.

**pastoral counseling**
Counseling performed by clergy, often with an emphasis on religion.

**pathological/pathology**
A disease or disorder. A client's chart might, for example, indicate that "she suffers from pathological gambling."

**patriarchy**
A society or organization run by men. Often contrasted with a *matriarchy,* which would be run by women.

**Pavlov, Ivan (1849–1936)**
A Russian physiologist who won the 1904 Nobel Prize for his work pertaining to the digestive system of dogs. In human services, Pavlov is known for the classical conditioning paradigm (also called Palovian conditioning and respondent conditioning) that he discovered after he noted that dogs would salivate when they saw the person coming into the room to feed them. In classical conditioning, a neutral stimulus known as a *conditioned stimulus* or *CS* is paired with an *unconditioned stimulus* also known as a *UCS* or *US* that normally produces a response. Pavlov discovered, for example, that if a bell (a CS) sounds just before a dog sees food (a US or UCS) that after a number of trials the bell (the CS) will cause the dog to salivate. When the dog learns to salivate to the sound of the bell without the meat the response is known as a *conditioned response* or *CR.*

**pediatric**
Anything pertaining to a child's physical/mental health or illness.

**pedophilia**
Occurs when an adult is sexually attracted to a child.

**peer counseling**
Occurs when people of the same age or status (usually adolescents or college students) counsel each other. Many schools and agencies provide training programs for the peer helpers.

**Per capita income**
The quotient when you divide the total household income by the number of persons living in the household.

**perinatal**
In developmental psychology, that which occurs at birth or immediately after birth.

**Personal Responsibility Work Opportunity Reconciliation Act of 1996 (PRWORA)**
*See TANF.*

**person-centered counseling/therapy**
A humanistic psychotherapeutic approach created by Carl R. Rogers. The approach was initially called *nondirective therapy,* then *client-centered therapy,* and most recently *person-centered therapy* to emphasize the power of the person. The term *self-theory* is also used in to describe his approach. Rogers felt that the term *patient* was demeaning and thus used the term *client* and later *person* for the individual in treatment. He also disliked formal diagnosis and psychological testing as he felt they were dehumanizing. Rogers emphasized the importance of the relationship between the counselor and the client. He felt an effective therapist needed to give the client unconditional positive regard (UPR), needed to be genuine or congruent, and needed to provide empathic understanding. The relationship is emphasized rather than techniques. Rogers (unlike the Freudians) felt that humans are innately good and that they would thrive and self-actualize if given understanding and love. In this approach the client directs the topics of the interview and very little if any advice is given. Often contrasted with active-directive approaches (such as Albert Ellis' REBT) in which the therapist is active, talking a lot and giving advice, and may direct the topics discussed.

**petit mal**
A mild seizure in which the person loses consciousness.

241

## phallic stage
In Freud's psychoanalytic theory the third developmental stage (i.e., oral, anal, phallic, latency, and genital) that occurs between ages 3 and 7. According to Freud the child would be preoccupied with his or her sex organs during this period.

## phantom limb
Often after a person loses a limb (e.g., an arm or a leg) they still claim to feel pain or other sensations from the limb.

## phenomes
The smallest unit of human verbiage that can be identified.

## phobia
An exaggerated, morbid, or irrational fear of something.

## photocounseling
The use of photography to enhance the counseling or psychotherapy process.

## physical therapy
Techniques intended to help those with orthopedic and muscular problems.

## physician
Another word for doctor of medicine (M.D.) or doctor of osteopathy (D.O.). Training includes a bachelor's degree, four years of medical school, and a hospital residency of approximately four years. All psychiatrists are medical doctors. *See psychiatrist.*

## Piaget, Jean (1896–1980)
A Swiss psychologist known primarily for his famous four-stage structuralist model of cognitive development. Piaget suggested four key stages or periods of development. (1) The sensorimotor stage (until 2 years of age) in which the child's reflexive behaviors such as sucking and grasping are strengthened. During this stage the child develops object permanence, which is the notion that an object exists even when you can't see it. (2) The preoperational stage (ages 2 to 7). The child learns language but is said to be egocentric (i.e., they cannot comprehend another person's point of view). The child also displays centration, in which he or she focuses on an outstanding feature such as a clown's red nose. (3) The concrete operations stage (ages 7 to 12) in which the child learns conser-

vation (e.g., that cutting a cake does not change the size of it, or that pouring a short squat pitcher of water into a tall skinny pitcher does not alter the volume). In this stage the child cannot grasp abstract concepts or what could be. (4) The formal operations stage (begins at age 11 at the earliest) in which the child acquires abstract thinking. This theory has been criticized by some experts because Piaget used his children for his theoretical observations. *See centration.*

### pica
A tendency for an individual to eat substances that are not food such as chalk or pencils. Children ingesting lead paint in older buildings is unfortunately common and is especially dangerous and can cause permanent neurological damage.

### placater
According to the experiential family therapist Virginia Satir, this is a person who tries to please everybody. This is seen as dysfunctional.

### placebo effect
Occurs when a substance that has no medicinal value, such as a plain gelatin capsule or a sugar pill, causes a person to feel better. For example, a patient is given a sugar pill and is told that it is an antidepressant. If the patient's depression lifts then the pill has worked as a placebo. The placebo effect is so common that prescription drugs are routinely tested against them. A researcher might feel that a given antidepressant is effective because it helped 100 out of 200 people. If, however, a placebo helped a similar number then the drug might merely be acting as a placebo. The placebo effect is often contrasted with the *nocebo effect,* which occurs when an inoccuous substance, say a sugar pill or a negative diagnosis (e.g., you have 2 weeks to live ) causes the person to get sick.

### placement services
(1) Finding an appropriate job for a client. (2) Finding appropriate living arrangements for a client (e.g., a homeless shelter, psychiatric facility, or a foster care home).

### plagiarize
The act of copying somebody else's writing and passing it off as your own. A student, for example, might turn in a paper with his or her name on it that he or she copied from a professional journal or an Internet site.

### pleasure principle
(1) The notion that people seek pleasure and attempt to avoid pain. (2) In Freud's structural theory the id is sometimes called the pleasure principle.

### Plessy v. Ferguson
A well-known 1896 Supreme Court case that resulted in the "separate but equal" concept of race relations. *See Brown v. the Board of Education, Topeka, Kansas.*

### poison-pen therapy technique
The client is instructed to write a letter to a person who is living or dead to express pent up feelings. The letter, nevertheless, is not mailed but the content of the letter and the feelings are discussed in the treatment sessions.

### policy
A set of rules or guidelines that is used to implement a plan.

### political activist
An individual who interacts with politicians and elected individuals (and urges others to do likewise) to change policies. Political activists often run for office themselves.

### politically correct
Acting or writing in a manner that will not offend anyone else.

### political practice
Occurs when human service workers assist politicians or hold political offices themselves.

### polygamy
Have multiple husbands or wives. This practice is illegal in the US but is permissible in some countries.

### polysubstance abuse/polysubstance abuser
The use of several addictive or mind-altering substances by the same client during a given period of time. Hence, a client might be drinking, taking amphetamines, and smoking marijuana.

### poorhouses
*See almshouses.*

**poppers**
Slang for inhaling amyl or butyl nitrates such as one drop room deodorizers. This practice is said to produce euphoric feelings and enhance sexual orgasm but is extremely dangerous as it lowers the individual's immune system. Some experts believe these inhalants are correlated with AIDS and Kaposi's sarcoma, a form of cancer.

**population**
(1) The number of people in a population. (2) A statistical analysis of the people in a population (e.g., 13% African American, 8% Asian, etc.). (3) In research, any person or animal that could be chosen to participate in the study or experiment.

**positioning**
A business concept. When it is applied to human services agencies it suggests that from a marketing standpoint an agency or practitioner should specialize (e.g., divorce counseling) rather than trying to be all things to all people. Thus, when a client or a worker thinks of a referral source they will think of a given agency or provider as an expert in this area (e.g., grief counseling or eating disorders).

**positive addiction**
Psychiatrist William Glasser, father of reality therapy and choice theory, believes that certain addictions like jogging and meditation can be healthy.

**positive regard**
*See unconditional positive regard (UPR).*

**positive reinforcement/reinforcer**
In behavior modification and Skinnerian operant conditioning theory, a stimulus that occurs after a behavior that raises the probability that the behavior will occur again or strengthens the behavior. Thus, if you give a child a piece of candy after he or she completes a math problem and this raises the number of problems that the child completes, then the candy is acting as a positive reinforcer. A reinforcer must come after the behavior, never before it. If you tell a child that you will give him or her a piece of candy and then the child must complete a math problem, he or she will often eat the candy and then not perform the task.

**positive transference**
*See transference.*

**postconventional morality**
In Lawrence Kohlberg's theory of morality the third or highest level of morality (i.e., preconventional, conventional, and postconventional level). A high level or morality that less than 25% of all adults reach in which moral decisions are made with the knowledge that laws are arbitrary to cultures. The individual makes decisions based on principles rather than rules. This is sometimes known as a *prior to society perspective.* An individual in this stage may be willing to break the law in the name of justice.

**postlingual**
That which occurs after the development of language. Often used to describe hearing loss that occurred after the individual began to speak.

**postnatal**
That which occurs after the birth of the child.

**postpartum depression**
The depression that occurs after the birth of a child. A slang term for it is *baby blues.*

**post-test**
A test given at the end of a study, course, or program to indicate how the individuals changed. Hence, an agency helping depressed clients might give the clients a pretest prior to the treatment and then a post-test after the treatment to ascertain whether or not the intervention was effective.

**post-transfer poor**
Individuals who are still living below the poverty level even after they are receiving public assistance. *See poverty line.*

**post-traumatic stress disorder (PTSD)**
An anxiety disorder, often accompanied by nightmares, that results from a traumatic event such as robbery, rape, being taken hostage, war, receiving a death threat, being diagnosed with a life threatening illness, experiencing a severe auto accident, witnessing someone else die violently, or perhaps a natural disaster such as a flood, tornado, or volcanic eruptions. The reaction may be acute (symptoms last less than 3 months), chronic (symptoms last 3 months or longer), or delayed onset (6 months pass before the onset of symptoms).

**Postvention**
Intervention that occurs after an event. Usually refers to intervention after a suicide or tragedy (e.g., a terrorist attack).

**poverty**
*See absolute poverty and poverty line.*

**poverty line**
Also known as the *poverty index* or *poverty threshold*, this is the minimum amount that the federal government believes is necessary in order to live at an acceptable standard. The concept was first used in 1964.

**practicum**
An educational service learning experience in a human services, social work, or related program; working in an actual work setting such as an agency, practice, residential treatment center, helpline, or hospital. Students in a practicum setting are generally placed in a practicum seminar where issues that come up in the fieldwork are discussed. Some advanced graduate programs refer to practicum experiences as *internships* or *clerkships*.

**Praxis/Praxis II**
Educational Testing Service (ETS) has created tests that some states use for a portion of the teacher certification (e.g., exams for school social worker, school guidance and counseling, or school psychologist).

**preconscious**
In Freud's topographic notion, the preconscious can recall things that are not on the tip of one's tongue but are not repressed either. Thus, most people could remember what happened during their last birthday but they would need to think about it for a moment to recall it.

**preconventional morality**
In Lawrence Kohlberg's three levels of morality (i.e., the preconventional, conventional, and postconventional) it is the first stage, in which people obey the rules to avoid punishment and secure rewards. Most children under age 9 fit into this category.

**predictive validity**
Also known as empirical validity, this refers to a test's ability to predict future behavior or events such as how a client will perform in school or whether a client will become suicidal. *See validity, construct validity, content validity, and face validity.*

**pregnenolone**
An over-the-counter nutritional supplement that can raise hormone levels. Thought to be beneficial in cases of depression, poor memory, and arthritis. Since this substance can impact hormones it can be dangerous in higher dosages and is generally never recommended for people under the age of 30 or 40. Hormone tests administered by a physician are advised to ensure safety.

**Premack principle**
In behavior modification, the notion that a low probability behavior (LPB) can be reinforced by a high probability behavior (HPB). A child who won't do his homework (LPB) is told that for each page he completes he gets to play a video game (HPB). Named after behavior modification expert David Premack.

**prenatal**
That which occurs before the birth of the child.

**preoperations stage**
*See Piaget, Jean.*

**presbyopia**
A common visual condition in which an individual cannot see objects well up close (e.g., trying to read a book). Considered a normal part of the aging process after approximately age 40. Presbyopia is caused by the loss of flexibility in the fibers of the lens inside the eye.

**pretest**
A test given prior to a class or intervention. For example, a human services class might be given a pretest before the class begins and then a post-test at the end of the semester to ascertain whether the students' level of knowledge increased.

**pretransfer poor**
Individuals who are living under the poverty level prior to receiving public assistance. *See poverty line.*

**prevalence**
The number of individuals who are afflicted by a given condition or situation.

**prevention**
Taking steps to stop a problem before it occurs.

**prevention approach to poverty**
Creating programs such as Social Security to prevent people from becoming poor.

**primal scream therapy**
A form of therapy created by psychologist Arthur Janov in which the client is asked to relive painful childhood memories and scream out his or her feelings in regard to the situation.

**primary group**
A group formed to prevent or ward off a problem before it occurs, for example, a group that teaches kids how to resist the peer pressure to take drugs.

**private practice**
Professionals who provide services who are not affiliated with an agency or government organization. Commonly refers to counselors and therapists who are licensed as social workers, counselors, or psychologists. These individuals either set their own fees or accept insurance plans.

**privatization**
When a private concern carries out the tasks that are delineated by a local, state or federal government policy. Hence, a state law might dictate that child abuse perpetrators receive counseling, but the state might contract with private agencies or therapists to perform this task.

**privileged communication**
A legal term suggesting that a mental health professional (e.g., a licensed social worker, counselor, psychiatric, or psychologist) cannot reveal information in court that the client conveyed in confidential sessions without the client's permission. Privileged communication varies from state to state. Privileged communication does not apply in cases regarding malpractice, child abuse, neglect, or exploitation, or if the client is a danger to self or others. Human service workers who are not licensed by a mental health profession would not have privileged communication.

**probability**
In statistics, the chance that something will occur (e.g., the chance of flipping a coin one time and having it be "heads" is 50%).

### probability level
In statistics and research, the probability that an alpha error, also called a type I error, will occur. In the social sciences the probability level of an experiment is usually set at the point .05 level ($p = .05$) indicating that if you replicate the experiment 100 times you will attain the same results 95 times. A probability level of .01 ($p = 01$) would lower your chances of a type I error so that if you would give the same experiment 100 times, you would receive the same results 99 times out of 100. Older texts often refer to this as the *confidence level.*

### process versus content interventions
This phrase usually applies to group work; however, it could apply to individual or marriage and family interventions. *Process* refers to the manner or the fashion in which people communicate. Thus, if a therapist remarks: "Every time Sam talks in group, Mary rolls her eyes," that is a *process statement. Content* refers to the actual material or information discussed. So, if a therapist said: "You seem very concerned about your father's health," then that would be a *content statement.*

### prognosis
Refers to the outcome of treatment (e.g., this client will probably attain gainful employment within three months).

### projection
An ego defense mechanism (i.e., a distortion of reality) in which the person attributes something he or she cannot accept about himself or herself to somebody else. Thus, a man who wants to leave his wife may accuse her of being distant and cold.

### projective tests
Subjective tests that do not have a certain right or wrong answer. Since there is no right or wrong answer the client is said to be revealing unconscious material. To accomplish this projective tests are specifically vague, a bit unstructured and amorphous. For example, in the famous Rorschach Ink Blot test the client is shown an inkblot and asked to tell the person administering the test what it is. In the well-known Thematic Apperception Test (TAT) the client is shown a vague picture and asked to tell a story about it. A happy person will tell a happy story while a depressed person will recount an unhappy saga. Both are looking at the same picture and revealing their inner personality. Some projective tests use incomplete sentences such as "whenever I think of

my mother I feel" and the client finishes the sentence. Projective tests are sometimes called *projective expressive* measures and are usually administered by clinical psychologists. Although projective tests were once the backbone of clinical psychology, they are now being criticized for possible lack of validity (i.e., not testing what they really say they test).

**Prometheus script**
In transactional analysis a life theme which gets its name from Greek mythology. An individual with a Prometheus script views himself or herself as a savior and/or rescuer and identifies with the underdog. An individual with this script often finds himself in trouble with authority figures at the expense of trying to save or rescue others.

**proprietary**
A for-profit agency, school, or practice.

**prosthesis**
A device that replaces a limb or body part.

**provider**
The person or agency who is providing the service. The term was popularized by insurance companies and managed care firms.

**proxemics**
The notion that how close or how distant people are can affect communication. Thus, a human service worker who is sitting too close to a client may be invading their space and making them feel uncomfortable.

**Prozac**
A trade name for the prescription medicine fluoxetine, currently the most widely prescribed selective serotonin reuptake inhibitor (SSRI) antidepressant in the world.

**psyche**
The mind.

**psychiatric emergency**
Connotes a situation where a person intends to harm himself/herself or others; hospitalization or immediate treatment is indicated.

**psychiatric nurse**
A nurse who works in mental health.

**psychiatric social worker**
A social worker (generally with a minimum of an MSW and a state social work license) who works in a mental health or psychiatric setting. The term *clinical social worker* is sometimes utilized.

**psychiatrist**
All psychiatrists are medical doctors (e.g., M.D. or D.O.). An individual can never become a psychiatrist with a nonmedical degree such as a Ph.D., Ed.D. or Psy.D. To become a psychiatrist you need a four-year college degree. Next you must attend medical school for four years, followed by 4 years residency in a hospital setting. Child psychiatrists will need 2 or 3 years additional residency working with children. Psychiatrists diagnose clients, prescribe medicines, admit and treat clients in hospitals, and perform electroconvulsive shock therapy (ECT).

**psychiatry**
A medical specialty that helps prevent, treat, and study mental illness.

**psychoactive substance abuse**
Drug and/or alcohol abuse.

**psychoanalysis**
(1) Also known as *analysis,* this is a long-term treatment model created by Sigmund Freud. The client (known as an analysand) comes to treatment for 3 to 5 years, for 3 to 6 sessions per week. The analyst has his or her back turned to the client and the client is lying on a couch. The client is told to free associate (i.e., say whatever comes to mind) and the analyst attempts to interpret the true unconscious meaning of the client's thoughts, feelings, and behaviors. Dreams and childhood memories are key sources of clinical information. Ultimately the client achieves insight or an understanding of his or her unconscious impulses. Psychoanalysis is best suited to bright, middle or upper class clients who possess good verbal skills. It is not the treatment of choice for those who are in crisis. (2) Sigmund Freud's theory of personality that emphasizes the psychosexual stages of childhood. *See transference.*

**psychoanalyst**
An individual who practices psychoanalysis after receiving training from an accredited psychoanalytic school, institute, or foundation. The analyst

goes through his or her own treatment known as a "training analysis." Most psychoanalysts are medical doctors; however, other experts who are not physicians can become analysts. They are referred to as *lay analysts*. *See psychoanalysis.*

**psychodietetics**
The study or practice of nutrition and its impact on mental health. Sometimes referred to as *orthomolecular psychiatry.*

**psychodrama**
A psychotherapeutic strategy created by Jacob Moreno (who coined the term *group therapy* in 1931) in which clients role play or create a drama related to parts of themselves or others in their life.

**psychodynamic**
The notion—popularized by Freud's structural id, ego, superego theory— that energy forces in the mind control our behavior.

**psychodynamic therapy**
Therapy that uses primarily psychoanalytic principles (e.g., the unconscious mind, dream analysis, and interpretation) but the client and helper sit face-to-face and generally meet only once or twice a week. *See psychoanalysis.*

**psychogenic**
Implies that symptoms are caused by psychological or emotional rather than physical difficulties.

**psychological autopsy**
A procedure used primarily in cases of suicide to investigate what factors may have led the person to act in this manner.

**psychologist**
An individual trained to study human and animal behavior. Human service workers work primarily with clinical and counseling psychologists who diagnose, test, and treat clients. Agencies also use psychologists as consultants to help staff who have less training than the psychologist. *See Licensed Psychologist.*

**psychology**
The scientific study of human and animal behavior.

### psychometrician
An individual who does psycho-educational testing usually employed in an elementary school, middle school, or high school. A masters degree in counseling or psychology plus state certification is generally required for psychomtricians.

### psychometrics
The study of psychological testing.

### psychopath/psychopathy
Also known as a *sociopath,* this term is refers to an individual who has little or no conscience. Therefore, this individual may commit crimes, physically hurt others, or otherwise take advantage of them without feeling guilty.

### psychopathology
(1) The study of abnormal behavior. (2) A mental illness. (e.g., "He has psychopathological symptoms of schizophrenia.").

### psychosexual developmental stage theory
Refers to Freud's oral, anal, phallic, latency, and genital theory. Often contrasted with ego psychologist Erik Erikson's psychosocial stage theory. *See anal stage, genital stage, latency period/stage, oral stage, and phallic stage.*

### psychosis/psychotic
According to the *DSM-IV-TR* this term has received a number of different definitions over the years; however, "none has achieved universal acceptance." When most experts use the term they are referring to a mental state characteristic of some severe mental disorders, such as schizophrenia, in which a person experiences a partial or complete loss of contact with reality and exhibits profound alterations in psychological, emotional, and cognitive functioning. The key features include extra-sensory experiences called *hallucinations,* which can affect any of the five senses, and *delusions,* which are false beliefs held firmly in spite of invalidating evidence. Other symptoms may include disordered thinking, incoherence, incoherent speech, inappropriate affect, and grossly disorganized behavior. Some sources site the brief definition that psychosis consists of hallucinations, delusions, and thought disorder, emphasizing that the key factor is that the individual is unable to separate reality from fantasy (sometimes known as *impairment of reality testing*).

**psychosocial developmental stage theory**
Refers to Erik Erikson's eight psychosocial stages. Often contrasted with Sigmund Freud's psychosexual stages. *See autonomy versus shame and doubt, identity versus role confusion, industry versus inferiority, initiative versus guilt, integrity versus despair, intimacy versus isolation, generativity versus stagnation, and trust versus mistrust.*

**psychotherapist**
A person who practices psychotherapy, usually a state licensed psychologist, psychiatrist, counselor, social worker, or psychiatric nurse.

**psychotherapy**
Specialized techniques, strategies, and interventions to help persons cope with everyday life or treat mental disorders. In recent years the term has become more synonmous with professional counseling. Popular methods of psychotherapy include: individual therapy, group therapy, marriage counseling, marriage and family therapy, and couples therapy. The major theories or so-called "schools of psychotherapy" are: brief solution-oriented therapy, cognitive psychotherapy, cognitive behavior therapy (CBT), conditioned reflex therapy, rational-emotive behavior therapy (REBT), rational self-counseling, behavior therapy, reality therapy, person-centered therapy, hypnotherapy, logotherapy, vegotherapy, transactional analysis (TA), multimodal therapy, gestalt therapy, neurolinguistic programming, and psychoanalysis.

**psychotic**
*See psychosis/psychotic.*

**psychotropic medicine/medicinal**
Also referred to as *psychotherapeutic drugs* or *psychoactive drugs,* these are medicines that are used to treat emotional or psychiatric conditions. Antidepressants, antianxiety (i.e., anxiolytic) drugs, antipsychotics, and antimanic medicines fall into this category.

**PTSD**
*See post-traumatic stress disorder.*

**public assistance**
Government programs providing assistance based on the need of the recipients. Entitlement to public assistance depends solely on means-testing. No work history is required. Funding comes from general revenues of the state or federal government, or from a combination of

state and federal funds. Examples of public assistance include these now-defunct programs—Old-Age Assistance (in some places called Old-Age Pensions), Aid for Families with Dependent Children (AFDC), and Aid to the Permanently-and-Totally Disabled—plus the present-day Supplemental Security Income (SSI), Temporary Assistance for Needy Families (TANF or TA), and Medicaid. *See TA, TANF, and Supplemental Security Income for the Aged, Blind, and Disabled (SSI).*

**punch-drunk**
Brain damage in boxers and others from traumatic blows to the head that leads to tremors, memory problems, and personality changes.

**punishment**
In behavior modification, any stimulus that occurs after a behavior that lessens the probability that the behavior will occur again or that weakens the behavior. Positive punishment occurs when something is added after the behavior (e.g., squeezing a child's hand). Negative punishment occurs when something is taken away and it lowers behavior (e.g., taking away a toy). Both types of punishment—positive and negative—lower behavior. Behavior modifiers prefer positive reinforcement over punishment to mold behavior. Many experts insist that punishment does not eliminate a behavior but rather just masks it temporarily.

**pycnogenol**
An over-the-counter nutritional supplement from the bark of the French Maritime Pine that appears to help clients with Attention Deficit Hyperactivity Disorder (ADHD). Additional research is necessary to prove whether this hypothesis is accurate.

**Pygmalion effect**
Also known as the *Rosenthal effect* (after psychologist Robert Rosenthal), the notion that the researcher's beliefs may impact the outcome of an experiment. For example, a researcher who believes that a child is very bright may inadvertently treat that child differently, and thus the child's school performance and even IQ could go up.

**pyromania**
A tendency or morbid impulse to start fires.

**pyromaniac**
A person who feels compelled to start fires.

## Q

In statistics and research $Q$ stands for quartile. A one, two, or three is sometimes placed after the Q to designate the quartile in question. *See quartile/quartile range.*

### Q data

Any data revealed via a questionnaire.

### Q method

Any methodology relying on a questionnaire.

### Q sort

An exercise in self-perception. The client is given numerous statements. Each is written on a card. The client is then asked to put them in piles (i.e., sort the cards) indicating "most like me" to "least like me." The client can also use the statements on the cards to create an "ideal self." The comparison can be used to assess self-worth/self-esteem.

### quack

(1) Unqualified medical or nonmedical helpers. (2) Helpers who use techniques which are not accepted by the professional community or who rely on unethical practices.

### quadriplegia

Paralysis of all four limbs/extremities.

**Qualified Clinical Social Worker (QCSW)**
A credential conferred by the National Association of Social Workers indicating expertise in clinical social work.

**qualitative analysis/research**
Studies where the researcher describes his or her observations without resorting to numerical data. Often contrasted with *quantitative analysis,* which uses numbers and measurements. *See quantitative analysis/research.*

**quality assurance**
Any set of procedures and/or programs intended to assure quality service delivery. Services that are not up to standards will be rectified or negated.

**quality circles**
A problem-solving activity in which a group of people in an organization get together to brainstorm about solutions to a problem. Participants often receive training in problem solving prior to the actual group experience.

**quality education**
William Glasser's model for creating an effective educational system based on choice theory and the management techniques espoused by Dr. W. Edwards Deming, who was instrumental in training Japanese auto and electronics plant managers. Lead-management and cooperation rather than punitive boss-management is suggested. The paradigm is outlined in his book *The Quality School, Managing Students Without Coercion.*

**quantitative analysis/research**
An entity that can be measured and/or counted. Often contrasted with a *qualitative entity.* The term is used primarily in research settings to describe a study depicting quantity. *See qualitative analysis/research.*

**quarantine**
The act of isolating an individual because he or she could be contagious and might therefore infect other individuals.

**quartile/quartile range**
In statistics, three points that divide a distribution into quarters. Generally the first or lowest quartile is at the twenty-fifth percentile, the second is at the median, and the third is at the seventy-fifth percentile, thus separating it from the top quarter.

**quartile deviation**
Also called the *semiquartile range,* the term describes one-half of the distance between the first and third quartiles (i.e., half the distance between the twenty-fifth percentile and the seventy-fifth percentile). It is a very quick though rough measure of the variability in a distribution since it does not take into account all the scores. The variance and the standard deviation are preferred. *See quartile/quartile range.*

**quasi-experimental research**
A research situation in which the researcher cannot positively conclude that the change in the dependent variable is caused by the independent/experimental variable. In such cases, the research is correlational; the researcher cannot control the status of the independent variable; random assignment/sampling is not possible; or the independent variable was administered prior to the beginning of the study (i.e., an ex-post facto design).

**queer**
A homosexual. Term has negative connotations. The term *gay* is preferred.

**questioning**
Any comment on the part of the human service worker that is intended to elicit information from the client. Close-ended questions (How old are you?) can be answered via "yes" or "no" answers, while open-ended questions ("What is it like living with your brother?") will draw more information from the client. Generally speaking, open-ended questions are preferred unless the client is very vague.

**questionnaire**
A set of questions designed to elicit specific information from a subject. Questionnaires are appropriate for biographical, clinical, and research purposes.

**quickening**
The first movement of the fetus noted by a pregnant mother.

**quid pro quo**
Literally means something for something. (1) In family therapy or relationships, the notion that I will do something for you if you do something for me (e.g., I will fill your car with gas if you clean the house). (2) In sexual harassment cases, the notion that a supervisor would ask a worker for a sexual favor in order to receive preferential treatment such as a raise, a promotion, or special work privileges.

### quorum
The minimum number of people required to have a meeting. An agency board of directors, for example, might stipulate that at least five board members need to be present in order to hold a board meeting.

### quota sampling
In statistics, a sampling procedure that ensures that various subgroups of the population are included in the sample. A researcher or agency plan could require that 25% of the individuals be Asian American.

### quotient
In statistics, research, and mathematics, the result when one number is divided into another. If, for example, six is divided by three, the the quotient/answer is two. Many years ago the IQ or Intelligence Quotient was computed by taking the child's MA (mental age) and dividing it by the CA (the actual or chronological age) and multiplying the figure by 100.

**r**
(1) In statistics and research, the symbol for correlation coefficient. *See correlation and correlation coefficient.* (2) In behaviorism, stands for the response (e.g., SR psychology means stimulus/response psychological theory).

**RA**
*See rheumatoid arthritis (RA).*

**race**
A subdivision of a given species based on minor genetic differences (e.g., Black, White, or Asian). Each race has certain physical characteristics such as skin color. Often contrasted with *ethnicity,* which implies a difference in customs rather than genetics.

**racism**
To stereotype or discriminate against an individual based on his or her race (e.g., all Asians are good at science and math). A generalization about a given race. Can be a form of prejudice (i.e., prejudging the person without really knowing him or her).

**racketeering**
Another word for organized crime, fraud, extortion, or, in the prohibition era, bootlegging.

**radical behaviorist**
Radical behaviorism was initially associated with John B. Watson. His "radical" environmental approach (hence the term *radical*) suggested that experiential factors contributed more or outweighed genetic or he-

reditary factors. Today the term refers to a helper or experimental psychologist who believes that if you can't observe it or measure it, then it doesn't exist or isn't scientific. In addition to Watson, radical behaviorists believe primarily in classical conditioning as set forth by Ivan Pavlov and operant conditioning as formulated by B. F. Skinner. These helpers often dismiss—or at the very least minimize—the concept of mental events.

**rage**
Intense anger that cannot be controlled.

**random sample**
In an experiment, subjects are chosen for either control groups or experimental groups via a procedure called *random sampling* that is analogous to putting names on sheets of paper and then picking them randomly out of a fish bowl. *Random* means that everyone in the population has an equal chance of being chosen. Rather than using a fish bowl, experimenters use random-number tables (often included in statistics books) and computer-generated random numbers.

**range**
In statistics, the difference or distance between the highest and lowest score in a distribution of scores. Hence, if the lowest highest score on an exam was 75 and the lowest score was 50 then you would subtract 50 from 75 to compute the range, which in this case would be 25.

**rank order**
To arrange data or test scores in order from the lowest to the highest (1, 5, 7, 9) or the highest to the lowest (9, 7, 5, 1).

**rape**
Sexual intercourse that occurs without the person's consent or against the person's will.

**rapid eye movements (REM)**
Quick vertical or horizontal movement of the eyes during sleep that is often said to occur when the person is dreaming.

**rapport**
Describes a situation in which a human services worker and a client have good open communication. A desirable, comfortable relationship.

**rate of behavior**
The incidence of a behavior during a given period of time expressed as a ratio. For example, the suicide rate in the US is approximately 12/100,000, meaning that for every 100,000 people in a population, 12 will kill themselves in the course of a year.

**rational behavior therapy (RBT)/rational self-counseling (RSC)**
A therapeutic approach created by psychiatrist Maxie C. Maultsby, Jr. Maultsby created Associated Rational Thinkers (ART), a self-help group who wanted to learn RET, now REBT. Maultsby now teaches the client to act as if he or she is his or her own therapist to contradict irrational beliefs. Maultsby's approach has been very successful with substance abusers and for multicultural counseling. *See rational-emotive therapy (RET)/rational-emotive behavior therapy (REBT).*

**rational-emotive therapy (RET)/rational-emotive behavior therapy (REBT)**
A system of counseling and psychotherapy developed by New York clinical psychologist, sexologist, and marriage and family therapist Albert Ellis. Ellis—a former psychoanalyst—rapidly became convinced that most human disturbance was not caused by unconscious processes (the Freudian/psychodynamic notion) or merely by the environment (as the radical behaviorists contend), but rather by our irrational thinking, cognitions, self-talk, or so-called "internal verbalizations." Ellis is very didactic and teaches clients to think in a more rational, logical, and scientific manner. Ellis' approach to therapy is very active-directive, meaning that the therapist often talks as much if not more than the client and gives numerous homework assignments in addition to the therapy sessions. In very early writings his approach was called *rational therapy*. *See A-B-C/ A-B-C-D-E theory* and *irrational beliefs (IB)/thinking.*

**rationalization**
An ego defense mechanism first coined by the psychoanalyst Ernest Jones to describe or justify one's conduct using socially acceptable reasons that are not the true reasons. In essence, the person defends his or her actions, but the defense is not the actual motive for the behavior. It is an intellectual excuse to minimize hurt feelings. The literature often cites two basic types of rationalization: the *sour grapes* and the *sweet lemon* variety. In the *sour grapes* version of rationalization, the person under-rates a reward, such as the fable in which the fox who couldn't get the grapes decided they were

probably sour anyway. A client might comment that he was glad he didn't get the promotion since he would just have to pay higher taxes. In the *sweet lemon* version of rationalization, the individual overrates a reward (e.g., I'm really glad I have a job working next to the high heat of a boiler since I sweat off a lot of water weight). *See defense mechanisms.*

### rationing
To give a fixed amount of a given resource that may be in limited supply (say gasoline, food, or water) to families or individuals in times of war or emergencies (e.g., a flood).

### ratio scale of measurement
The highest scale of measurement (i.e., out of nominal, ordinal, interval, and ratio). The only one with a true zero point where ratios are mathematically accurate. A person who is 6 feet tall, for example, is actually twice as tall as a person who is 3 feet tall. Unfortunately, this scale can rarely be used in the human services field since most variables are not like this, e.g., a person with a 140 IQ is not twice as smart as a person with a 70 IQ. *Also see interval scale of measurement, nominal scale of measurement, and ordinal scale of measurement.*

### ratio schedule of reinforcement
In behavior modification, the act of giving a reinforcer after a certain number of responses. Ratio schedules are based on work output. Thus, if a child is given a piece of candy after each math problem, then he or she is being reinforced on a ratio schedule. This is often contrasted with *interval schedules of reinforcement* in which the reinforcer is given after a period of time (say, after the child works on the math problems for five minutes).

### raw score
A score that is not converted, transformed, altered, or standardized. It is merely the score as it is recorded. If a student gets 23 correct on a test, then 23 is the raw score. If we express it as 2 standard deviations above the mean, then it is not a raw score as it has been analyzed and transformed.

### RDA
Short for recommended daily allowance of nutrients as set forth by the U.S. Food and Drug Administration (FDA). Recently, alternative practitioners have suggested that the RDAs of many nutrients (e.g., vitamins and minerals) are set too low and are not conducive to optimal health.

**reaction formation**
An ego defense mechanism that unconsciously occurs in which the individual acts in a manner that is totally the opposite of a threatening unconscious impulse. Thus a person who fears gay impulses might castigate gays or attempt to date numerous persons of the opposite sex. *See ego defense mechanism.*

**reaction time**
How long it takes a person to respond to a stimulus.

**reactive disorder**
A disorder (e.g., reactive psychosis or reactive alcoholism) that occurs after an event. Often contrasted with a *longstanding disorder,* which cannot be traced to a given life circumstance.

**reactive effects**
Refers to the fact that generalizability may be limited when an experiment is conducted since experimental situations are not the same as real life situations. Say, for example, that an experiment conducted in a treatment center showed that behavior modification curbs alcoholism. Although the laboratory setting (i.e., in this case the treatment center) had alcohol available it isn't identical to an actual bar, where there are other factors (such as the fact that you have consumed alcohol there before and friends are urging you to drink).

**reality principle**
Another name for the ego. *See Ego and structural theory of the personality.*

**reality therapy**
A treatment approach created by psychiatrist William Glasser. Reality therapy is implemented using eight steps: (1) Make friends with the client to create a relationship. (2) Focus on the present. (3) Help the client evaluate current behavior. (4) Work with the client to create a plan of action. (5) Get a commitment from the client to follow the plan. (6) Accept no excuses. (7) Use no punishment. (8) Refuse to give up. The individual must take responsibility for his or her behavior as behavior is internally motivated. Glasser uses the concept of *choice theory* to explain behavior. This concept states that all of our behavior is chosen and it is our best attempt to satisfy our needs.

**recall**
The ability to remember something. In human services the term usually refers to an event that is significant or therapeutic.

**recency effect**
The tendency to learn or remember that which was presented last.

**recidivism**
A tendency to relapse or to begin engaging in a behavior again. Especially applies to addictions (e.g., giving up drinking and then starting to drink again) or criminal behavior (e.g., an individual gets out of a corrections facility and begins breaking the law again).

**reciprocity**
Occurs when one state accepts another state's license or practice credentials. Hence, if a person is licensed and moves to another state that does not grant reciprocity, the person might need to take courses, supervision, or further testing stipulated by the new state before he or she could practice as a psychologist, counselor, or social worker.

**red-light district**
Refers to an area of a city where prostitution and sex-oriented adult clubs and businesses are common.

**red tape**
Slang for procedures and operations set by organizations, agencies, or government that make a project or task difficult to complete. A human service worker, for example, might have to fill out a tremendous amount of paper just to get a client something small such as a food order or a pair of shoes.

**reel therapy**
The use of movies or videos in therapy to help the client understand his or her behavior or predicament.

**referral**
Suggesting a provider or service to a client. As a simple example a client might be referred to a physician who is a specialist or to a food pantry. Whenever possible, human service workers should provide more than one provider as the client might find one more convenient than another or that one provider has a better rapport than another. *See resources and resource and referral coordinator.*

**reflection**
An interviewing technique in which the helper repeats what the client has said (i.e., paraphrasing) with an emphasis on the emotional aspects of the message.

**reflex**
*See Pavlov, Ivan.*

**reformer**
Someone who changes a system, policy, organization, industry, or field.

**reform school**
An old term for a residential center that attempted to help youth and teens who got in trouble with the law. Also called a *reformatory*, these institutions were intended to reform the person and keep them out of prisons or corrections facilities.

**reframing**
The notion that a helper can help a client view an issue in a different manner. Often by redefining or relabeling a problem a whole new set of emotions will be evident. A glass of water can be described as either half-full or half-empty. In a similar fashion, a client might be told that she really doesn't have a psychiatric eating disorder, but just doesn't eat enough. This technique was popularized by Milton H. Erickson and Jay Haley.

**regression**
An automatic unconscious ego defense mechanism in which an individual who is experiencing anxiety reverts back to an earlier infantile pattern of behavior (e.g., curling up in a fetal position or sucking one's thumb).

**regression to the mean**
The notion that a person who receives an extremely low score, or an extremely high score, on a test most likely regress or go toward the mean if the test is administered again. Say the mean or arithmetic average on a human services test is 100 and that 200 is the highest possible score on the exam. If Sam takes the test and scores a 5 he will most likely score much higher if he takes the exam again. If Mary scores 200 the first time she will probably score lower if she takes the exam a second time.

**rehab**
Short for rehabilitation or treatment. Generally refers to the fact that the person is receiving treatment for an addiction (i.e., she's in rehab).

**rehab center**
Short for a treatment center, generally one that treats addictions.

### rehabilitation
To help a person achieve the highest possible level of functioning. The term is mainly used to describe interventions provided to the disabled. *See rehab and rehab center.*

### Reich, Wilhelm (1897–1957)
A controversial psychiatrist who created vegotherapy. Reich helped spawn the body therapy manipulation movement and believed that repeated successful sexual orgasms were necessary for mental health. Reich was convinced that an energy called "orgone" determined mental and physical well-being. He was placed in jail and died after the FDA made him destroy orgone boxes that he created to heal people. Debates still rage as to whether Reich was simply a madman or a genius years ahead of his time.

### Reik, Theodor (1888–1969)
A famous analyst who never broke away from Freud. Freud wrote a book *The Question of Lay Analysis* that defended Reik's qualifications to be a psychoanalyst although he did not possess an an M.D. Traditionally, many analytic institutes would only accept medical doctors into their training programs. This trend continues to change. Analysts who are not M.D.s are still referred to as *lay analysts.*

### reinforcement/reinforcer
*See positive reinforcement/reinforcer and negative reinforcement.*

### relabeling
*See reframing.*

### relapse
*See recidivism.*

### relative poverty
*See absolute poverty.*

### reliability
The ability of a psychological, physical, or educational test to provide the same results if the test is taken again and again. Reliability measures the consistency of the test score. Hence, if a client took an IQ test on one day and scored 93 and then scored 137 on the test the next day, the test would have low reliability assuming the client's mental and physical status did not change. Reliability is considered the second most important factor when evaluating the usefulness of a measure. The first is validity. A valid test is al-

ways reliable, but a reliable test is not always valid. A scale may be consistent and always say you weigh 2 pounds more than you really weigh, nevertheless, the scale is not accurate (i.e., valid). Finally, the term can also refer to whether an experimental finding can be replicated. *See validity.*

**reluctant client**
A client who does not really want the human service worker's help.

**remission**
Occurs when a disease or disorder is no longer evident (e.g., her cancer is in remission).

**REM**
*See rapid eye movements.*

**replication**
Recreating an experiment step by step to ascertain whether the results will be the same.

**report writing**
Any writing that will result in a document that is used in the client's record or sent to another source (i.e., agency, hospital, etc.).

**repression**
According to Freud the most important unconscious ego defense mechanism. Repression occurs when something is so painful that the mind blocks it out (i.e., represses it). For example, a child who is the victim of severe physical or sexual abuse may not be able to remember it, or an adult in a terrible auto accident may not be able to recall the occurrence of the accident even though he or she was conscious at the time. Although the repression may temporarily protect the individual so he or she can continue to function, the Freudians believe that in the long run the repression causes symptoms, and it must be remembered (or lifted) in order to ameliorate the symptoms.

**rescuer**
*See Karpman's triangle.*

**research**
(1) Any procedure conducted to add to our knowledge. (2) Using experimentation to discover why or how something occurs. (3) Gathering data to make comparisons regarding different situations (e.g., will alcoholics who receive six sessions of cognitive therapy drink less than those who do not?).

### resentful demoralizing of experimental subjects
Occurs when subjects in an experiment give up or stop trying and thus confound the experiment.

### resident
(1) A person living in a home, treatment center, nursing home, etc. (2) A physician who is receiving practical training and work in a medical setting after graduation from medical school.

### residential treatment center
A center where the client lives during the treatment.

### resistance
(1) A client or an employee who refuses to follow directives and rules. (2) In Freudian psychoanalysis, the notion that the client will resist material and interpretations regarding the unconscious mind. Understanding id material is said to be threatening to the ego.

### resource and referral coordinator
A job position in an agency in which the individual works to keep the resource files updated so staff and volunteers will be capable of referring clients to the most appropriate place. This position is very common at helplines and mental health associations. *See resources.*

### resource seekers
Slang for a client who really doesn't want to change his or her behavior but wants a resource to solve a current problem (e.g., wants shoes and clothes when employment is really the issue or wants a homeless shelter when finding suitable housing is necessary). Clients of this ilk rarely return for services once they receive the referral.

### resources
Any goods (e.g., clothes, food, shoes, or shelter) or services (e.g., medical care, family counseling) that can help a client.

### respondent conditioning
Another name for classical conditioning or Pavlovian conditioning. Often contrasted with operant or instrumental conditioning popularized by B. F. Skinner. *See Pavlov, Ivan.*

### response burst/response bursting
In behavior modification, this principle states that when you use extinction (i.e., a lack of reinforcement such as ignoring a behavior) it will generally get worse before it gets better. Also called an *extinction burst. See extinction.*

**responsive listening**
Also called attending or active listening, this occurs when a worker is attuned to the verbal and nonverbal messages of the client.

**restate**
Occurs when a counselor uses different words to capture the essence of a client's message. Often contrasted with *parroting,* which occurs when a helper uses the identical words that the client says. In nearly every case, restating is preferred. If the restatement focuses on affective or emotional aspects rather than the cognitive factors, the term *reflection* is used.

**retarded**
*See mental retardation.*

**retrograde amnesia**
Occurs when an individual cannot remember anything that took place prior to a tragedy or trauma that caused the amnesia.

**reverse tolerance**
In addiction studies, the notion that at first an alcoholic will brag that he or she can drink an inordinate amount of liquor without acting or feeling drunk. In this phase the alcoholic is desensitized by a process known as *satiation* or *habituation.* As the alcoholism progresses, however, the liver breaks down and is less able to detoxify the system and thus the person can get drunk on an extremely small amount of alcohol. *See tolerance.*

**revolving door**
(1) Slang for an agency that continually runs ads for employment because human service workers do not stay at the facility as an employee very long. (2) The notion that a lot of clients (especially in the area of addictions) relapse and return for treatment a short time after discharge.

**reward**
Anything that is pleasant or satisfying for the person. Often used in popular literature to mean positive reinforcement, although some experts feel this is not scientifically accurate since a stimulus that is not pleasurable can be a positive reinforcer.

**rheumatoid arthritis (RA)**
A type of autoimmune disease that causes a person's immune system to attack the tissues that line their joints. The disturbance of the synovial membranes surrounding the joints causes inflammation of the tissues around the cartilage and joints, which over time can lead to destruction

271

of the tissues and lead to disability. Most cases of RA appear in individuals between the ages of 40 and 60.

### RIASEC
A popular memory device for remembering John Holland's *typology* career theory that asserts that there are stereotypical jobs/personality types: realistic (e.g., a mechanic), investigative (e.g., a computer programmer), artistic (e.g., a poet), social (e.g., a human service worker), enterprising (e.g., a saleswomen), and conventional (e.g., a file clerk). A client should secure a job type that matches or is *congruent* with his or her personality type.

### rickets
A disease caused by a vitamin D deficiency that makes bones soft. In the US some foods, such as milk, are vitamin D-fortified to prevent this malady. Vitamin D can be acquired via sunlight and thus is often referred to as "the sunshine vitamin." The literature often mentions the fact that Alfred Adler, the father of individual psychology, suffered from rickets and perhaps that is why his theory focused so heavily on the inferiority complex.

### right brain
A theory that posits that people who are controlled mainly by the right side of their brains are emotional and creative. Often contrasted with *left brain* people, who are thought to be factual and scientific thinkers.

### right-to-die
Refers to a patient's right to refuse life support equipment to stay alive.

### right wing
Slang for someone who is extremely conservative, especially in terms of political and social issues. Often contrasted with *left wing,* which describes an individual who is very liberal.

### risk taking
(1) A positive behavior that is scary to the client but can move the person to a higher level of functioning. (2) In suicidology, the tendency of a person to do risky things (e.g., repeatedly driving in a daredevil manner) which might indicate that the person has suicidal or self-destructive impulses. Often seen as a warning sign of suicide.

### risky shift phenomenon
The idea that a group decision is generally riskier than a decision made by an individual.

**ritual**
A pattern of behavior that a person repeats before he or she engages in a given act. A golfer might always stretch her arms before hitting a shot or a speaker might tug on his tie before going on stage.

**Rogers, Carl R. (1902–1987)**
Father of humanistic nondirective therapy, later called client-centered therapy, and then person-centered therapy or self-theory. *See person-centered counseling/therapy.*

**role model**
Refers to a high visibility person such as a rock star, athlete, or television personality who others (usually young people) will try to emulate or model their behavior after. Thus, depending on their behavior, role models can have a good or bad influence on society.

**role playing**
A popular technique used in many forms of counseling and psychotherapy, but popularized mainly by the behaviorists and practitioners of psychodrama. The client and therapist role play a difficult situation. The client can play himself or herself and the helper can play the other person (e.g., a client who is afraid to ask for a raise plays himself or herself and the therapist plays the boss). The opposite therapeutic arrangement can also be used (e.g., the client plays the boss and ther therapist role plays the client asking for a raise). In a group setting other members may play either or both roles. Role playing is intended to give the client feedback, insight, and role models after which to pattern behavior.

**role reversal**
(1) A form of role playing generally used in groups where a client is asked to play the direct opposite of his or her personality. A client, for example, who is a people pleaser and acquiesces with everybody is asked to disagree with everything that is said. (2) A form of role playing in which the client plays somebody else in his or her life, for example, a friend he or she is experiencing difficulties with. The therapist or another group member (if it is group therapy) would play the client. *See role playing.*

**roles of human service workers**
*See human service worker roles.*

## Rorschach Inkblot Test

A projective test created by the Swiss psychiatrist Herman Rorschach that utilizes ten 6⅝ by 9½ inch cards. Five of the cards are grey or black and five are colored. The examinee is asked to describe what he or she sees or what the card brings to mind. The test is appropriate for ages three and beyond and is difficult to fake since the client is not certain what type of response is desirable. *See projective tests.*

## Rosenthal Effect

*See Pygmalion effect.*

## rote learning

Memorizing material without understanding it. A young child, for example, memorizes a famous presidential speech to give to his class but does not truly comprehend what he is saying.

## rounds

(1) Occurs when a doctor (e.g., a psychiatrist) goes from hospital room to hospital room to visit each patient for the day. (2) In group counseling and therapy, the act of going around the group and letting everybody talk for a given length of time to make certain that group members have roughly equal participation. Some of the literature refers to this technique as "making the rounds."

## rumination

A condition in which the person keeps having the same thought over and over and continues to dwell on it. Considered a sign of obsessive-compulsive disorder (OCD).

## runaway

A minor child who leaves home without the consent of his or her parents or legal guardians.

## rural

Living in the country or on a farm. Often contrasted with living in a highly populated area.

## Rush, Benjamin (1745–1813)

Called the Father of American Psychiatry. He wrote about medical treatment and diseases of the mind.

## SAD

Abbreviation for *Seasonal Affective Disorder.* This is a mood disorder in which the individual feels depressed (usually in the winter months). Seventy to eighty percent of those afflicted are female. The current hypothesis is that sunlight or full spectrum lighting can help abate this condition.

## sadism/sadistic

(1) Occurs when an individual derives pleasure by being mean or cruel to others. (2) A paraphilia in which a person receives sexual gratification by humiliating or hurting a sexual partner.

## sado-masochism

A condition in which the individual derives pleasure via inflicting hurt or pain (i.e., sadism) and receives satisfaction from being hurt or humiliated (i.e., masochism).

## Salvation Army

An international organization that works in over 100 countries using over 140 languages to accomplish their interventions. They currently have over 14,000 Corps (i.e., centers). The organization provides numerous services, including accommodation for the homeless (including soup kitchens), occupational centers, providing food for the hungry, care for elderly, day care and nurseries for children and infants, help for alcoholism and drug addiction, services for the blind and the disabled, involvement with military personnel, tracing missing relatives, care for offenders and visits to prisioners, suicide prevention, health care clinics, education programs, counseling, convalescent homes, and treatment for leprosy. The Army uses militaristic uniforms and titles.

## SAMe
Short for *S-Adenosyl-Methionine,* a natural mental health remedy for depression that is also used for arthritis and fibromyalgia. In 1952 in Italy it was discovered that the human body produces this substance; however, supplemental dosages seem to be necessary in order for it to have an antidepressant effect. The substance helps manufacture and maintain healthy levels of brain neurotransmitters such as serotonin and dopamine. Most of the research on this product has been conducted in Europe.

## sample
In research, the individuals chosen from the population who are being studied or observed. These individuals are intended to represent the population.

## sampling bias/sampling error
Occurs in research when the sample does not accurately represent the population.

## sanatorium
In older literature, a mental hospital for someone with a chronic illness.

## sanction
(1) To authorize a service. For example, an insurance company might sanction six sessions of group therapy for a client. (2) A penalty (e.g., losing your license to practice) for violating a law or ethical guideline.

## sanguine
Optimistic, energetic, and free of worries.

## satyriasis
The male equivalent of *nymphomania* in which a man has unsatiable sexual desires.

## scapegoat
An individual in a group (e.g., the family group) who is blamed for the problem.

**scattergram / scatter diagram/scatter plot**
In statistics, a pictorial graph that depicts a correlation (i.e., relationship or association) between two variables. A scattergram that goes up from left to right is indicative of a positive correlation, while a scattergram that goes down from left to right shows negative correlation. A perfect correlation (i.e., $-1.00$ or $1.00$) would be a straight line.

**schedule of reinforcment**
In behavior modification, refers to the pattern that a reinforcer is given. In continuous reinforcement the reinforcer is given after every desired behavior. In a ratio schedule of reinforcement the reinforcer is administered after a given number of desired behaviors, and in interval reinforcement the reinforcer is administered after a given time has elapsed. When a reinforcer is not given after every desired behavior it is known as an *intermittent schedule.*

**Schein Consultation**
Edgar Schein created a typology of consultation models based on assumptions regarding what is helpful: the purchase-of-expertise model (the client or organization pays an expert to remedy or fix the difficulty), the doctor-patient model (goes beyond the purchase-of-expertise model since the consultant diagnoses the difficulty and provides a solution/prescription), and the process consultation model (a joint relationship between the consultant and the consultee in which the manner in which problems are solved is examined). Schein's 1969 book *Process Consultation* has been a primary reference for counselors acting as consultants.

**schema/schemata**
The cognitive way one mentally perceives the environment.

**schism**
In family therapy, a division in the family in which groups of individuals are antagonistic or compete with each other.

**schizophrenia**
A psychotic disorder characterized by a loss of contact with reality. Hallucinations, delusions, and thought disorder are present, resulting in bizarre behavior. Schizophrenia is not synonymous with multiple personality disorder (MPD) or a so-called *split personality,* although the term is often used in this incorrect manner in the popular press.

### schizophrenogenic
A factor or experience that contributes to schizophrenia. Genetics and double-bind communication via parents and caretakers are commonly cited as examples.

### schizotypical personality disorder
*See latent schizophrenia.*

### school counselor
*See guidance counselor.*

### school phobia
A morbid or exaggerated fear of school that generally leads to attendance problems.

### school psychometrician/psychologist
A professional who works in a school and administers psychoeducational tests to children with difficulties. Generally a battery of tests will be given and then a report with recommendations will be completed. A certification via the state department of elementary and secondary education is generally required and a master's degree in counseling or psychology with specific course work is mandatory.

### school social worker
A social worker who is employed to perform social work duties in a school setting. Depending on the state in question, the department of education may or may not have a certification requirement for this position. The National Association of Social Workers (NASW) does have a School Social Work Specialist (SSWS) credential that designates expertise in this area.

### screening
(1) The process of initially evaluating a client to see what services or referrals he or she needs. A hospital, for example, might need to screen a new client to see whether he will be best served via their psych unit, chemical dependency unit, or dual diagnosis unit. The term is often used to describe the process of selecting persons who will be appropriate for group counseling or therapy. (2) Selecting items to be used on a psychological or educational test.

### script/script analysis
In Eric Berne's transactional analysis, the notion that a person's life is like a fairy tale or script. The therapist examines the script and if it is dysfunctional, contracts with the client to create a new healthy script.

**sculpting**
A nonverbal experiential family therapy strategy, the family members place themselves in physical positions that indicate their relationship and feelings toward other family members. Also known as *family sculpting.*

**scurvy**
A disease caused by a deficiency of Vitamin C. The first sign is often bleeding gums.

**Seashore Test**
A measure used to test musical aptitude.

**secondary gain**
The theory that a client secures an advantage (i.e., a gain) from his or her physical or mental illness, such as receiving more attention or not attending work.

**secondary group**
A group set up for people who already have a minor problem or a concern. Often contrasted with a *preventive group,* which tries to ward off a problem, and a *tertiary group,* which treats people with severe, longstanding issues.

**secondary labor market**
Part-time, irregular, or seasonal jobs with low pay, and few if any benefits, that do not lead to an ongoing career.

**secondary reinforcer**
Something that is not a reinforcer itself but can be used to acquire reinforcers. Hence, a residential center for children may give children plastic tokens that can be traded in for goods (e.g., a pizza) or an activity (e.g., a trip to the ballgame). Money is sometimes viewed as the most common secondary reinforcer in the world. Secondary reinforcers are often called *back-up reinforcers.*

**secondary school**
High school, either grades 9 through 12 or grades 10 through 12.

**second-degree games**
In Eric Berne's transactional analysis a social game that is more serious than a first-degree game but not as serious as a third-degree game (where someone is physically hurt or killed). Second-degree games lead to very bad or negative feelings.

**second opinion**
Occurs when a client or patient seeks out the advice of a second practitioner. Thus, a patient who is told that he or she needs surgery that could be fatal would seek the guidance of another expert to see if that expert agrees that the surgery is necessary.

**second-order cybernetics**
In family therapy, the assumption that anybody who tries to counsel the family becomes a part of the family system itself.

**second-order qualitative change**
In family systems theory and brief solution-focused therapy, the notion that the family or organization has actually changed in terms of structure and the way it maintains stability. Often contrasted with *first-order change* in which a change in behavior is made but the structure or rules of the family remain the same. Second-order change is necessary for lasting results.

**selective eligibility**
Another term for *means test. See means test.*

**selective serotonin reuptake inhibitors**
*See SSRIs.*

**self-actualized**
Kurt Goldstein's, and later Abraham Maslow's, term for an individual who is using his or her abilities/potential to the fullest extent. Someone who surpasses the tendency to merely cope well with the environment. Often the literature uses the phrase *transcending the environment* to describe an individual who has reached this level of autonomy. This term was popularized by humanistic psychology.

**self-awareness**
Self-understanding. Knowledge of one's own behavior, thoughts, feelings, motives, and emotions.

**self-concept**
*See self-awareness.*

**self-control procedures**
Strategies (usually but not always based on behavior modification) that help the individual control or change an overt or covert behavior.

**self-defeating behavior**
Anything the person does to hold himself or herself back (i.e., work against a goal) or harm himself or herself. Older literature uses the term *masochism*.

**self-disclosure**
Occurs when a helper reveals personal information to enhance the therapeutic process. The consensus is that while a little self-disclosure promotes treatment, a lot will hinder the process.

**self-efficacy theory**
(1) The notion that our choices are based on whether we feel we can or cannot accomplish something. A popular term in career counseling. Hence, the theory predicts that an individual who feels he does not have the ability to perform a certain job probably wouldn't apply for that position. (2) Recently used in place of the term *self-esteem*.

**self-esteem**
Refers to how one perceives oneself (e.g., good, bad, not worthy of love, etc.).

**self-fulfilling prophecy**
Occurs when a client or a researcher believes so strongly that something will happen that he or she inadvertently makes it come true.

**self-help groups**
A group in which everyone has the same basic problem or concern (e.g., alcoholism or cocaine addiction). The members of the group try to help each other rather than relying on a professional helper as the leader. Alcoholics Anonymous (AA) is the most popular self-help group in the world.

**self-help materials**
The use of books, tapes, computer programs, videos, etc. to help ameliorate problems and abet coping skills. When a helper assigns a client to utilize self-help materials the process is often called *bibliotherapy*.

**self-hypnosis**
To hypnotize one's self. Also known as *autohypnosis*.

**self-image**
The way a person perceives himself or herself which may or may not be accurate (e.g., a very successful individual might view himself or herself as a failure). Sometimes referred to as the *self-concept*.

**self-instructional training**
*See stress inoculation technique/training (SIT)*

**self-monitoring**
Sometimes known as *self-rating* this occurs when a client keeps a record, graph, or journal of his or her thoughts, feelings, and behaviors. A helper, for example, might have a client monitor his or her smoking behavior for a given period of time. Very popular with behaviorists and cognitive-behaviorists.

**self-theory**
Another name for the personality theory of Carl R. Rogers' person-centered approach.

**semantic differential**
The notion that different people react differently to the same message.

**semantics**
An analysis of the meaning of words within a given language.

**senescence**
The changes in the body and organs as a result of aging.

**senile/senile dementia**
A state of old age. When the person's memory, perceptions, and grasp of reality are diminished then it is known as *senile dementia.*

**senium**
Age 65 and beyond.

**sensate focus**
A well-known sex therapy procedure created by William Masters and Virginia Johnson that helps eliminate performance anxiety by instructing the couple to engage in nonerotic touching.

**sensitivity groups**
Often known as *T-groups* or *training groups,* these encounter groups focus on improving human relations and fostering growth.

**sensorimotor intelligence/sensorimotor stage**
The first stage of Swiss psychologist Jean Piaget's four-stage theory of cognitive development. It occurs from birth to two years during which time the infant learns about objects and events by interacting with them,

although the child does not think about what he or she is doing or why he or she is doing it. *See Piaget, Jean.*

**serendipity**
In research, this occurs when a researcher sets out to discover one thing but in the process makes an unexpected discovery that can be much more important.

**serotonin**
A chemical (5-Hydroxytryptamine or 5 HT) that helps control numerous bodily processes including mood, sleep, and sexuality. A lack of this neurotransmitter is thought to cause depression. Antidepressant medicines (often referred to as *selective serotonin reuptake inhibitors* or *SSRIs*) and natural remedies are often utilized to keep serotonin in the brain or increase the amount the body produces.

**service learning/service-learning cycle**
Work at an actual community service organization, school, or business that is related to what the student is learning in the classroom. For example, a student in a college-level literacy class might be assigned to tutor a child at a local school. Service learning is often contrasted with *volunteer work*, which would not necessarily have an academic component in addition to the service. Additionally, authentic service learning has four distinct and necessary phases. (1) *Preparation:* when students and teachers identify a community need, conduct research, create learning objectives, and make preparations for the service activity. (2) *Service:* the service must be meaningful to both the community and to the student and must address a genuine community need. (3) *Reflection:* the opportunity for students to think about and learn from their experiences (e.g., the student may keep a journal); and *Celebration/recognition:* students are recognized for their efforts and the valuable service they provided (e.g., each student may be honored and receive a certificate). The four phases are sometimes known as the *service-learning cycle.*

**settlement house**
A facility that is generally staffed with volunteers who provide human services to people who reside in the neighborhood.

**sex role**
Expectations for a person of a given sex (i.e., male or female).

### sex therapy
Any counseling or therapy procedure that helps clients who are experiencing difficulties in the area of sexuality. Albert Ellis, William Masters, and Virginia Johnson are considered three of the major pioneers in this area.

### sexual orientation distress
A person who is upset regarding his or her sexual orientation (i.e., preference). In most of the literature it refers to a homosexual person who wishes he or she possessed heterosexual desires.

### shadow
In Carl Jung's analytic psychology, the shadow is the "dark side of the personality" in the unconscious that is the opposite of what the person consciously shows the world. The shadow encompasses everything an individual refuses to acknowledge. The role we present to others to hide our true self is termed the *persona*.

### shame
When you feel badly because another individual is critical of your behavior, claiming that it is embarrassing or that it causes others to lose respect for you (i.e., "you should be ashamed of yourself for talking that way in front of a teacher"). Often contrasted with *guilt*, where the aforementioned feelings are self-induced.

### shaping/shaping with successive approximations
In behavior modification, the practice of reinforcing small chunks of behavior that approximate the ultimate desired behavior. For example, a mentally challenged client cannot spell his name "Tom." You would first reinforce him for drawing a vertical line and then crossing it to make a "T." Next the "o," and so on. The key concept is that you only reinforce responses that lead to the ultimate target behavior.

### shock therapy
Short for electroconvulsive shock therapy. *See electroconvulsive shock therapy (ECT)/electroshock therapy (EST).*

### shoplifting
The act of stealing from a store rather then purchasing the item at the checkout counter.

**short-term memory (STM)**
A memory that does not last over 30 seconds (some sources say less than 10) and has a limited storage capacity of 7 to 9 items, such as a phone number. During the short-term period the individual decides whether to commit the information to long-term memory.

**sibling rivalry**
(1) Occurs when a child attempts to draw the parents' attention to himself or herself rather than the other brothers and sisters. The child is competing for the parents' attention. (2) Fighting, arguing, or discord among children of the same parent or parents.

**siblings**
Refers to brothers and sisters.

**sickle-cell disease**
The most common inherited blood disorder. The disease involves the oxygen-carrying capacity and shape of red blood cells. An individual with sickle-cell has an abnormal type of hemoglobin (HbS), which is made up of proteins and iron. Hemoglobin is important for carrying oxygen throughout the body to the interstitial fluid. In sickle-cell disease, once the oxygen is transferred, the red blood cell becomes stiff and takes on a sickle shape. Since this is hereditary, the severity is determined by whether one or both genes for sickle-cell are present. This disease is most commonly found in individuals of African American descent, but it can be encountered within any racial or ethnic background.

**side effect**
An effect of the treatment that is not intentional. For example, a person on a given psychiatric medicine might experience weight gain or headaches.

**sidetracked**
Occurs when a client and human services worker stray from the intended subject of the interview. This can be caused by (1) poor interviewing techniques, (2) conscious or unconscious resistance on the part of the client, or (3) countertransference on the part of the helper (i.e., the helper has issues and doesn't feel comfortable discussing the issue).

## significance level

In research, the probability that an experimental result is due to chance factors, random occurrences, or something other than the independent variable (IV) or experimental variable. In the social sciences a significance level is set at .05 or lower (i.e., .01 or .001). The significance level is often designated by the letter $p$. The .05 significance level indicates that if a researcher runs the experiment 100 times, the results will occur by chance 5 times. The significance level is equivalent to the *alpha error* or Type I error. *See alpha level, beta error, Type 1 error, and Type 2 error.*

## significant other

(1) A person you are married to or dating. (2) Anthropologist Margaret Mead's term to describe anyone who is very important to us or anybody who has a strong impact on our self-image.

## signing off

This refers to the practice of putting a mental health practitioner's name on an insurance claim form when the practitioner did not actually treat the client. Say, for example, that the client actually saw a social worker but the insurance company will not pay a social worker, therefore a psychiatrist who the company will pay signs off on the insurance form. In some cases the practice of signing off is used not because the practitioner in question cannot be paid, but rather that the professional signing off receives a higher fee (e.g., a social worker might get $60 for a counseling session while a psychologist might be paid $80 a session). Both practices are considered unethical and forms of insurance fraud.

## silence

Occurs when the helper intentionally does not rush in with a verbalization so that a client can assimilate what has been said. Some helpers believe that a client's most significant comments will be verbalized after a period of silence. Some textbooks refer to silence as *wait time.*

## single-parent family

A family with one parent. Often the result of a divorce, death, or the fact that the child was born out of wedlock.

## single-subject research design

Also called the $N = 1$ design, this paradigm is very popular in behavior modification studies where a single individual is monitored during a baseline (i.e., no treatment) and during treatment. In psychodynamic literature this is known as a *case study. See AB/ABAB design.*

## site visit
A visit made at the actual agency or school site for the purpose of evaluating a person (e.g., a human services practicum student) or a program. An accreditation team, for example, would make a site visit to assess a university program to ascertain if the institution is meeting the required standards. United Way and other institutions that provide money often have teams make visits to agencies to help make decisions related to funding and contributions (i.e., How much money does this agency really need to operate?).

## skeleton keys
Steven deShazer's brief therapy approach that assumes that some interventions will work for a host of different problems and thus have more or less universal application.

## skewed distribution
In statistics, a curve that leans left or right and is not symmetric like the normal bell-shaped curve. When a skewed curve is graphed and the tail points to the left then the curve is said to be *negatively skewed* (i.e., has lots of high scores). When the graphed curve has a tail that points to the right then the curve is said to be *positively skewed* (i.e., has lots of low scores).

## skid row
Slang for a poor, run-down, or impoverished area.

## Skinner box
An experimental boxlike apparatus created by B. F. Skinner to study operant conditioning with pigeons and rats. The animal presses a lever to control the reinforcement or other characteristics in the environment.

## Skinner, Burrhus F. (1904–1990)
The father of operant/instrumental conditioning, which became the bedrock of behavior modification. The most important factor in this theory is that environmental stimuli that come after the behavior control that particular behavior in the future. Simply put: behavior is molded by its consequences. A child, for example, who receives a toy he likes after reading a paragraph is more likely to read another paragraph. Skinner popularized the use of positive reinforcement.

### slander
A written document containing false statements that are injurious to a person's character. Often contrasted with *libel* in which a verbal communication contains false statements that are injurious to the person's reputation.

### sleeper effect
The notion that a message a person receives may change his or her attitude but it will not do so immediately, but only after a period of time has elapsed. It also suggests that the individual may recall the message but will be unable to remember the source of the message.

### snorting
To use a drug (e.g., cocaine) by inhaling the substance through the nose.

### snow
A street name for cocaine.

### social and human service assistants
*See human service assistants.*

### social class
Describes how a group (i.e., class) of people are different from others in the society based on their education, material possessions, values, occupations, or prestige.

### social exchange theory
In social psychology, the belief that rewards and costs can be analyzed to determine human interaction and relationship dynamics. A client might remark that, "I pay the bills, as long as my husband cuts the lawn."

### social inequality
A situation in which some members of a society are treated in a different manner.

### social insurance
Refers to government programs providing benefits to people who have earned the right to those benefits through their work. Typically, funding for social insurance comes from earmarked payroll taxes levied on workers and their employers. These taxes are often called *contributions*, and a term frequently associated with social insurance is *contributory*. Social insurance is not means tested: both rich and poor workers, and their families receive payments from social insurance if they fulfill a set of

predefined requirements. Examples of social insurance in the United States include Social Security, Medicare, Railroad Retirement, unemployment insurance, Black Lung benefits, and workers' compensation. The first social insurance program was created in 1889 by Chancellor Otto von Bismarck in Germany.

**socialization**
The process of learning what is and what is not appropriate in a given culture.

**social justice**
An attempt to assure that all members of a given society have the same opportunities and benefits.

**social learning theory**
(1) Based on the work of Albert Bandura, the notion that an individual who sees another individual being reinforced for a given behavior will then model or imitate the behavior. (2) Receiving reinforcement via the act of observing another individual being reinforced. (3) An individual has been reinforced for imitating a model's behavior in the past and thus continues to imitate the behavior. *See vicarious conditioning/learning.*

**social mobility**
A change in social, residence, or economic status often determined by the rules or policies of a society.

**social policy/social welfare policy**
(1) A society's policies and plans for dealing with social welfare, housing, mental health, hunger, child care, health care, education, criminal justice, public assistance, and energy programs. (2) Any action or lack of action taken by a government (e.g., taxation) that will have an impact of the citizens by providing them with income (e.g., temporary assistance) or services (e.g., vocational rehabilitation). Major social welfare programs include: temporary assistance or related welfare benefits, social security, supplemental security income (SSI), workers compensation, food stamps, school lunch and breakfast programs, special supplemental food program for Women Infants and Children (WIC), meals on wheels, Medicare, Medicaid, family preservation and child protective services, job training and employment services, day care and preschool programs, and vocational rehabilitation.

**social science courses**
Generally includes courses that investigate the manner in which humans live and work together as a group (i.e., anthropology, economics, human services, psychology, sociology, history, geography, and political science).

**Social Security**
Social insurance programs administered by the Social Security Administration (SSA) including retirement (old-age) insurance, disability insurance, and survivor insurance. OASDI (old age, survivor and disability insurance) and RSDI (retirement, survivors, and disability insurance) are common acronyms. Most of the funds for Social Security come from earmarked earnings taxes levied on employees, employers, and the self-employed. Social Security eligibility is not means tested: There are no income or asset limitations, therefore even a very wealthy person could secure benefits. Surviving spouses, ex-spouses, children, and parents may draw Social Security survivor benefits. The deceased worker must have worked in Social Security-covered work. A surviving spouse or ex-spouse may draw at age 60, or 50 if disabled, or at any age if taking care of a child of the deceased worker. A surviving child may draw while under 18, between 18 and 19 if in high school, and at any age if unable to work due to a childhood disability. Surviving parents may draw at age 62 if they were financially dependent on the deceased child. Social Security also pays monthly cash benefits to disabled workers and their families. The disabled worker must have a recent work history in Social Security-covered work. A common acronym for Social Security Disability Insurance is SSDI. The original U.S. Social Security law (public law 74-271, which was fueled by the hardships of the Great Depression) was signed by President Franklin Delano Roosevelt on August 14, 1935, and provided old age insurance. The 1939 Amendments to the Social Security Act added survivor insurance. Disability insurance was added in 1956.

**Social Security Administration (SSA)**
An independent agency in the executive branch of the federal government. SSA administers Social Security and Supplemental Security Income through 1300 field offices, hearings offices, and telephone service centers. In the early days of the program, SSA was called the *Social Security Board*.

**social service technician**
Refers to helpers with an Associate's degree in human services.

**social service worker**
(1) Agencies often use this title for workers who perform social work duties but cannot legally use the title *social worker* because the individual lacks a social work license. (2) A worker who deals primarily with child abuse, neglect, exploitation, and sexual abuse.

**social work/social worker**
A helping profession that uses community resources and information amassed from social work research and by other social science disciplines (i.e., psychology, counseling, sociology, etc.) to help the client or the family. In most states a licensed social worker must have a Master's Degree (M.S.W.) from a social work program accredited via the Council for Social Work Education (CSWE). In some states persons with accredited bachelor's programs (e.g., B.S.W. or B.S.S.W.) can be licensed and may thus call themselves social workers. To become a licensed social worker, the individual must generally complete a test and a supervision requirement; master's level licensing is required for private practice.

**sociogram**
A pictorial or graphic representation of the interaction and relationship between individuals. Often used to help understand dynamics when conducting group work by mapping the members' attraction and rejection patterns.

**sociology**
The scientific study of society.

**sociometry**
The study of person-to-person relations created by Jacob Moreno who coined the term *group therapy. See sociogram.*

**solution-focused therapy**
Brief treatment that focuses on exceptions to typical behavior that can be curative. A mother may protest that she never gets along with her daughter. Rather than analyzing the problem, the helper probes to see if there was ever a time when they did get along. The mother admits they get along well on the child's birthdays. The helper then helps mom discover what is different on those occasions and how to use it in the present moment. Also called *brief solution-focused therapy,* this approach was pioneered by William O'Hanlon and Steven deShazer.

**somatic complaints**
Complaints about one's body.

**SOS**
*See survivor of suicide.*

**soup kitchen**
A church or social service agency that provides food or meals to the hungry. Many experts believe that the concept of soup kitchens was popularized by the work of Salvation Army. *See Salvation Army.*

**spaced practice**
Brief periods of practice or trials of learning that are used to reduce fatigue. Often contrasted with *massed practice* or longer practice sessions without a rest. When spaced versus massed are compared, spaced practice is generally more effective. Hence, short study sessions with breaks would prove superior to long marathon study sessions. Spaced practice is also known as *distributed practice.*

**specialist**
Someone who has a high level of education and experience related to a given discipline (e.g., a physician who specializes in laser surgery for the eye) or problem (e.g., eating disorders). Often contrasted with a generalist, who works with a wide range of problems. Currently, most human service workers view themselves as generalists with a multitude of skills, who can work with a vast range of difficulties and perform numerous jobs (also known as *diversity of employment*).

**speed**
Slang for amphetamines or *uppers.*

**speed freak**
Slang for a drug user who regularly takes amphetamines.

**speed test**
A timed test.

**spina bifida**
A malformation of the spine and vertebrae which causes severe lower body weakness and loss of sensation.

**split-half reliability**
A method of examining the reliability of a test by putting test items into two separate categories (e.g., even questions and odd questions) and then correlating the scores obtained from the categories. Often the categories are picked via random number generation.

**spontaneous remission**
Emotional or physical recovery that occurs without treatment.

**SR psychology**
Abbreviation for *stimulus response psychology*. Treatment models based on SR psychology emphasize behaviorism over cognitive or psychoanalytic models.

**SSRIs**
Stands for *selective serotonin reuptake inhibitors,* a class of prescription medicines that are used primarily for depression but can also be prescribed for eating disorders, panic disorder, and obsessive compulsive disorder (OCD). SSRIs include Celexa, Luvox, Paxil, Prozac, and Zoloft.

**staff development**
Also sometimes referred to as *in-service training,* this occurs when the staff of an organization receives training to enhance the staff's ability to handle the existing job or to teach them changes that are taking place in the job.

**stage**
(1) In developmental psychology, a period in a person's life (e.g., the oral stage). (2) In group work, the phase or period the group is going through (e.g., the termination stage).

**standard deviation (SD)**
In statistics, a measure of dispersion from the mean. In a normal distribution, 68.2% of the cases fall between plus or minus 1 SD from the mean; 95.4% of the cases fall between plus or minus 2 SD of the mean; and 99.7% of the cases fall between plus or minus 3 SD of the mean.

**standard error of measurement (SEM)**
A statistic that reveals what would most likely occur if a client would take the same test over and over again. For example, if a client scores 100 on an IQ test and the SEM is plus or minus 3 then the client would score between 97 and 103 about 68.2% of the time. *See standard deviation (SD).*

**standardized test**
A test (that a helper usually purchases from a test publisher) that has standards (guidelines) for administering the test, scoring it, and interpreting what the results mean. These tests generally have good validity (i.e., they truly test what they purport to test) and reliability (i.e., they are consistent and will yield the same results again and again). The person can then be compared to a large number of persons who have normed the test.

**standard scores**
*See T-score and Z-score*

**Stanford Binet Intelligence Scale**
A popular individual IQ test that received its name from the fact that it was originally created by Alfred Binet and revised by experts at Stanford University. *See resources section of the text for more information on intelligence tests.*

**statistics**
Using mathematics to collect, analyze, and utilize data for research or experiments.

**status offense**
A behavior, such as skipping school, that is not desirable but would not be considered a violation of the law if the person in question was legally an adult. Juvenile and family courts often deal with status offenders.

**statutory rape**
This term is used to describe a sexual encounter where both people consent to have sex, nevertheless, one of the parties is below the legal age of consent.

**stimulant**
A drug or natural substance such as an herb that increases alertness. Caffeine is considered the most popular stimulating substance.

**stimulus**
Anything in the environment that has an impact on the person.

**stimulus discrimination**
The ability to react differently to stimuli that are similar. For example, a mentally challenged individual must know that his bus is number 95

rather than number 59, or perhaps that he steps into the yellow bus and not a yellow car. Stimulus discrimination is usually taught to clients using a behavior modification or behavior therapy approach. A dog, for example, who has undergone classical Pavlovian respondent conditioning who was successfully taught to salivate to a door bell, but not a bell on a child's toy, has mastered stimulus discrimination. Often contrasted with *stimulus generalization. See stimulus generalization.*

## stimulus generalization
Occurs when a stimulus that is similar to a learned response (not but exactly the same) elicits the same response. A dog, for example, who has undergone classical respondent Pavlovian conditioning is taught to salivate to a bell. If a car horn or a piano note elicits the salivation response then stimulus generalization has set in. Often contrasted with *stimulus discrimination. See stimulus discrimination.*

## stereotype a person
To judge a person on based on generalizations about his or her social status, race, culture, ethnicity, job, education, etc. For example, all Asians want to major in fields related to math, science, and technology. To go beyond this tendency the person must be viewed as a unique individual.

## steroids
A class of substances that are often abused by bodybuilders, powerlifters, wrestlers, and athletes who want to gain a significant amount of muscle in a short period of time. Steroids (also called *anabolic steroids* or *roids*) have been implicated in serious life-threatening diseases. Moreover, the term *roid rage* has been coined to describe the violent, angry behavior that some experts feel is caused by taking these drugs. It should be noted that physicians do use steroids to combat asthma, muscle loss in AIDs, and inflammatory conditions.

## St. John's Wort
Also known as *hypericum,* this compound is a natural herbal antidepressant. Some studies indicate that St. John's Wort is as effective as prescription antidepressants, with fewer side effects. Until further research is conducted this natural remedy should be avoided by people who spend an inordinate amount of time in the sun, those who are taking AIDS medications, those who are already taking prescription antidepressants, and those who are taking organ transplant medicinals.

### strategic therapy/strategic family therapy

A term coined by Jay Haley to describe the therapeutic approach of the late great psychiatrist/psychologist Milton H. Erickson, who focused on symptoms and not insight. Paradox, hypnosis, and story telling using metaphors are used in this approach.

### stress

Mental or physical strain or tension. Stress may be created via negative events, such as caring for a sick relative, or positive events, such as getting married.

### stress inoculation technique/training (SIT)

(1) Coping skills the helper teaches the client to help the client deal with future stress. (2) Part of Donald Meichenbaum's *self-intructional therapy* in which stress inoculation is taught in three basic phases. First the client is taught to monitor the impact of inner dialogue on behavior in a stressful situation. Next the client is taught to rehearse new self-talk. Finally, the client implements the new self-talk during an actual stressful event.

### stressor

Anything that causes stress (e.g., having to ask for a raise).

### strokes

In transactional analysis, biological and/or psychological hunger which can be satisfied via recognition from others. The recognition is termed a *stroke*. According to the theory, strokes can be positive ("I think you're terrific"), negative ("I hate you"), or conditional ("I like you when you do exactly what I want"). Many counselors who don't practice transactional analysis use the word *strokes* loosely in place of the word *reinforcement*.

### structural theory

Freud's notion that the mind is composed of three entities: the id, the ego, and the superego. These are hypothetical constructs and not actual biological stations in the mind. Hence one could not see these structures under a microscope or dissect them. *See id, ego, and superego.*

### structured exercise

A specific technique or strategy prescribed by an individual or group counselor (e.g., role playing or a group activity).

**structured group**
A group that focuses on a given topic (e.g., self-esteem or assertiveness training). Most psycho-educational groups are structured groups. The term has also been used to describe groups that rely primarily on group exercises (i.e., a highly structured group).

**subconscious**
A term used in the popular press for the term *unconscious*. *See unconscious.*

**subgoal**
Steps involved in reaching the desired goal once a problem has been identified. For example, a student whose goal is to secure a master's degree would have a subgoal of attaining a bachelor's degree.

**subgroup**
A group within a group, such as all pregnant teens in a high school.

**subjectivity**
A private, personal and unique way of experiencing situations; a private reaction or feeling about someone or something. Being subjective suggests that one's experience is unique and thus not directly observable via another person.

**subjective units of distress scale**
*See SUDS.*

**sublimation/subliminal perception**
An unconscious ego defense mechanism in which a socially acceptable goal is substituted for a socially unacceptable unconscious wish. For example, according to this theory, a person who wants to cut or hurt others may become a surgeon. The term is popular with psychodynamic career theorists. This term should not be confused with the term *subliminal perception,* which implies that something one can only perceive unconsciously (e.g., words that can't be consciously heard that are imbedded in rock music) impacts one's behavior. Subliminals in advertising are supposed to be illegal and there is an intense debate as to whether or not they are effective.

**subpoena**
A legal document stipulating that an individual must appear in court on a certain date and time.

## substance abusers
Persons who misuse substances such as alcohol, street drugs, prescription drugs, or inhalants for the purpose of altering mood or psychological state.

## successive approximations
*See shaping/shaping with successive approximations.*

## SUDS
Subjective units of distress scale. A client rates situations on a scale of 0 to 100 (100 is the most anxiety provoking) in order to create a treatment hierarchy. *See systematic desensitization.*

## suggestion
To give the client advice, directives, prescriptions for change, or delineate a plan of action. Very common in hypnosis and directive, didactic approaches to treatment, and not very popular with nondirective or person-centered paradigms.

## suicide
Intentionally killing oneself. Approximately 30,000 individuals take their own lives each year in the US. Due to problems in reporting and coding such deaths, suicidologists estimate that the actual number of suicides in the US could be nearly triple this official figure. Suicide is usually the second or third leading killer of teenagers (about 6000 teens per year between the ages of 15 and 24 take their own lives) and the geriatric suicide rate is approximately double what it is for the general population. Suicide is primarily a male phenomenon, while suicide attempts are more prevalent in females. Guns and firearms generally account for more suicides than all other methods put together. Seventy to eighty percent of the individuals who commit suicide give warning signs. These signs include: talking, joking, or obsessing about suicide or death; giving away prized possessions; clinical depression (often the most serious time is when the depression is lifting); a change of behavior that is out of character; risk taking behavior; and a history of suicide attempts. Human service workers should take suicide threats seriously.

## suicide prevention
The act of preventing suicide or a suicide attempt by (1) asking the client if he or she is suicidal, (2) inquiring about the plan, (3) realizing that the more specific the plan is the greater the likelihood of an attempt, (4) inter-

vening to interfere with the plan such as removing a gun or bullets or contacting a significant other who can accomplish this, (5) contracting with the person to stay alive, (6) giving the person the number of the suicide prevention hotline, and (7) helping the individual to secure ongoing counseling and psychiatric help. If the person will not agree to a written or verbal contract hospitalization must be seriously considered.

### suicidologist
An individual who studies or does research on the phenomenon of suicide and suicidal behavior.

### suicidology
Edwin Shneidman's term for the study of suicide and suicidal behavior.

### summarize
The human service worker and the client discuss the most important points covered during an interview or other intervention.

### summative evaluation
Refers to an evaluation that takes place at the end of a study or treatment. Often contrasted with *formative evaluation*, which takes place during a study or implementation of treatment or a program.

### superego
In Freudian theory, one of the three subsystems of the personality (i.e., the id, the ego, and the superego). The superego houses the conscience and thus is compose of values, morals and ideals of parents, caretakers, and society. The superego is mainly concerned with what is ideal rather than what is real. It is often said to house the *ego ideal.* The superego is roughly analogous to the Parent ego state in Eric Berne's transactional analysis. *See id, ego, and structural theory.*

### Supplemental Security Income for the Aged, Blind, and Disabled (SSI)
A public assistance program administered by the Social Security Administration and funded by general revenues of the federal government. SSI recipients must be 65 or older, or blind, or disabled. They must also be residents of the United States, and generally must also be a US citizen. SSI is means-tested: Income and resources (assets) cannot exceed limits set in the Social Security Act. SSI pays monthly benefits up to a maximum of $545 (in 2002), depending on the recipient's other income. In fifteen states and the District of Columbia, SSI payments sometimes exceed the

maximum because the state or District has opted to supplement the federal SSI payments. SSI started in 1974. Before that time, each state ran its own programs to aid its "old-age," "blind," and "permanently-and totally-disabled" residents.

### support group
Often called self-help groups, these groups are made up of individuals who all share the same problem (e.g., overeating, shyness, alcoholism, etc.). The leader has the same difficulties as the rest of the group and thus would not necessarily be a professional. In other support groups, there is no official leader. 12-step groups like Alcoholics Anonymous (AA) are generally called *self-help groups*.

### support system
Friends, religious institutions, resources, helpers, or agencies that a person can turn to during a crisis or a time of need.

### suppression
An ego-defense mechanism sometimes known as *denial* in which the person intentionally tries to put a negative thought or experience out of his mind. Often contrasted with repression that is automatic or unconscious forgetting.

### survey research
Conducted via information gathered from questionnaires.

### survivor of suicide (SOS)
An individual who has lost a loved one through the act of suicide (e.g., a parent whose child killed himself). Often confused with the term *attempter*, which refers to an individual who made a suicide attempt and lived. It is generally accepted that the grief and bereavement following a suicide is more difficult to cope with than that associated with other forms of death or loss. Counseling provided for survivors of suicide is often termed *postvention services*.

### sweatshirt message
In transactional analysis, the Child ego state, often with the help of the Little Professor, conveys a message to others in order to *play games, initiate rackets,* or *collect stamps.* The person's verbal and/or nonverbal communication is seen as if the person is wearing a sweatshirt with a saying printed on the chest. Hence, a woman who dresses and acts ex-

tremely seductive sends the message "I'm available." An adolescent who looks very nonassertive, droops his shoulders, and shakes, has a sweatshirt that says, "Don't kick me, I'm a victim." *See games, and trading stamps.*

## symbiosis
(1) A normal mother/child attachment in infancy. (2) In family therapy, two people who are so close that neither has a healthy identity.

## sympathy
Feeling sorry for somebody. Often contrasted with *empathy*, which is defined as the act of attempting to understand another person's world (i.e., feelings, thoughts, etc.).

## symptom substitution
The psychoanalytic/psychodynamic theory that if you merely treat the symptom or problem and not the unconscious conflict, a similar symptom will appear. Thus, if you teach an alcoholic to stop drinking he or she will become addicted to smoking or perhaps attending twelve-step groups such as Alcholics Anonymous (AA). The behaviorists, who treat the symptom, totally disavow this theory.

## syntax
Analyzing the arrangement of words within a given language.

## syphilis
A sexually transmitted disease that can cause serious physical and mental problems if not treated.

## systems theory
The notion that a system is composed of interlocking elements and thus the change of one person will necessarily influence the other persons in the system. This theory is extremely popular with family therapists who want to work with the entire family system (or even the extended family) rather than simply focusing on the identified patient or so-called person with the problem. A systems theorist working with an alcoholic, for example, would note that when he comes home drunk his behavior may be affected by whether his wife ignores him, castigates him, or greets him with open arms at the door each night with a drink. His behavior is influenced by other people and things (e.g., his physiological reaction to alcohol) in the environment.

**301**

**systematic desensitization**

A therapy technique based on classical conditioning created by psychiatrist Joseph Wolpe. In this technique the client is taught to relax. Then the client imagines anxiety-provoking situations beginning with those that evoke the least anxiety and gradually working up to situations that provoke the most anxiety in a step-by-step hierarchy. The client imaginings are paired with the relaxation to counter-condition (i.e., remove) the fear. This approach was extremely popular in the 1970s for dealing with phobias and fears. It is still used by some behavior therapists today. Older literature may refer to the procedure as *reciprocal inhibition.*

## TA

(1) Stands for *Temporary Assistance*. A program that replaced Aid to Families of Dependent Children (AFDC) welfare payments. The term is favored in some states over the term *TANF,* or *Temporary Assistance for Needy Families. See TANF.* (2) Abbreviation for a form of therapy known as *transactional analysis,* created by the psychiatrist Eric Berne. *See Transactional Analysis (TA).*

## taboo
Something which is forbidden or unacceptable within a given culture.

## tabula rasa
From latin "blank tablet," the notion that the mind is empty or like a blank slate at birth. John Locke emphasized this point, which later became popular with the behaviorists.

## TANF
Stands for *Temporary Assistance for Needy Families.* Refers to new programs that replaced Aid to Families of Dependent Children (AFDC) welfare payments, which were previously called Aid to Dependent Children (ADC) welfare payments. TANF became a reality after the Personal Responsibility Work Opportunity Reconciliation Act of (PRWORA) was signed on August 22, 1996 by President Bill Clinton and became a law (PL 104-193). Unlike earlier programs, clients usually have a five-year lifetime eligibility for which they can receive benefits. The new program also stipulated that able-bodied adult cash recipients must work or be engaged in work activities (e.g., a job search or job readiness training) after two years of receiving assistance. Can also be referred to merely as *TA* or *Temporary Assistance.*

## Tarasoff decision/duty
Refers to a landmark California Supreme Court case in which it was decided that counselors and therapists have a duty to warn an intended victim when his or her life is in danger. Ethical guidelines in the behavioral sciences are supportive of this position, suggesting that confidentiality must be breeched when a client is a danger to the self or others.

## tardive dyskinesia
Uncontrollable movements such as facial contortions, sticking out one's lips or tongue, or leg or trunk jerks caused by side effects of antipsychotic medications.

## target behavior
In behavior modification, the behavior that needs to be changed or altered. Strictly speaking, target behaviors must be measurable. Hence, a client who says, "I don't want to be so codependent," has not expressed a target behavior. A behavior modifier would help this client operationally define her problem in a measurable manner; for example, "I call my boyfriend three times per hour at work."

## target population
(1) Those individuals who are selected for help by human services. (2) A policy term indicating the people who can benefit from the program (e.g., male alcoholics over the age of 65, families at risk for sexual abuse, or pregnant teens).

## task-centered/focused treatment
A paradigm of treatment in which the human service worker and the client select a problem and then create specific tasks and activities to reach the goal. Often a contract is utilized that outlines a timetable for the implementation of each task.

## task force
A committee set up to analyze a problem or a program and come up with strategies to improve it or reach a given goal. A college, for example, might set up a task force to discover why retention in their human service program is so poor, set a goal for acceptable retention, and specify steps to keep students from dropping out of the program.

## task-oriented roles
In group counseling, specific tasks, projects, jobs, or problems which the group is working on. Group members performing such tasks are said to

be in task roles. Information providers, opinion givers, data analyzers, and opinion/information seekers are considered task-oriented roles. Task roles are often contrasted with *maintenance-oriented roles* which focus on enhancing group interactions. *See maintenance-oriented roles.*

**TAT**
Abbreviation for the *Thematic Apperception Test. See Thematic Apperception Test (TAT).*

**taxonomy**
The science of classification.

**Tay-Sachs disease**
A hereditary disease that is characterized by the absence of an enzyme (HEX-A) needed to bread down fatty waste material, known as ganglioslide GM2, found in neuronal cells of the brain. Infants born with this disease appear normal at birth, but as the fatty deposits begin to accumulate there is a noticeable impact on physical and mental capabilities. Within a short time after birth, the infant becomes mentally retarded and loses control of all motor functions. Most children born with Tay-Sachs do not live past the age of five, and there is no current cure for the disease. It is most commonly found in families of Eastern Jewish descent.

**tea head**
Slang for a person who smokes a lot of marijuana.

**technical/apprentice level**
Those workers who have one or two years of formal training or experience; sometimes they possess an associate's degree.

**technique**
A strategy or method for instilling behavior change or reaching a goal.

**teleological**
Goal directed.

**temperament**
Strictly speaking, the term refers to genetic makeup which predisposes one to have certain personality traits and reactions to the environment. Counselors sometimes use the term in a looser fashion to describe one's personality or emotional responses without implying that such traits are the result of genetic disposition.

**temperance**
Movements whose goals are the reduction or elimination of alcohol consumption.

**tenement house**
Large antiquated homes that are in poor shape; nevertheless, they are rented to the poor.

**tenet**
A belief or a notion in regard to a principle or theory. A tenet of cognitive counseling, for example, would be that thoughts influence emotions.

**tentative interpretation/directive**
The helper presents the client with an insight, analysis, or assignment in such a manner that the client can provide feedback and/or reject what the helper has said. Tentative interpretations/directives are less threatening to most clients. A direct interpretation might be, "You need to assert yourself with your mother." A tentative directive might be, "Have you ever thought about what life would be like if you asserted yourself with your mother?" or "I wonder if your situation would change if you asserted yourself with your mother."

**terminal illness**
A disease or condition that generally results in death.

**termination**
To stop providing services or treatment.

**tertiary**
A term commonly used in group psychotherapy, crisis intervention, and preventive mental health, it is the notion that a substantial problem that already exists will be treated. Often contrasted with *primary prevention,* which attempts to ward off a problem before it starts (e.g., a group to warn children about the dangers of smoking), and *secondary prevention,* which attempts to limit the duration of a difficulty by intervening before it becomes a severe tertiary problem.

**test anxiety**
Extreme or exaggerated fear related to test-taking or examination situations.

**test battery**
The act of giving a client several tests (rather than a single measure) in order to come up with an assessment, diagnosis, and treatment program.

**test bias**
A test that is unfair to certain individuals. Hence, a test that uses only middle-class language might be biased toward poverty-stricken individuals.

**test of significance**
In a true experiment a statistical test of significance is utilized to determine whether the results occurred via chance or due to the experimental/independent variable. In the social sciences the level of significance is generally .05, meaning that 95 out of 100 times the experimenter will achieve the same results.

**test retest reliability method**
Test reliability refers to a test's ability to consistently provide the same results. In the test retest method, the reliability of a test is assessed by having the same individual or group of individuals retake the same test. If the test is reliable then the score/scores should remain constant. Thus, if you step on your scale and weight 120 pounds, wait one minute, and then step on the scale again and it registers 135 on the same surface, the scale is not reliable.

**thanatologist**
A counselor or related professional who specializes in the study of death and dying and the reaction of survivors after the tragedy. *See postvention.*

**thanatophobia**
A fear of death or dead bodies.

**Thanatos**
In Greek, the god of death. Freud used the term to describe the death instinct in the personality. Often contrasted with *Eros,* the life instinct. *See Eros.*

**Thematic Apperception Test (TAT)**
A projective-expressive test first used in 1935. The client is shown a series of 20 cards (the test has a pool of 30 cards plus a blank card to choose from) with ambiguous pictures and asked to tell a story about what is going on in the picture. The test is popular with psychodynamic/analytic helpers who believe that the measure reveals unconscious motives.

**theory**
An assumption used to explain phenomena. Theories help explain the world and bring the facts into a sensible overall picture. Psychoanalytic theory, for example, assumes that the unconscious regulates our behavior, while cognitive theory postulates that our thinking controls our actions.

**therapeutic**
Any factor or intervention that is helpful and curative.

**therapeutic recreation**
The selected use of recreational activities as an aid in the treatment, correction, or rehabilitation of physical or mental disorders. The primary focus of this form of treatment is corrective or rehabilitative.

**therapist**
Short for psychotherapist. An individual who helps others ameliorate or cope with problems. *See psychotherapist.*

**therapy**
(1) Short for psychotherapy or counseling. In the older literature *therapy* often meant long-term in-depth therapy, as opposed to counseling which focused only on conscious issues. Today the terms are usually synonymous. (2) In medical settings or healing, any procedure that is used as a treatment or a cure. *See counselor.*

**therapy group**
Although the terms "counseling" and "therapy" are more or less synonymous when describing individual treatment, when these terms are used in relation to group work the term "therapy" usually refers to longer more in-depth treatment than would result in a counseling group.

**third ear**
A term popularized by Theodor Reik, a famous lay analyst who worked with Freud. The notion that counselors and therapists can often help clients best when they use clinical intuition and hunches that go beyond what the client has literally communicated. The act is often called *listening with the third ear.*

**third-degree games**
In Eric Berne's transactional analysis, the most serious type of communication game (i.e., more harmful than a first- or second-degree game) in which somebody gets physically hurt or killed.

**third-force psychology**
Refers to humanistic/existential approaches to treatment. The first major force was psychoanalysis while the second was behaviorism.

**third-party payer**
An organization such as an insurance company or Medicaid that pays for the client's counseling and/or medical services.

**third revolution in mental health**
The notion that institutionalized people can be served by moving them back into the community.

**Thorazine**
A prescription medicine known as an anitpsychotic that helps to reduce the symptoms of schizophrenia. The generic name for Thorazine is Chlorpromazine and it is in a class of drugs known as Phenothiazines.

**thought disorder**
A feature of schizophrenia wherein the client cannot think or communicate in a coherent manner. *See word salad.*

**thought stopping**
A technique popularized by behavior therapists in which the client is mentally taught to mentally shout "stop" when he or she is thinking or emoting in a dysfunctional manner.

**tic**
Involuntary movements of muscles which do not seem to be caused by environmental stimuli.

**time out**
An operant conditioning behavior modification technique in which the person is removed from a reinforcing environment (e.g., a child is placed in a room without other children or toys) in order to lessen or ameliorate a target behavior.

**time-series design**
A research design used primarily with a single subject or a small number of subjects; however, it has also been utilized for program evaluation. Also known as a *continuous measurement design,* it is when numerous (nearly continuous) measurements and/or observations are taken. Hence, progress is monitored via repeated observations before, during, and after a treatment or program. This is sometimes contrasted with the traditional pre-post experiment in which observations are not continually conducted throughout the course of the research. *See AB/ABAB design.*

**timing**
(1) Refers to the fact that what the helper says is not always as important as when he or she says it. Confronting a client during the first few minutes of the initial interview might prove counterproductive, but the same confrontation could be beneficial during a later session. (2) In behavior modification, refers to the time a reinforcer is administered.

**tinnitius**
Ringing in the ears.

**Title XVIII**
*See Medicare.*

**Title XVIX**
*See Medicaid.*

**toddler**
Refers to children from approximately 1 to 3 years of age.

**token economy**
An operant conditioning behavior modification system that uses tokens (also called back-up or secondary reinforcers) to increase the probability that a target behavior will occur. A token is an innocuous item that is not reinforcing itself (e.g., plastic chip, gold stars, points) but represents a primary reinforcer that does increase behavior (e.g., one's favorite food). Generally a prescribed number of tokens must be accumulated before the individual receives the primary reinforcer.

**tolerance**
Occurs when an individual needs increased dosages of a given drug to experience the original response. A problem drinker, for example, generally goes through a phase in which he or she needs more alcohol to get drunk. *Also see reverse tolerance.*

**tolerant**
The helper's ability to maintain a nonjudgmental stance, to be patient and fair about the client's thoughts and activities.

**Topdog**
In gestalt therapy, the part of the personality that houses the "shoulds," "oughts," and "musts." Theorists claim it is similar to Freud's superego and Berne's Parent ego state.

**Tourette's Disorder/Syndrome**
A condition named after the French physician Gilles de la Tourette, characterized by involuntary tics and foul language. Generally, begins in childhood.

**toxic**
Any substance that can physically harm the body. Some of the literature uses the term *toxic thoughts,* to refer to pernicious cognitions.

**trading stamps**
In Eric Berne's transactional analysis, the notion that the Child ego state collects feelings called "trading stamps." The term gets its name from the practice of collecting trading stamps received from purchases to redeem for goods and services. The theory suggests that people collect these stamps for a psychological payoff or prize such as tremendous anger ventilated toward another person. When a person manipulates, imagines, or invites others to do things so he or she can get this psychological payoff, transactional analysis calls it a "racket." *See Transactional analysis (TA).*

**Trait Factor Vocational Guidance**
An approach popularized by Frank Parsons (the Father of Guidance) which uses self-knowledge and information about job characteristics to match the individual with the ideal job.

**tranquilizer**
A drug that reduces anxiety and agitated states. In recent years, the term *antianxiety* medicine is preferred.

**transaction**
Communication that occurs between two or more individuals.

**Transactional Analysis (TA)**
A cognitive school of psychotherapy created by psychoanalytically trained psychiatrist Eric Berne. The theory uses nomenclature that is easily understood by lay persons. In TA, for example, the personality is broken down into the Parent, Adult, and Child ego states, which roughly correspond to Freud's superego, ego, and id. The theory focuses heavily on one's life scripts and games, and it has often been combined with Fritz Perls' gestalt therapy, especially within a group setting. Books such as Bernes' 1964 *Games People Play,* his 1974 *What Do You Say After You Say*

*Hello?*, and Tom Harris' 1967 *I'm Ok—You're Ok*, acquainted the public with this approach. *See Adult ego state, Child ego state, and Parent ego state.*

**transcend**
To go beyond or surpass one's current level of functioning. The term has been popularized by humanistic theorists and practioners.

**transcendence**
To reach one's highest level of functioning and maximize potential.

**Transcendental Meditation**
A yogi named Maharishi Mahesh is given credit for bringing this technique (usually referred to as TM) to Western society. The individual is given a mantra which is a sound or a word that has no real meaning. The individual focuses on repeating the mantra silently again and again. The technique has been useful for individuals who need to relax or reduce their blood pressure. Some human service workers prefer biofeedback for the same purpose since it provides the helper and the client with more objective feedback.

**transcript**
A verbatim written account of what occurred during a session, meeting, or consultation. Also called a *typescript* in some of the older literature.

**transcultural counseling**
To counsel someone from another culture. Synonymous with multicultural, cross-cultural, and intercultural counseling.

**transferable skills**
Skills that an individual has learned that can be used in another job or educational setting. Generally, skills can only be transferable if the original skill is somewhat similar to the skill required in the new setting.

**transference**
Occurs when a client unconsciously expresses positive, negative, or ambivalent feelings toward the helper. It is assumed that the client is acting as if the helper is a significant other from the past. Psychodynamic and Freudian practitioners assume that an analysis of transference is extremely significant in terms of the treatment process.

**transfer summary**
A report that a human service worker writes to summarize the highlights of the case and the client's current situation when the case is turned over to

another helper. As an example, a child abuse intake worker would give a transfer summary to a treatment worker who will be taking over the case.

**transients**
Persons with no permanent address or who move on a regular basis.

**transition stage**
In group work, the notion that a group progresses from the initial stage in which people get to know each other to the transition stage in which participants test the safety level of the group, decide if they are willing to totally commit to the group, evaluate whether they feel comfortable with the group leaders, and deal with ambivalence to promote cohesiveness.

**transparent**
The ability of a counselor to be conguent or genuine.

**transracial adoption**
When a child of one race is placed with adoptive parents of a different race (e.g., an Asian-American Child is placed with an African-American family).

**transsexual**
An individual who constantly feels he or she would like to be the opposite sex. In extreme cases the person may secure surgical procedures and hormone treatments. Some of the literature refers to this as a problem of *gender identity.*

**transvestite**
An individual who gains sexual pleasure by dressing and/or acting like a person of the opposite sex. Some of the literature uses the term *cross dresser.*

**Tranxene**
An antianxiety prescription medicine. The generic name for Tranxene is Clorazepate.

**trauma**
A profound negative experience, such as rape or robbery, which can abet or intensify an emotional problem.

**triad**
(1) Three people. (2) The relationship/interaction between three people such as a father, a mother, and a child. (3) A theory with three key points (e.g., Freud's structural theory postulating that the mind is composed of the id, ego, and superego).

### triad training model
A paradigm used to help counselors improve their multicultural counseling skills. A counselor works with a client of a different culture. Then, an anticounselor illuminates the differences in their values and expectations. Lastly, a third member (hence the term "triad"), known as a procounselor, notes the similarities.

### triage
In a crisis or disaster situation, the act of sorting out those who can benefit most from immediate care while weeding out those who cannot.

### triangulation
In family therapy, the notion that when two people are experiencing discord, one may confide in a third party to secure that person as an ally (say a friend or a secretary), and this generally makes the problem worse.

### trichotillomania
The compulsion to pull out one's hair and in some cases eat the hair strands. The act of pulling one's hair is usually from the scalp; however, in some cases individuals will pull at other hair sites, such as the hair under their arms or their eyebrows. About 8 million individuals in the US suffer from this compulsive disorder.

### tricyclics
A popular class of drugs used to treat depression such as imipramine and amitriptyline.

### trimester
Used to describe whether a pregnant woman is in the first three months (first trimester), second three months (second trimester), or third three months (third trimester) of pregnancy.

### truancy
The act of missing school without permission.

### true experiment
An experiment utilizing random assignments to groups where the researcher can control the independent variable and a dependent variable measure is calculated. Hence, correlational research would not be considered true experimental research. When intact groups are used the term *quasi-experiment* is technically more appropriate.

**trust exercise**
Used in group settings to help the members rely and trust one another. The most popular trust exercise is performed by having a client fall into the arms of another group member (or members), who will catch the client.

**trust versus mistrust**
The first of Erik Erikson's eight psychosocial stages. In this stage (from birth to one year) the infant either develops optimism/trust (i.e., he or she can rely on the caretaker) or mistrust (i.e., he or she is taken care of poorly and cannot trust others).

**trustworthiness**
The client's perception that the helper is honest, will not mislead the client, and will not do any harm.

**T-score**
A transformed standard score using 50 as the mean and each standard deviation equals 10 (e.g., 2 standard deviations below the mean equals a T-score of 30, while 1 standard deviation above the mean equals a T-score of 60). T-scores are desirable since they eliminate negative integers.

***t*-test**
A statistical test used to determine if the means of two groups are significantly different. A researcher, for example, might wish to know whether a group of alcoholics who goes through a treatment program drinks significantly less than a group of alcoholics that does not receive the treatment.

**tumor**
*See cancer.*

**turf battles**
Refers to the conflicts between the various professional human service groups. For example, psychologists might not want counselors to administer certain personality tests, while the counselors might assert that psychologists should not be giving various career inventories. Psychologists and counselors might balk at the idea of social workers calling themselves therapists or counselors, while the social workers might take offense when the other professions are engaged in strict social work tasks. The current *turf battle* involves whether psychologists should be allowed to administer prescription drugs like psychiatrists.

**tutor**
An individual who helps another individual learn a subject. The term is usually used to describe someone who is helping an individual who is having difficulty in a class. Hence, a student who is having difficulty with math may see a math tutor for supplementary instruction between classes.

**twin study**
The use of twins to help determine what factors are influenced by heredity and what factors are determined by the environment.

**Type I (juvenile diabetes)**
*See diabetes mellitus (DM).*

**Type II diabetes**
*See diabetes mellitus (DM).*

**Type I error**
In statistics and research, rejecting the null hypothesis when true. Also called an *alpha error.*

**Type II error**
In statistics and research, accepting the null hypothesis when it is actually false. Also called a *beta error.*

**Type A personality**
According to cardiologists Meyer Friedman and Ray Rosenman, a person who is competitive, driven to succeed, very controlling, and is impatient. Early research indicated that such an individual is at greater risk for heart disease; nevertheless, current data seems to show that anger and hostility, rather than competitiveness are the culprits. *See Type B personality.*

**Type B personality**
According to cardiologists Meyer Friedman and Ray Rosenman, an easy-going, relaxed individual who is not very competitive. Not as likely to develop coronary heart disease as the Type A personality. *See Type A personality.*

**typescript**
A typewritten verbatim account of a session, meeting, or consultation; also called a *transcript.*

**UCR/UR**
*See unconditioned response (UCR/UR) and usual, customary, and reasonable (UCR).*

**UCS/US**
*See unconditioned stimulus (UCS/US).*

**umwelt**
In existential therapy, one's relationship to the natural, biological environment.

**unauthorized session/visit**
A session with a doctor or a mental health professional that has not been approved by a third-party payer such as a managed care company. In many cases if the provider does not receive the proper authorization (i.e., approval), then the provider will not be paid for the service.

**unbalancing**
A technique in which a family therapist allies himself or herself with an individual or a subsystem of the family. The strategy cajoles the rest of the family to act differently toward the individual or subsystem. Generally the therapist will support an underdog to change the hierarchical structure of the family.

**uncomplicated bereavement**
Normal grief after a death, loss, or abandonment that is not indicative of a mental disorder or pathological condition.

### unconditional positive regard (UPR)
In Carl R. Rogers person-centered therapy (also referred to as nondirective or client-centered therapy), the notion that total nonpossessive acceptance of the client is a necessary condition for efficacious helping. The acceptance is not conditional; that is to say, the helper accepts the client regardless of what the person says or does.

### unconditioned response (UCR/UR)
In classical conditioning theory (also known as *respondent* or *Pavlovian conditioning*), a response that naturally occurs when an unconditioned stimulus is presented without learning or conditioning trials. A dog will salivate (an unconditioned response), for example, when the animal smells meat (an unconditioned stimulus). In the literature, the process is often termed a *reflex* since it occurs automatically. *See Pavlov, Ivan.*

### unconditioned stimulus (UCS/US)
In classical conditioning theory (also known as *respondent* or *Pavlovian conditioning*), a stimulus that elicits an unlearned or so-called unconditioned response (UCR/UR). Meat or meat powder, for example, can cause a dog to salivate without conditioning or learning trials, thus it is acting as an unconditioned stimulus. In the literature, the process is often termed a "reflex," since it occurs automatically. *See Pavlov, Ivan.*

### unconscious
(1) The portion of the personality that is out of awareness. According to Freud's psychoanalytic theory, the unconscious houses repressed memories and id impulses. It is assumed to be the largest portion of the personality (i.e., larger than the conscious or preconscious). Most scholars agree that Freud's conceptualization of the unconscious mind was his greatest contribution. The unconscious cannot be directly observed, but is evident in parapraxes (i.e., slips of the tongue), dreams, posthypnotic suggestions, free associations, and projective measures. (2) A state void of conscious awareness such as when one faints, has a blackout due to alcohol intoxication, or is in a coma.

### unconscious motivation
A driving force unknown to the person. Thus, the individual does not truly understand why he or she wants to engage in a given act. Ego defense mechanisms, for example, are fueled via unconscious motivation.

**underachiever**
(1) A person who does not try hard enough or does not live up to his or her potential. (2) An individual whose performance is significantly below others who have the same aptitude.

**underclass**
(1) Families or individuals, generally living in an urban setting, who have been poor for a long period of time. (2) The lowest socioeconomic class that remains poor even when the economy is favorable.

**Underdog**
In gestalt therapy, the portion of the personality that wishes to fulfill instinctual needs. *See Topdog.*

**underemployment**
The act of taking a job which is below an individual's level of skill or training. A Ph.D. counselor, for example, who takes a job sweeping floors would exemplify this concept.

**underemployment neurosis**
Viktor Frankl's term indicating that an unemployed individual often thinks life has no meaning. Frankl feels that his existential logotherapy can help the person understand that the world does indeed have meaning despite this unfortunate situation.

**underground railroad**
Helping slaves escape to the Northern areas where slavery was illegal.

**understanding**
(1) Refers to a helper's ability to accurately comprehend the meaning of the client's verbal and nonverbal behavior. (2) Empathy.

**underworld**
Refers to organized crime such as the Mafia.

**undoing**
In psychoanalysis, an ego defense mechanism aimed at abating an earlier unacceptable behavior. This is a form of irrational, magical thinking often seen in obsessive-compulsive clients. The classical example would be an individual who feels terribly guilt-ridden over a given act and thus engages in repeated showers or hand washing.

**unemployment**
(1) Being out of work. (2) Being out of work when one wants a job and is capable of working.

**unfinished business**
(1) In gestalt counseling and therapy, the hypothesis that unexpressed feelings from past situations linger on and get in the way of effective present moment living and awareness. Expressing these emotions is seen as curative. (2) Any uncompleted task which is still causing concern, relationship difficulties, and/or stress.

**unfinished story technique**
The client is given an incomplete story and told to finish it via role playing, verbalizations, or writing. This is an expressive-projective technique.

**unfreezing**
The act of helping a client change long-standing beliefs, notions, attitudes, feelings, and perceptions that are counterproductive. The term has traditionally been used in relation to group counseling and therapy.

**unimodal**
In statistics, a distribution of scores characterized by a single mode or peak. Often contrasted with a *bimodal* distribution of scores, which will have two peaks when graphed, or a multimodal distribution, which has a number of peaks or high points. *See mode.*

**United Way Of America**
A national organization founded in 1918. Their 1400 independent community-based United Way Organizations help to raise funds for non-for-profit, tax exempt, social service agencies that are governed by volunteers. Agencies that receive United Way status must also submit to an annual independent financial audit, have a policy of nondiscrimination, and provide services at reasonable rates. United way refers to themselves "as the nation's leading community solutions provider."

**unipolar**
A major depression mood disorder. Can be contrasted with a bipolar disorder (e.g., manic-depression) in which there are two phases or poles.

**univariate**
In statistics and research, a study concerned with a single variable.

**universal eligibility**
Conveys the notion that all clients will receive the same services regardless of their income, possessions, or means.

**universality**
In group counseling and therapy, the client's discovery that others are experiencing similar problems and difficulties. Generally this is seen as therapeutic inasmuch as clients entering treatment often feel that they are the only one in the world with a given problem.

**universal program**
A social policy term. Refers to programs open to anybody who falls into a given category. Universal programs do not have needs, means, or income testing. Social Security, for example, is said to be a universal program since individuals can be recipients whether they need the income or not.

**unlearned behavior**
Behaviors that occur without training, conditioning, learning, or instruction. Can also be called *unconditioned behaviors* or *reflexes*. Innate, instinctual behaviors fall into this category.

**unlearning**
Refers to the process of trying to eliminate a previously learned behavior. Extinction and counterconditioning are procedures intended for this purpose.

**unlust**
A psychoanalytic term meaning pain, discomfort, or a lack of satisfaction. Synonymous with the term *unpleasure.*

**unprofessional behavior**
Actions on the part of a human service worker or other professional who violates ethical guidelines.

**unreliable measure/test**
A test or measurement instrument that does not give consistent results. A bathroom scale, for example, which registered 150 lbs. and 155 lbs. when weighing the same person would be unreliable. Tests with reliability coefficients below .90 are often considered unreliable.

**unspaced practice**
Also called *massed practice,* the term implies that one engages in an activity without breaks or rest periods. Often contrasted with *distributed practice* in which breaks or rest periods are utilized. In most instances (e.g., studying for a test) distributed practice is more effective.

**unstructured group**
(1) A group that has no set agenda. Many general counseling and therapy groups are unstructured in this sense. (2) A group that does not utilize structured group exercises, topics, or activities. Some experts take issue with this term, pointing out that a group cannot not have structure. They point out that structure versus a lack of structure occurs on a continuum and thus it should not be conceptualized as a dichotomous property of the group. *See structured exercise and structured group.*

**unstructured test**
Any projective or expressive measure which uses ambiguous stimuli (e.g., ink blots) and allow test takers to respond in any way they wish. Thus, a multipoint format using a multiple choice answer format would be considered structured rather than unstructured.

**upgrading jobs**
The act of moving to a higher- and/or better-paying job often in the same setting.

**uppers**
Slang for speed or amphetamines. These drugs heighten energy and alertness and have been abused for the purpose of weight control.

**urban**
A city or densely populated area.

**user**
Slang for a person who is chemically dependent and has used or is presently using drugs, including alcohol.

**user-friendly**
Counseling and helping materials, especially computer programs, which are easily understood, simple to use, and do not require extensive training.

**usual, customary, and reasonable (UCR)**
In physical and mental health treatment, the standard fee in a given area for a specific treatment or intervention. Insurance companies and managed care firms often look at data of this nature to determine payment rates. Thus, if a group therapist is charging $175 per hour and the UCR in that community is $60 per hour, then the charges would not be usual, customary, and reasonable.

**U-test**
Short for the *Mann-Whitney U-test.* A nonparametric statistical test used to determine whether a significant difference is present between two uncorrelated/unmatched means. Can be used in place of the *t* test for uncorrelated, unmatched independent means when parametric assumptions cannot be met. A Whitney Extension allows the test to be used with three sample groups. *See t test.*

**utilitarian marriage**
A couple who gets married and/or stays married for practical rather than emotional purposes. Often contrasted with the *intrinsic marriage,* which is based on emotional reasons such as intimacy and sex.

**utilization review**
An investigation and/or analysis of a treatment provider's services. The government and/or third-party payers often use utilization review to determine whether their money is being wisely spent on effective client services.

**vaccine**
A substance (e.g., a flu shot) that lowers the probability that an individual will get a certain disease. Vaccines can be controversial since some of them have side effects that can be as serious as the condition that the substance is intended to prevent.

**validity**
The extent that a test or assessment measures what it purports to measure. Validity is the most important property of a test. Validity is often contrasted with reliability, which refers to the test's propensity to give the same basic results again and again. *See content validity, construct validity, face validity, predictive validity, and reliability.*

**Valium**
A prescription benzodiazepine drug (its generic name is Diazepam) utilized as a tranquilizer for conditions such as anxiety and panic. Individuals can become addicted to this drug and withdrawal symptoms can occur when the medicine is discontinued.

**value conflict**
(1) Differences in values between people. (2) Different or contradictory values that cause conflict within the same individual.

**values**
The criteria one uses to make choices or take action.

**values clarification**
Any technique or exercise that helps the client become more aware of the role values play in his or her life.

**variability**
In statistics and research, a measure of the spread of scores from the mean. Examples include the range, the variance, and the standard deviation (SD).

**variable**
(1) A factor or attribute which is free to vary and can exist in at least two different numerical values. (2) A factor or attribute that can change.

**variable interval reinforcement**
In operant/instrumental conditioning, the act of reinforcing a target behavior after a time interval which varies. Often contrasted with *variable ratio reinforcement,* which is based on the number of correct responses. *See ratio schedule of reinforcement and intermittent reinforcement.*

**variable ratio reinforcement**
In operant/instrumental conditioning, the act of reinforcing a target behavior after a number of correct responses. The number will vary but will be based on an average number. Often contrasted with *variable interval reinforcement* based on time intervals. *See ratio schedule of reinforcement and intermittent reinforcement.*

**variance**
In statistics and research, a measure of the spread of scores computed by squaring the standard deviation (SD).

**variate**
In statistics and research, the value of a variable.

**vascular**
Anything having to do with blood vessels.

**vasoconstriction**
In biofeedback or medical settings, the ability to constrict or reduce the diameter of a blood vessel.

**vasodilation**
In biofeedback or medical settings, the ability to dilate or increase the diameter of a blood vessel.

**V Codes**
Categories listed in the American Psychiatric Association's *Diagnostic and Statistical Manual Of Mental Disorders (DSM-IV-TR)* that are not attributed to a mental disorder but for which treatment may be necessary. V Codes include relational problems (e.g., Partner Relational Problem), problems related to abuse or neglect (e.g., Sexual Abuse of Child), or additional conditions that may be a focus of clinical attention (e.g., Bereavement or Occupational Problem). Human service workers need to be aware that third-party payers such as insurance companies and managed care firms usually will not pay for treatment if a V Code is the only disorder.

**vegetative nervous system**
Older literature uses this term for the autonomic nervous system (ANS).

**vegotherapy**
A technique created by psychiatrist Wilhelm Reich to deal with character-amouring (inappropriate muscular rigidity) to restore orgiastic potency. Also called *the technique of character-analytic vegotherapy.* Reich's book *Function of the Orgasm* delineates his theory.

**vendor**
Refers to a counselor, agency, hospital, or other treatment provider who sells (i.e., a vendor is someone who sells) a therapeutic service or product (e.g., gambling addiction treatment or a relaxation tape).

**ventilate/ventilation**
To express feelings during a counseling or therapy session. Also known as "catharsis" or "abreaction." *See abreaction.*

**veracity**
In ethics, the notion that a helper will be truthful with clients.

**verbal IQ**
The Wechsler intelligence tests are divided into two scales, a verbal and a performance IQ. The verbal assesses intelligence via verbal feedback.

**verbalization**
To express oneself using words rather than actions.

**verbal reinforcement**
The act of using verbalizations (i.e., words, sentences) to reinforce a target behavior. *See reinforcement/reinforcer.*

**verbatim account**
An exact or word-for-word transcript or recording of the interview or counseling session. Ideally such an account will include nonverbal factors such as silence, body language, and tone of delivery.

**verification**
The process of testing an experimental or clinical hypothesis.

**vernacular**
In multicultural work, pertains to colloquial verbiage used by persons living in a given area.

**vertical career move**
The act of taking a job that is higher or lower in terms of salary and/or prestige. Often contrasted with a *horizontal career move,* which does not raise or lower one's salary and/or prestige.

**vertical intervention**
In group counseling, the act of working with an individual client within the group. Often contrasted with "group-as-whole" or "horizontal intervention" strategies.

**vertigo**
The sensation that the world is spinning around you; dizziness.

**vested interest**
When an individual or an organization has a personal interest in a decision or an outcome. A vested interest can often limit objectivity. Hence, if a computerized interview were proven superior to an intake worker's sessions, the intake worker might still oppose the agency going to computerized interviews.

**Veterans Administration (VA)**
A federal program that helps individuals who previously served in the military. VA hospitals provide a myriad of physical, mental, and social services. Other VA services include loans and insurance plans.

**VI**
Abbreviation for *variable interval reinforcement.*

**VIB**
Abbreviation for *vocational interest blank,* usually the Strong Interest Inventory (SSI). *See resources section of the text.*

**vicarious**
The act of substituting observation and/or imagination for behavior. A person receives gratification or negative feelings from the behavior of others. A coach, for example, might experience gratification when his athletes perform well. Codependents often rely on vicarious experiences. *See vicarious conditioning/learning and vicarious reinforcement.*

**vicarious conditioning/learning**
A type of learning that occurs when an individual observes someone else's behavior (i.e., a social role model) and notes the consequences. When it is used therapeutically, some of the literature refers to this process as *spectator counseling/therapy* or *vicarious counseling/therapy.* If the status of the model is high, the likelihood that the individual will imitate the behavior increases. Observational learning of this nature can take place even if the individual observing a model is not reinforced. A popular behavior modification term. The process is often referred to as *Bandura's social learning theory* and models or symbolic models are often used to act out the desired behaviors. *See vicarious and vicarious reinforcement.*

**vicarious counseling/therapy**
*See vicarious conditioning/learning.*

**vicarious liability**
In ethics, the notion that a supervisor may be ethically or legally responsible for a supervisee's actions.

**vicarious reinforcement**
This is a social learning/behavior modification term that has a number of accepted meanings. (1) An individual sees another individual being reinforced for a given behavior and then models/imitates the behavior. (2) Receiving reinforcement via the act of observing another individual being reinforced. (3) An individual has been reinforced for imitating a model's behavior in the past and thus continues to imitate behavior. *See vicarious and vicarious conditioning/learning.*

**vice squad**
A law enforcement unit that focuses on crimes related to gambling, illegal drug sales, prostitution, and pornography.

**victim compensation**
When a person is the victim of crime he or she is often entitled to services (e.g., counseling) or financial payments. Most individuals are unaware of this fact. Victim service agencies have been very useful in informing clients of this fact and helping them receive the benefits they to which they are entitled.

**victimless crime**
A crime such as gambling that does not harm another individual.

**victimology**
A fairly recent term for the study of individuals who have been the victims of crime or have otherwise been harmed.

**victim role**
An individual who blames others for his or her difficulties. Can also describe a person who others often take advantage of.

**video counseling/therapy**
Using a video system to give a client objective feedback (e.g., a counselor might videotape a couple trying to solve a marital difficulty). A video can also be used to help the client model appropriate behavior. This technique is popular with assertiveness trainers and counselors who favor a behavioristic model of intervention.

**video feedback training**
A human service worker, practicum student, or classroom student is videotaped with an actual client or in a role play situation and then the video is played by to secure feedback from the class members, supervisor, or instructor.

**Viennese School**
In older literature, a helper who adheres to Freudian psychoanalytic principles. Generally a Freudian analyst.

**vigilante**
An individual who takes the law into his or her own hands. An individual may feel that a criminal should have been convicted and was not, and therefore decides to punish or harm the criminal in some manner.

**virile**
To have masculine qualities. Loosely used to refer to a man's potency.

**visitation**
This term is used when a parent or caretaker loses custody and the court legally stipulates when, where, and how long visits with the child can occur. The term is commonly used in foster care cases.

**visual cliff**
In child development, a device used to test for depth perception. The infant crawls along a glass apparatus that appears to fall off at a given point. If the infant stops at the beginning of the cliff, which is actually an illusion, then depth perception is evident.

**vitamin therapy**
*See orthomolecular psychiatry.*

**vocabulary subtest**
On the Wechsler IQ tests, the vocabulary subtest is often considered the finest single predictor of school performance.

**vocation**
(1) An occupation. (2) A number of jobs in a given field or area.

**vocational counseling/guidance**
Also referred to as "career counseling" or "career guidance." A set of interventions that help individuals to address one or more of the following issues: finding appropriate employment; explore lifestyle and leisure concerns; conduct a job search or interview; match qualifications to suitable lines of work; manage one's own career development; adjust to a new job; assist with job relocation; improve social skills related to work or job search activities; use career testing data, occupational resource guides, and computer programs; and focus on psychological, emotional, family, and economic issues related to one's career.

**vocational maturity**
One's level of maturity in relation to a job, career, or occupational situation. Making responsible career choices based on accurate information about jobs as well as one's own skills, knowledge, experience, and feelings. Vocational maturity, also called *career maturity,* is stressed in Donald Super's model of career development.

**volition**
Purposely or willfully behaving or attempting to behave in a given manner. Also called *active volition* in some of the literature.

**voluntary**
A movement or act that is consciously enacted or caused via the central nervous system. Can be contrasted with acts that occur unconsciously or via the autonomic nervous system. Current research shows, nevertheless, that autonomic nervous system functions can be brought under voluntary control. *See biofeedback.*

**voluntary admission/treatment**
An individual who willingly admits himself/herself to a hospital or facility or who engages in treatment by choice.

**voluntary stable singles**
Persons who have always been single or who have been divorced yet do not intend to marry, including priests and nuns.

**voluntary temporary singles**
Persons who never married or divorced individuals or who are postponing marriage or remarriage. Such individuals often emphasize another area of their lives, such as a career, that might not lend itself to marriage.

**volunteer**
A helper who offers services to an agency, practice, or treatment facility free of charge.

**volunteer bias**
The notion that individuals who volunteer for experimental research are not representative of the population at large due to their high level of cooperation. This would thus suggest that the results will be skewed.

**von Restorff effect**
Items that "stand out" or appear "distinct" are better learned and easier to remember.

**voucher**
A stamp or a coupon that can be redeemed for a good or a service. For example, a food stamp voucher could be taken to a store to purchase food and related items allowed via the food stamp program. Recently, more and more programs have turned to electronic benefit transfer cards (EBT) to reduce the fraud associated with voucher systems.

**voyeurism**
The act of looking at others (e.g., who are undressed or engaging in sexual acts) to gain sexual satisfaction. Voyeurs are sometimes referred to as *Peeping Toms.*

**VR**
Abbreviation for *variable reinforcement* or *vocational rehabilitation.*

**vulnerable**
Someone who is likely to succumb to a physical or emotional difficulty. *See at-risk.*

**wage control**
Any policy that regulates the salary workers are paid.

**WAIS-R**
*See Wechsler Adult Intelligence Scale–Revised.*

*Walden Two*
A novel written by B. F. Skinner about a utopian society that operated on the principles of operant conditioning (i.e., behavior modification).

**War on Poverty**
*See Great Society.*

**warm up**
Refers to "get acquainted" exercises used in the initial stage of group counseling or therapy which help members feel more comfortable and less anxious. In individual treatment the term describes helper/helpee conversation unrelated to the presenting problem (e.g., the weather or a client's hobby).

**washout**
In gambling addiction treatment, the notion that a client broke even (i.e., didn't make any money gambling and also didn't lose any money).

**Watson, John Broadus (1878–1958)**
The American psychologist who founded *behaviorism*. He coined the term behaviorism in 1912. Watson believed that conditioning (i.e., learning) molded the individual. His feeling was that, "men are built, not born," and thus a young child could be trained to behave in any manner. He is famous for his so-called Little Albert experiment in which he and Rosalie Rayner conditioned an eleven month old (Albert B.) to fear a white rat, cotton, a rabbit, fur coats, and a Santa Claus mask. The experiment was intended to show that phobic behavior is merely the product of learning. There is no need for a psychodynamic interpretation of the unconscious mind. Although Watson proposed a strategy to ameliorate the experimentally induced phobia, the child was released from the hospital before it could be implemented. Watson ultimately left academia for a career in advertising.

**wave frequency**
In biofeedback, the number of waves present in a specific period of time expressed in cycles per second (CPS) or Hertz (Hz). *See biofeedback.*

**waxy flexibility**
Sometimes referred to as *catalepsy*, the term is intended to describe a state in which the client stays in a motionless body position. The symptom is manifested in catatonic schizophrenia.

**weak family**
Describes a family that feels they have little control over their destiny. When a family member in a weak family is experiencing difficulty coping he or she will not turn to other family members for support and will even avoid other members of the family.

**weaning**
(1) In human growth and development, the process of reducing and ultimately not consuming mother's milk. (2) Breaking one's dependence on a parent, addictive substance, therapist, or dysfunctional behavior.

**Web counseling**
*See Internet counseling.*

**Wechsler Adult Intelligence Scale–Revised (WAIS-R)**
A very popular individually administered adult intelligence test (named after it's creator, David Wechsler) that yields a verbal IQ, a performance IQ, and a full scale IQ. Initially this test was called the Wechsler-Bellvue

Scale. The average (i.e., the mean) IQ on this test is 100 with a standard deviation of 15. The test is intended for persons 16 and older.

**Wechsler Intelligence Scale for Children–Third Edition (WISC-III)**
An individually administered intelligence test for children ages 6 to 16 years, 11 months created by David Wechsler. The test yields a verbal IQ, a performance IQ, and a full scale IQ.

**Wechsler Preschool and Primary Scale of Intelligence–Revised (WPPSI-R)**
An individually administered intelligence test for children ages 3 to 7 years, 3 months.

**weekend hospital program**
Refers to programs where the client or patient only goes to the hospital on weekends.

**welfare**
Used to describe public assistance programs such as Aid To Families With Dependent Children (AFDC) or Temporary Assistance (TA)/Temporary Assistance to Needy Families (TANF) that help serve the poor. *See TA and TANF.*

**welfare reform**
Programs to change the welfare system with the ultimate goal of reducing the number of individuals receiving public assistance while helping them to become self sufficient. Recent welfare reform programs have limited the time individuals can secure public assistance and/or stipulated that recipients can only receive assistance for a limited number of children. Training programs to help welfare recipients become employed have been utilized.

**Welfare to work**
*See TANF.*

**wellness**
Conveys the notion that individuals can take charge of their own physical and emotional health by learning and practicing preventive measures (e.g., healthy eating, exercising, and stress-reduction techniques). Often contrasted with the medical model, this approach is seen as antideterministic.

**Weltanschauung**
German for *world view.*

**Wernicke-Korsakoff syndrome**
Nervous system dysfunction due to a vitamin B-1 deficiency (i.e., Thiamine) that occurs in chronic alcoholism, which depletes this vitamin. The syndrome is characterized primarily by a deterioration in one's memory.

**"what if" strategies**
Any technique that urges the client to project or fantasize about the future. In cognitive therapies it is especially desirable to help clients catastrophize or awfulize. The counselor might say: "What if you did lose your job and also flunked out of school?" Such interventions can also help clients who are afraid to behave in a novel manner (e.g., "What if you did ask your boss for a raise?").

**whistle-blowing**
Occurs when someone in authority is informed about an illegal, unethical, or wasteful act. Thus, a caseworker might report to his supervisor that other caseworkers are not really making mandated home visits to clients' houses, yet they are reporting that they had been doing so in their agency records.

**WHO**
*See World Health Organization.*

**why questions**
Questions used when interviewing or counseling a client. Why questions are intended to elicit information about the reason, purpose, or cause of a behavior or a situation. For example, a human service worker might ask, "Why are you afraid to apply for food stamps?" Since why questions can abet defensiveness, many helpers prefer what questions.

**WIC**
*See Women, Infants, and Children Program.*

**widow**
A women whose husband has died and she has not remarried.

**widower**
A man whose wife has died and he has not remarried.

**willful**
A behavior, feeling, and/or thought that an individual purposely does or does not engage in.

**willpower**
Self-control.

**will to power**
Alfred Adler's term for the striving for superiority and domination over others.

**wired**
Slang for someone under the influence of a drug.

**WISC-III**
*See Wechsler Intelligence Scale for Children–Third Edition.*

**wish fulfillment**
A psychoanalytic concept which suggests that we reduce psychic tension of id impulses via dreams, parapraxes (slips of the tongue), and neurotic symptoms.

**Whitmer, Lightner (1867–1956)**
Student of Wilhem Wundt; founded the first psychology clinic in 1896.

**withdrawal**
A tendency to isolate one's self from others or society.

**withdrawal syndrome**
Used to describe the physical and emotional impact of discontinuing an addictive substance or behavior.

**Women, Infants, and Children Program (WIC)**
A U.S. Department of Agriculture program that began in 1972 in order to provide healthy food to low-income pregnant women, women who are breastfeeding, and children up to age five who are deemed to be at nutritional risk. Research indicates that the WIC program is effective. Participation in WIC is associated with a decrease in infant mortality and improved IQ, visual motors skills, and school performance.

**word association**
A projective/expressive technique created by Carl Jung in which a client is given a word and asked to reveal the first word that comes to mind. The strategy is intended to elicit unconscious material.

**word salad**
A chain of words that do not have meaning. This pattern of communication sometimes occurs in persons with schizophrenia.

**workfare**
Any program that requires the welfare recipient (e.g., AFDC or TA) to secure employment or training in order to receive benefits. Sometimes known as *welfare to work.*

**Work Incentive Program (WIN)**
A federal program that encouraged public assistance recipients to receive training and go to work.

**working class**
A social class comprised of blue-collar families who are not wealthy, yet they have steady jobs and thus retain their social status.

**working hypothesis**
A guess concerning a given hypothesis before it is scientifically tested.

**working poor**
Individuals who are employed but still earn less than the poverty level.

**working stage**
In group work the third stage (i.e., after the initial stage and the resistance or transition stage) in which the group is cohesive, works together, and is very productive.

**working through**
(1) A psychoanalytic concept which suggests that a client can learn to cope with current difficulties by exploring and analyzing problems from the past as well as noting the transference relationship with the counselor. Ultimately, the unconscious significance of the behavior is discovered. (2) The process of discussing difficulties to gain insight and improve coping skills. Working through problems is roughly the opposite of ignoring them or denying their existence.

**work participation rates**
The percentage of individuals on public assistance that are required to be participating in the workforce under TANF guidelines. *See TA and TANF.*

340

**workplace**
The actual building or environment where the person carries out his or her job duties.

**work psychology**
A term sometimes used in place of the term *industrial/organizational psychology.*

**work release**
When an individual who is incarcerated or in a half-way house is allowed to leave the facility to engage in paid employment.

**work samples tests**
Refers to the use of actual work procedures to test one's level of skill in a given job.

**workshop**
A training session related to a human service topic led by an individual with expertise in the area of study.

**Works Progress Administration/Works Projects Administration (WPA)**
A New Deal program created in 1935. Many individuals were still out of work from the great economic depression of 1929 and the WPA literally created jobs for millions. The program ended in 1943.

**work up**
The use of testing and/or interviewing to acquire information to diagnose a client.

**World Health Organization (WHO)**
Created in 1948 by the United Nations, WHO produces a disease classification guide (*The International Classification of Diseases/ICD*). A diagnosis from this guide is generally required for third-party payment of physicians, dentists, and licensed social service/ mental health providers such as psychologists and counselors.

**world view**
One's personal philosophy or understanding of life.

**worthy poor**
Describes individuals who truly deserve assistance due to their disability or unfavorable circumstances. Although the term was once popular, it is rarely used in current literature.

## WPPSI-R
*See Wechsler Preschool and Primary Scale of Intelligence–Revised.*

### Wundt, Wilhelm (1832–1920)
Created the first psychology laboratory in 1879 at the University of Liepiz, Germany. Wundt felt that psychology could be accepted as a legitimate science if consciousness could be measured. In America, E. B. Tichner, a student of Wundt's, opened an experimental psychology laboratory at Cornell University and this approach came to be known as *structuralism*. Structuralism emphasized the measurement of mental elements using self-reports given by subjects.

**X**
(1) The experimental variable. Can also signify a raw score. (2) The mean also known as the arithmetic average. *See mean.*

**$x$ axis**
The horizontal reference line on a graph often used to plot the independent/experimental variable. Also known as the *abscissa* or the *$x$ coordinate*.

**xenophobia**
An intense, morbid, or exaggerated fear of strangers.

**Y**
The dependent/outcome variable in an experiment.

**Yalom, Irvin D. (1931–)**
A professor of psychiatry at the Stanford University School of Medicine. He is primarily known for his work as an existential therapist who was influential in the group counseling and psychotherapy movement. He is the author of *The Theory and Practice of Group Psychotherapy,* and *Inpatient Group Psychotherapy.* Both are classic texts used to teach group intervention. He is also the author of *Love's Executioner and Other Tales of Psychotherapy,* that depicts some of his most interesting psychotherapeutic encounters.

**yantra**
A visual pattern that one concentrates on in meditation such as a light or a candle.

**YAVIS**
A young, attractive, verbal, intelligent sexy (or successful) client.

**y axis**
The vertical reference line on a graph often used to plot the dependent variable. The y axis is also called the *ordinate* or the *y coordinate* or the *y value.*

**yellow jackets**
A street name for barbiturates, especially Nembutal.

**Yerkes-Dodson law**
Asserts that while very high levels of arousal and stress can deteriorate performance, a moderate amount leads to optimal performance. Hence, a minute degree of test anxiety might actually improve a student's performance on an exam. As the exam became more difficult, the level of arousal for optimal performance would decrease. It is also important to note that the optimal level of arousal is different for every person.

**York retreat**
One of the first mental hospitals opened in 1792 in York, England, by the Quakers.

**young adult**
Persons 20 to 40 years of age.

**young old**
Persons 65 to 74 years of age. Often contrasted with middle old (75–84) and oldest old (85 and over).

**yuppies**
Slang term for young urban professionals.

### Zeigarnik effect
Named after Bluma Zeigarnik, who discovered in 1927 that unfinished tasks are recalled better than finished tasks if the subject is motivated to complete the task or concerned about the outcome.

### zeitgeist
In German the word literally means *the spirit of the times*. In human services the term is intended to describe the overall social climate (e.g., sociological, political, economic, philosophical, etc.) that characterizes a given era. It is assumed that the Zeitgeist affects each individual's behavioral and emotional responses. Hence, each historical era has a unique impact.

### Zen Buddhism meditation
A form of meditation which purportedly allows the person to transcend rational thought in order to reach an enlightened state of mind known as *satori*.

### zero population growth
Occurs when the number of births is equal to the number of deaths.

### zero-sum approach
The notion that a gain for one individual will result in a loss for another individual, therefore some people will always have more than others.

### Zeus script
In transactional analysis, Greek myths often provide examples of typical life themes. Eric Berne, the father of this model felt that myths explain personal-

ity prototypes. Zeus was the "father of the gods" and punished Atlas to carry the weight of the heavens on his shoulders. Individuals with Zeus scripts set rules, use threats, and have persecutor personality tendencies.

### Zionism
The movement to preserve Israel.

### Zoloft
A popular antidepressant medicine prescribed for clinically depressed individuals.

### zombie
Slang for an individual who uses a lot of drugs.

### zoning
When a city, state, or nation stipulates who can use a given plot of land or address. Thus, an area that is zoned strictly as residential would not permit an agency to operate there.

### zooerasty
To engage in sexual intercourse with an animal.

### zoophobia
An exaggerated fear of animals.

### Z-score
A standard score that expresses the number of standard deviations that a raw score is from the mean. Thus, numerically, Z-scores are the same as standard deviations (e.g., 3½ standard deviations below the mean is a Z-score of $-3.5$). Z-scores always sport a mean of zero and a standard deviation of one and can be positive or negative. Some texts refer to a Z-score as a *standard score* or a *sigma score.*

### Zurich school
Refers to practitioners who use Carl Jung's school of analytic psychology, which was created in Zurich, Switzerland. Helpers who use this model are also called *Jungians.*

### zygosity
In twin studies, refers to whether the children are monozygotic identical twins (from a single ovum) or dizygotic fraternal twins (from two ova).

### zygote
The cell (i.e., ovum) formed by a sperm and an egg.

# RESOURCES

This chapter lists resources frequently used by human services workers. The first list is of statistical tests used in counseling research. Parametric and nonparametric tests are listed alphabetically. Explanations of each test are in brief summary form. For a more complete explanation, please refer to a statistics book.

The second list consists of major psychoeducational diagnostic tools. These are listed alphabetically. In each brief explanation is the kind of instrument, the age range (in most cases), and the general construct of each. The manual for the specific diagnostic tool and/or a comprehensive psychological testing text would be excellent references for more information.

Each professional group of mental health practitioners has a code of ethics. These codes are reviewed regularly and updated frequently. Therefore, each professional needs to keep abreast of the ethical codes applicable to him or her. The third list in this chapter provides the names and addresses of major organizations that provide ethical guidelines as well as other pertinent information.

Finally, a list of popular prescription medicines for psychiatric conditions, natural remedies for mental health, and common prescription medicines for general medical conditions are included as a quick reference source.

## STATISTICAL TESTS USED IN RESEARCH

### Parametric Tests

**Analysis of Covariance (ANCOVA or ANACOVA)** An extension of the ANOVA that controls the impact that one or more extraneous/unstudied variables (covariates) exert on the dependent variable.

**Analysis of Variance (ANOVA)** Also called a *one-way analysis of variance*, this test is used to determine whether two or more mean scores differ significantly from each other. The ANOVA examines a null hypothesis between two or more groups.

**Factorial Analysis of Variance** Used to describe an ANOVA that is used to compare two or more independent variables. When two independent variables are utilized, the term *two-way ANOVA* is used; with three independent variables, the term *three-way ANOVA* is used; and so on.

**Multivariate Analysis of Variance (MANOVA)** Used to describe an ANOVA when a researcher examines more than one dependent variable.

**Pearson Product-Moment Correlation (r)** Used with interval and ratio data, this statistic examines the direction and magnitude of two variables. Correlation describes a relationship or association between variables. When relying on correlational research, variables are merely measured, not manipulated by the researcher.

**Phi-Coefficient/Tetrachoric Correlation Coefficient** Used to assess correlation when both variables are dichotomous (i.e., binary or two-valued). Also known as a *fourfold-point correlation.*

**Point Bi-Serial/Bi-Serial Correlation** Used when one variable is continuous and the other is dichotomous (i.e., placed in two classes), for example correlating IQ with sex.

**Scheffe's S Test/Newman-Keuls/Tukey's HSD/Duncan's New Multiple Range Test** Used after a researcher discovers a significant $F$ ratio in an ANOVA to test the differences between specific group means or combinations of group means. Such measures are known as *a posteriori tests* or *post-hoc tests* for the ANOVA.

*t* **test.** Used to ascertain whether two means or correlation coefficients differ significantly from each other. The $t$ test procedures can be employed for correlated/related/matched samples and for uncorrelated/independent/unmatched samples. The $t$ test is used also to determine whether a single sample or correlation coefficient differs significantly from a population mean.

# Nonparametric Tests

**Chi-Square Test** Used to assess whether an obtained distribution is significantly different from an expected or theoretical distribution.

**Kruskal-Wallis Test** Used as a nonparametric one-way analysis of variance. The Kruskal-Wallis statistic is called $H$; hence researchers sometimes refer to it as the $H$ Test.

**Mann-Whitney U-Test** Used to test whether a significant difference is present between two uncorrelated/unmatched means. Can be used in place of the $t$ test for uncorrelated/independent/unmatched means when parametric assumptions cannot be met. A "Whitney Extension" allows the test to be used with three samples.

**Spearman Rank-Order Correlation (rho)/Kendall's tau** Used in place of the Pearson correlation coefficient when parametric assumptions can't be met (i.e., ordinal data are involved).

**Wilcoxon Matched-Pairs/Signed-Ranks Test** Used to determine whether two correlated means are significantly different. Can be utilized in place of the related sample's *t* test when parametric assumptions cannot be met.

## MAJOR PSYCHOEDUCATIONAL DIAGNOSTIC TOOLS

### Contributed by Peggy Grotpeter, M.Ed., Arthur C. Myers, Ed.D., and Howard G. Rosenthal, Ed.D.

**Bayley Scales of Infant Development (BSID-II)** A test that evaluates children from 1 month to 42 months. Test items measure responses to visual and auditory stimuli, manipulation, play with objects, and discrimination of sounds and shapes. The test is comprised of a Mental Scale, a Motor Scale, and a Behavior Rating Scale.

**Beery Developmental Test of Visual-Motor Integration (Beery VMI)** A test consisting of geometric shapes that the person reproduces. The test, which takes about 20 minutes to administer, measures visual perception and eye/hand coordination to identify difficulties which may lead to learning and behavior problems.

**Bender-Gestalt Test of Visual-Motor Integration (Bender)** An expressive test with no time limit consisting of nine stimulus cards with geometric figures that the person copies. It assesses visual perception and perceptual motor integration. It can be used also to detect the presence of underlying emotional difficulties, brain damage, and memory. Suitable for ages 3 or 4 and beyond. When a client rotates a figure in his or her copy then organicity (i.e., a neurological difficulty) may be present.

**California Psychological Inventory (CPI)** A test intended for reasonably well-adjusted individuals that focuses on the assessment of personality characteristics that are important for social living and interaction. It has been used with ages 12 and older. The inventory relies on 434 test items that yield 20 scales of individual differences.

**Career Decision Scale (CDS)** This is a 19-item, self-reporting measure suitable for high-school and college-aged students. It can be used in both individual and group settings.

**Children's Apperception Test (CAT)** A downward extension of the TAT that is utilized with children ages 3 to 10. It consists of 10 picture cards depicting animals in various situations that a trained examiner uses to reveal dominant drives, emotions, sentiments, and personality characteristics.

**Comprehensive Test of Nonverbal Intelligence (CTONI)** A language-free measure of intelligence and reasoning. It consists of 50 abstract symbols in patterns with a variety of problem-solving tasks presented. The tasks increase in difficulty. The administration does not require reading, writing, listening, or speaking on the part of the individual evaluated. The test is suitable for those 6 and over and takes about 1 hour to administer. The CTONI-CA version is computer administered.

**Draw-A-Person Test (DAP)** A norm-referenced projective/expressive test in which the person is asked to draw human figures. It is a nonverbal measure of intellectual ability and can be used as a projective measure of personality. Suitable for ages 3 to 16.

**General Aptitude Test Battery (GATB)** A multiaptitude test battery consisting of 12 tests developed specifically for vocational counseling in schools and job placement settings. The test focuses on in-depth measurements of aptitude and skills that relate to potential occupational success. The test takes about 2½ hours to administer and is designed for use with students in grades 9 through 12 as well as with adults.

**Guilford-Zimmerman Temperament Survey (GZTS)** This inventory is designed to be used with normally functioning individuals. It was initially developed to assess Carl Jung's constructs of introversion and extroversion. It can be used in a variety of settings, but it has been used most frequently with the college-aged population.

**Halstead-Reitan Neuropsychology Battery** This test is used not only to diagnose neuropsychological dysfunction but to establish a baseline of function against which to measure future functioning. It consists of three batteries, one for children ages 5 to 8, one for children ages 9 to 14, and one for adults. Each battery includes a minimum of 14 separate tests which are scored as 26 variables.

**Holtzman Inkblot Technique (HIT)** Initially developed in an attempt to improve the reliability of the Rorschach Test. There are two parallel forms (A and B), each consisting of 45 inkblot cards. There are two practice blot cards that are identical for each test. The client is encouraged to give only one response for each card. Parallel forms allow for test-retest reliability. Suitable for ages 5 through adult.

**House-Tree-Person (HTP)** A projective/expressive drawing test that provides the examiner with information pertaining to intrapersonal, interpersonal, and environmental adjustment of the individual evaluated.

**Kinetic Family Drawing (KFD)** This instrument is a supplement to the DAP in which the person is asked to draw everyone in his/her family doing an activity. It is used as a projective measure of personality to assess the individual's perception of themselves as well as their family.

**Kuder Career Inventory** An interest inventory that makes the assumption that a person will find satisfaction in an occupation where workers have similar interest patterns. This is a 100-triad inventory in which the respondent must choose between three activities, stating the one activity preferred the most and the one activity preferred the least. It takes approximately 12 minutes to complete and can be taken and scored online.

**Kuder Occupation Interest Survey (KOIS)** An interest survey that makes the assumption that a person will find satisfaction in an occupation where workers have similar interest patterns. It takes about 30 minutes to complete and must be scored by computer. Primarily suited to those in the tenth grade and beyond.

**Leiter International Performance Scale (LIPS)** A completely nonverbal measure of intelligence used with individuals from age 2 to adult. It is most often used to evaluate individuals who are deaf, nonverbal, non-English-speaking, culturally deprived, or have severe medical complications. The test consists of 54 subtests that increase in difficulty at each age level.

**Minnesota Multiphasic, Personality Inventory (MMPI-2)** A test that was designed to assess some major personality characteristics that affect personal and social adjustments. It contains 567 true/false statements covering a range of subject matter including physical conditions, moral attitudes, and social attitudes. The test is individually administered and is suitable for persons 18 years of age who have completed at least up to the sixth grade in terms of years of schooling.

**Myers-Briggs Type Indicator (MBTI)** A widely used measure of personality disposition and preferences that utilizes 166 items. It is based on Carl Jung's theory of perception and judgment. Four bipolar scales are used, resulting in 16 individual personality types, each of which are given a four-letter code used for interpreting personality type. It is suitable for use with upper elementary-aged children as well as adults.

**Otis-Lennon School Ability Test (OLSAT-7)** A group-administered multilevel mental ability battery designed for use in grades K through 12. The tests results are often used to predict success in school. It takes about 60 to 75 minutes to administer.

**Peabody Individual Achievement Test (PIAT)** This test is designed to measure the level of educational achievement in the areas of basic skills and knowledge. It does not require written responses and can be used with individuals from K (kindergarten) through adult.

**Piers-Harris Children's Self Concept Scale (PHCSCS)** This is an 80-item scale that provides a self-descriptive scale entitled, "The Way I Feel About Myself." This test yields a self-concept score as well as six subscores. It takes just 15 minutes to administer and can be used for ages 8 to 18.

**Portage Guide to Early Education Checklist** A developmentally-sequenced, criterion-referenced checklist used as a measure with infants, children, and developmentally disabled individuals with functional age levels from birth to 5 years. It is used to measure skills in the cognitive, language, self-help, motor, and socialization areas.

**Rorschach Inkblot Test** A projective test that utilizes 10 6⅝ by 9½ inch cards. Five of the cards are grey or black, and five are colored. The examinee is asked to describe what he or she sees or what the card brings to mind. The test is appropriate for ages 3 and up.

**Rotter Incomplete Sentence Blanks (RISB)** A projective method of evaluating personality. The person is asked to complete 40 sentences for which the first word or words is/are provided. It is assumed the individual reflects his or her own wishes, desires, and fears.

**Self-Directed Search (SDS)** A self-administered career interest assessment that is available in several forms, which addresses the needs of a variety of clients, both students and professionals. It is a self-scoring instrument that can be completed and scored in approximately 35 to 45 minutes.

**16 Personality Factor Questionnaire (16 PF)** An 187-item, normal adult personality measure that can be administered to individuals age 16 and above.

**Slosson Intelligence Test (SIT-R)** A verbally administered measure of intelligence utilized to gain a quick estimate of intellectual ability. This test can be utilized from ages 4 to 65 with a test time of approximately 10 to 20 minutes.

**Stanford-Binet Intelligence Scale (4th ed.)** A 45–90 minute intelligence test designed to measure cognitive ability as well as provide analysis of the pattern of an individual's cognitive development. A fifth edition is in the works.

**Stanford-Binet Intelligence Scale (form L-M)** The best test for ferreting out children above the ninety-ninth percentile. Since it has a higher ceiling than the Wechsler or the Binet listed above, it is the best test for the extremely gifted. An age scale using standards of performance to measure intelligence regarded as general mental adaptability.

**Strong Interest Inventory (SII)** This career inventory is based on the career theory of John Holland and can be used with anyone who can comprehend the test items, that is, most people over age 16. The SII compares a person's interests with those of persons who have been in their occupation for at least 3 years and state that they enjoy their work. The test consists of 325 items and can be completed in approximately 35 minutes.

**Thematic Apperception Test (TAT)** A projective test consisting of a pool of 30 picture cards (and one blank card) for which the individual is asked to make up emotions, sentiments, complexes, and conflicts of the individual's personality. Generally, a full TAT consists of 19 picture cards and one blank card.

If more than 10 cards are used, then it is appropriate to have test sessions on different days. It is suitable for age 4 and older.

**Vineland Adaptive Behavior Scale (VABS)** This is a survey form that assesses the individual's personal and social sufficiency. This instrument measures adaptive behavior from birth to adulthood.

**Wechsler Adult Intelligence Scale–Revised (WAIS–III)** This is the most popular adult intelligence test in the world. It is comprised of verbal and nonverbal scales designed to measure intellectual functioning of adolescents and adults based on a capacity to understand and cope with the world. The test takes 60 to 90 minutes to give and can be used for ages 16 to 89.

**Wechsler Intelligence Scale for Children (WISC–III)** An individual test comprised of verbal and nonverbal scales designed to measure intellectual functioning of children based on capacity to understand and cope with the world. Appropriate for ages 6 to 16 years, 11 months. The test takes approximately 50 to 70 minutes.

**Wechsler Preschool and Primary Scale of Intelligence–Revised (WPPSI–R)** A test comprised of verbal and nonverbal scales designed to measure intellectual functioning of young children based on capacity to understand and cope with the world. Appropriate for ages 3 to 7 years, 3 months and takes about an hour and a half to administer.

**Wide Range Achievement Test–Revised (WRAT–3)** An instrument used to measure reading, spelling, and arithmetic skills. Often utilized for a quick estimate of academic achievement. Suitable for ages 5 to 75 and can be administered in just 15 to 30 minutes.

## SOURCES FOR OBTAINING ETHICAL GUIDELINES

**Counselors** can secure *ACA Ethical Standards* from the American Counseling Association, 5999 Stevenson Avenue, Alexandria, Virginia 22304– 3300. Phone: (703) 823–9800 or (800) 347–6647. www.counseling.org

**Human Service Workers** can secure *Ethical Standards of Human Service Professionals* by contacting Naomi Wipert, 5326 Avery Road, New Port Richey, FL 34652. Phone (813) 929–2363. www.nohse.org. College and university programs wishing certification may contact the **Council For Standards in Human Service Education** at www.cshse.org. The **National Human Services Honor Society, Alpha Delta Omega** can be contacted at 118 Birchwood Lane, Mocksville, NC 27028. Phone: (336) 751–1970.

**Marriage and Family Therapists** can secure the *AAMFT Code of Ethics* from the American Association for Marriage and Family Therapy, 1133 15th Street, NW, Suite 300, Washington, DC 20005–2710. Phone: (202) 452–0109. www.aamft.org

**National Certified Counselors** can secure the *NBCC Code of Ethics* from the National Board for Certified Counselors, 3 Terrace Way, Dept. D, Greensboro, NC 27403. Phone: (336) 547–0607. www.nbcc.org

**Psychiatrists** can secure *Principles of Medical Ethics, with Annotations Especially Applicable to Psychiatry* from the American Psychiatric Association, 1400 K Street, NW, Washington, DC 20005. Phone: (888) 357–7924. www.psych.org

**Psychoanalysts** can secure the *Code of Ethics* from the American Psychoanalytic Association, 309 East 49th Street, New York, NY 10017. (212) 752–0450 www.apsa.org

**Psychologists** can secure *Ethical Principles of Psychologists* from the American Psychological Association, 750 First St. NE, Washington, DC 20002. Phone: (202) 336–5500 or (800) 374–2721. www.apa.org

**Social Workers** can secure the *NASW Code of Ethics* from the National Association of Social Workers, 750 First Street, NE, Washington, DC 20002 Phone: (202) 408–8600 or (800) 638–8799. www.naswdc.org

**Sociologists** can secure the *Ethical Standards of Sociological Practitioners* from the Sociological Practice Association. Phone: 320–255–3428. www.socpractice.org

## MEDICATIONS FOR PSYCHIATRIC CONDITIONS

Adapin—depression and anxiety
Adderall—ADHD
Anafranil—depression
Asendin—depression
Ativan—anxiety
Buspar—anxiety
Celexa—depression, anxiety, OCD, and eating disorders
Centrax—anxiety
Clozaril—psychotic conditions
Cylert—ADHD
Depakote—mania
Desyrel—depression
Effexor—depression and anxiety
Elavil—depression
Eskalith—bipolar disorder
Haldol—psychotic conditions
Klonopin—anxiety
Librium—anxiety
Loxitane—psychotic conditions
Luvox—depression, anxiety, OCD, and eating disorders
Mellaril—psychotic conditions

Moban—psychotic conditions
Nardil—depression
Navane—psychotic conditions
Norpramin—depression
Orap—psychotic conditions
Pamelor—depression
Parnate—depression
Paxil—depression, anxiety, OCD, and eating disorders
Prolixin—psychotic conditions
Prozac—depression, anxiety, OCD, and eating disorders
Restoril—insomnia
Ritalin—ADHD
Serax—anxiety
Sinequan—depression and anxiety
Stelazine—psychotic conditions
Tegretol—mania, psychotic conditions, and alcohol/cocaine withdrawal
Thorazine—psychotic conditions
Tranxene—anxiety
Valium—anxiety
Vesprin—psychotic conditions
Wellbutrin—depression
Xanax—anxiety
Zoloft—depression, anxiety, OCD, and eating disorders
Zyprexa—psychotic conditions

## Natural Remedies for Mental Health

Colloidal Lithium—bipolar disorder
DHEA—depression
5 HTP(5-Hydroxytryptophan)—depression and cocaine withdrawal
Ginkgo—memory
Grapeseed Extract—ADHD
IP-6 Inositol—depression
Kava—anxiety
L-Tyrosine—depression
Omega 3—depression and bipolar disorder
Pregnenolone—memory and depression
Pycnogenol—ADHD
SAMe—depression and bipolar disorder
7-Keto DHEA—depression
St. John's Wort—depression

## Common Prescription Medicines for General Medical Conditions

Allegra—allergies
Amoxicillin—antibiotic
Cipro—antibiotic
Claritin—allergies
Dyazide—blood pressure
Lasix—diuretic/water pill
Lipitor—cholesterol
Norvasc—blood pressure
Ortho Tri-cyclen—birth control pill
Premarin—female hormone for menopause
Prevacid—acid reflux/heartburn
Prilosec—ulcers
Synthroid—low thyroid
Tenormin—blood pressure
Vicodin (i.e., Hydrocodone and Acetaminophen)—pain
Vioxx—osteoarthritis and severe menstrual cramps
Zithromax—antibiotic
Zocor—cholesterol

# About the Author

*Dr. Howard G. Rosenthal, Ed.D.,* is the coordinator of the Human Services Program at St. Louis Community College at Florissant Valley and teaches graduate classes for Webster University in Webster Groves, Missouri. He has over 20 years experience doing psychotherapy, including his work at the Midwest Stress Center. He is the author and editor of a string of successful books. His book *Favorite Counseling and Therapy Techniques: 51 Therapists Share Their Most Creative Strategies* is an academic bestseller, while the sequel *Favorite Counseling and Therapy Homework Assignments: Leading Therapists Share Their Most Creative Strategies* features contributions from more famous helpers than any book of its kind. Most counselors are familiar with Dr. Rosenthal, as helpers from coast to coast have used and praised his academic bestseller the *Encyclopedia of Counseling* and his 15-hour audio licensing preparation program for the National Counselor Examination and state licensing exams.

Dr. Rosenthal's humorous, reader-friendly writing style landed him an interview—along with other influential authors such as Barry Sears of *Zone Diet Books* and Mark Victor Hansen, coauthor of the *Chicken Soup for the Soul* series—in Jeff Herman's recent book, *You Can Make It Big Writing Books: A Top Agent Shows You How to Develop a Million Dollar Bestseller.*

Some of his other popular books include *Not With My Life I Don't: Preventing Your Suicide and That of Others, Before You See Your First Client: 55 Things Counselors and Human Service Providers Need to Know,* and *Help Yourself to Positive Mental Health* (with Joseph W. Hollis). His video *Suicide Prevention Techniques that Work: Critical Information for Teachers* showcases his dynamic style of lecturing and was filmed in front of a large audience. Dr. Rosenthal has now lectured to over 100,000 people, making him one of the most popular speakers in the Midwest.

He has been the recipient of awards for his teaching as well as his clinical work. He lives with his wife and two sons in Saint Charles, Missouri. Dr. Rosenthal's website is www.howardrosenthal.com